MY LITERARY PROFILE:
A MEMOIR

MY LITERARY PROFILE:
A MEMOIR

Helene Pilibosian

Ohan Press
Watertown, Massachusetts

Library of Congress Control Number 2010903739
ISBN 978-1-929966-08-0
Designed by Hagop Sarkissian
Manufactured in the United States of America
Printed on acid-free paper

ON THE COVER: The Watertown Bridge over the Charles River in Watertown Square was originally built in 1647 and rebuilt later. It marks the place where Sir Richard Saltonstall's boat filled with settlers landed. It provides the backdrop for two inset photos of the author. The bridge appeared in the 1994 film "The River Wild," starring Meryl Streep and Kevin Bacon.

Preface

The author presents a highly detailed account of the lives of her Armenian immigrant parents and of her life in Watertown, Massachusetts as a youngster. This includes an ethnography of the village in historic Armenia her parents came from after the Armenian Genocide as well as descriptions of East Watertown and Watertown High School.

She continues with her study of humanities in Harvard's Division of Continuing Education, including the study of literature with Howard Mumford Jones and Paul Engle, presenting many anecdotes and descriptions in a tract that becomes a tribute to the art and the craft of poetry and prose.

After suffering a depressive illness, she has physical problems with a cardiac arrest during a routine surgery. Dwight E. Harken, M.D., an outstanding thoracic surgeon, saves her life with the best medical skill available in 1963. The book thus bears the marks of oral history, Harvard history, and medical history.

Travel to Europe and the Middle East with her husband adds to the action, as do hundreds of names of people and places she encounters in all phases of her experience. She learns a great deal about many kinds of people.

Later she reads the theories of Carl Gustave Jung and becomes a follower. In a complicated way, the memory of her surgery and these theories lead her to a mystical experience, which in turn fires her literary inspiration. She follows her inclination and writes and publishes a number of books of poetry and prose.

Acknowledgments

Sincere gratitude is extended to Hagop Sarkissian for his technical, factual and editorial help as well as the Index, and to the first readers including ice dancer and Harvard University student Loren Galler-Rabinowitz and tech writer and satirist Robert Sarkissian for encouragement.

Thanks also to Professors Lizabeth Cohen of Harvard University and Raymond V. Ingersoll of UCLA for their assistance with photographs as well as to Anne Covell of the University of Iowa Libraries.

꙰ Gratitude is extended to *The Armenian Mirror-Spectator* for publication of the articles entitled "A Journalist in the 60s" and "Why Details of the Armenian Genocide Are Necessary" with slightly different titles.

꙰ Gratitude is extended for permission to reproduce the following illustrations:

› Jones, Howard Mumford. HOWARD MUMFORD JONES: AN AUTOBIOGRAPHY. © 1979 by the Regents of the University of Wisconsin System. Reprinted by permission of The University of Wisconsin Press

› Howard Mumford Jones. Caricature by Charles C. Hefling, Jr., first published in *Harvard Magazine*, then in the above-mentioned autobiography

› Professor Paul Engle and Students. Frederick W. Kent Collection of Photographs, The University of Iowa Libraries, Iowa City, Iowa

› Dwight Emary Harken, M.D. © Louis F. Bachrach

꙰ The picture of Leon Surmelian is taken from his book *Daredevils of Sassoun*, a publication of the Armenian General Benevolent Union of America, Alan Swallow: Denver, Colorado, 1964

꙰ The picture of Jakob Kuentsler is taken from *The Armenian Mirror-Spectator*, Nov. 24, 2007

꙰ The picture of Dr. Clarence D. Ussher is taken from his book *An American Physician in Turkey*, Houghton Mifflin Company: Boston and New York, 1917

꙰ The following pictures are taken from Wikimedia Commons, a freely usable database of media files:

Arshile Gorky's *Abstraction with a Palette*, c. 1930; Carl Gustave Jung; Edgar Allan Poe; Walt Whitman

Table of Contents

Beginnings and Endings

Stories often start at the beginning, and my beginning was birth at St. Elizabeth's Hospital in Brighton in 1933 to live in nearby Watertown, Massachusetts, the second daughter of Khachadoor or Archie and Yeghsa or Elizabeth Pilibosian. I was never informed of the particulars of the birth like height or weight or difficulty, but my mother had mentioned that she took a taxi to the hospital because my father was at work with the car. In those days we were lucky to have one car, and many women didn't drive. The omitted detail was a matter of the name, which I discovered many years later when I needed a birth certificate from the city of Boston.

"I got the certificate in the mail."

"Let me see it."

"To think I never saw it until long after I was married."

"But you did need it when you went to school."

"There was a card from the town with my name on it. I always used that as a birth certificate because it was acceptable."

"There's no name on this."

"No, just 'female Pilibosian'."

"There must have been some confusion."

"Maybe in those days it wasn't necessary to give the name at the time of birth."

"That seems unusual."

"I read about such an incident in the book called *the namesake* written by an immigrant from India named Jhumpa Lahiri. It was a much more recent incident, and the officials at the hospital said they wouldn't release the child until there was a name given. According to their traditions, the grandmother chose the name. Her letter hadn't reached them yet, but they did choose a name since they were not in a hurry for the name but the hospital was. The coincidence struck me."

"Maybe the hospital you were born in didn't require the name immediately."

"It must have been the era."

"Of many immigrants, and I guess their rights to delay naming were respected. There still are many immigrants, but the authorities are stricter now."

Of course I don't remember the first few years of what turned out to be a fairly long life, but I do remember Hosmer Street where my family lived until I was five years old. It's a small street next to the Hosmer School, the elementary school I attended for a few days before we moved and quite near the building of the East Junior High School now used as a senior facility called Brigham House Assisted Living. The building had been designed by architect Charles Brigham, and was indeed sturdy enough to last a very long time with some internal updating. It had been the high school in the 1920s.

My aunt and uncle, newlyweds Arshalouys and Mesrob Haboian, were living in that house with us temporarily. The Star Market had given my father one of its small trucks to drive back and forth to work and had supplied driving lessons. I recall as one of my earliest memories seeing my father and uncle clinging to the porch rail due to the horrendous wind that was blowing there when they started to go out on September 21, 1938. The very dangerous wind was part of the New England Hurricane of 1938, which uprooted many trees in the town.

Also called the Big Blow, its winds measuring 121 mph with gusts to 186 mph, the hurricane killed more than 600 people and destroyed thousands of buildings in a matter of hours. Other states involved were in New York, Connecticut, and Rhode Island, sharing the worst natural disaster in America's history up to that point. The Connecticut River flooded disastrously, and at least 50 percent of trees in New England's forests were toppled. Many areas were left without drinking water, electricity, telephone or fire protection. The storm did much damage partly because the lack of weather analysis and communication at the time left many people in the middle of the day engaged in their work and activities exposed to the storm with no special precautions taken.

I didn't understand what a hurricane was at that age. I had begun kindergarten in that school and very vaguely remember a few scenes of being in a group of children. I also recall a great interest in the milk bottles the milkman left on the back stoop every day. They were glass bottles, and the cream in them rose to the top so that they had to be shaken for the milk to be used. Another scene that fascinated me was the sight of the iceman wearing a rubber cape and carrying a huge block of ice on his back with large tongs to put it into the ice box. That happened before refrigerators came into use, and it was taken for granted that a number of ice companies in the town would serve many customers with ice cut from the frozen Charles River.

We lived on the first floor of a two-story house, and across the street were family friends with a daughter who was about the same age as my sister Lucia and me. One's first memories begin at about four or five years of age, and I can only recall a few scenes of being on the first floor, looking down at the steep steps and going across the street to be with our friend Sona Haidostian. Her father Sam played the *saz*, an ancient Armenian string instrument, in the group that made some recordings of music by Sayat Nova, a medieval Armenian troubadour. Another friend named Yenovk Der Hagopian (the Der in front of his surname indicates that someone in his line of heredity had been a priest in the Armenian Church) sang those lovely songs, so different from the Armenian popular or even a classical music of that time or any other time.

Then we moved to a house on Kimball Road, also in East Watertown, where we would live quite near to the Coolidge School my sister and I would be going to. The building has now been renovated and is being used for rental apartments and condominiums called The Apartments at the Coolidge School. My life with Watertown as home base led me to travels downtown to Cambridge and Boston and eventually much farther on a temporary basis. But I always came back to familiarity that meant a great deal to me.

To Start a New Life

My grandfather, Dickran Pilibosian, became a citizen of the United States in 1895, then a few years later returned to his native village Ichmeh, near Kharpert in historic Armenia, where he married and had five children, then returned to America to work in the hopes that he could soon bring his family. Many Armenians immigrated under similar circumstances.

In 1915, however, the deportations wiped out all of the family except my father, who was kidnapped and enslaved by Kurds until the end of World War I, when he escaped by walking and by train to Aleppo, Syria. On the death march he had been taken from his mother, his brother and two sisters by a Kurd who sold him to another Kurd for a goat. After his escape four years later on the pretext of collecting cow dung, he was able to contact his father, who brought him to this country after gaining proof of his identity. My father entered the country from Rhode Island as an American citizen because he was the son of an American citizen at the time of his birth, a fact he had been unaware of when he went to Whitinsville, Massachusetts to join his father.

With an unusual zest for life, he soon had his first Thanksgiving dinner with relatives and worked at a various jobs, one of which was a temporarily digging graves during the Depression when any job was welcome. He tried opening a small grocery store in Providence, Rhode Island, and failed. As he worked and was paid the low wage of the day, he turned over his salary to his father with a small amount left for himself. He was dissatisfied with this old Armenian custom and took easily to American ways, such as exercising in the gymnasium.

In 1930 he sailed to Gardanne in France after a courtship by mail with Yeghsa Haboian during which it was agreed that the couple would marry sight unseen with only a recommendation from my uncle, who was in America. Though they had never met, it had seemed a good idea because my father needed a wife and family to root him down to one job, but due to the problems of that orphan generation, there were not enough Armenian women left to go around. The fact that the marriage was quite unsuitable because my father was a very friendly, outgoing man and my mother was very much the opposite does not seem to matter now, for the marriage lasted almost 60 years in spite of many disagreements.

From left, Yeghsa, her brother Mesrob Haboian and Khachadoor Pilibosian. Seated is Khachadoor's father Dickran

"Why didn't he search for his brothers and sisters?"

"When, where, how?"

"By going through a Turkish agency."

"There was no such thing to search out and resettle Armenian orphans, except what the American and European missionaries and Armenian organizations did at the time."

"Couldn't he go there and look for them?"

"He wouldn't be likely to go back to where his agony had been, and it would have been dangerous. His brother and sisters had been very young, and if they were left alive and taken into families, they were brought up as Muslims and wouldn't remember who and what they were. They might not remember him."

"Were there many children forcibly taken and converted?"

"Yes. It is estimated that about a million Turks have Armenian ancestors, and Kurds have a larger number of Armenian ancestors."

"How could he stand not knowing and doing nothing about it?"

"I also wondered about that. But conditions decided that, not my father. Even if he had wanted to, for years they were living from week to week on his paychecks that were hardly adequate for

Khachadoor Pilibosian
in 1929

their living. There was no money to take trips. I guess the only way he could live happily was to put the past behind him and try not to think about it. Though he often thought about it."

I write this not for any kind of vengeance but only for truth with much sympathy for the sufferings of my parents and a great deal of interest in their relatives and friends. Their attitudes and expressions, their way of living and their adjustment to this country, their stories and their anger, their relationships to one another were all sources of attraction to me, for as I was watching them I was studying their behavior and wondering how all this affected me. That history unravels in this book.

However, after all the distortions I have seen, I find that the truth has a cleansing effect, and all the moods that have gone under the bridge over the years are just an essential part of the way we have all related to each other and influenced each other. It could have been otherwise only if the world and human nature had been otherwise. But I am realistic because it is necessary to be.

Yeghsa Haboian in Marseille,
France, 1929

A Thimble Ethnography

My mother told me little about her early life, then only in the last couple of her 92 years. I had interviewed her extensively quite a few years before that for information about Ichmeh, her hometown and also my father's. Based on what she and my father told me as well as some research, I wanted to compile an adequate description of the town that was such a mystery to me and my modern life to comprehend its perennial shadow.

So the facts that follow about the history, manners, and customs of Ichmeh will fill a thimble with a brief ethnography about the background our lives were played against, the Armenian lives of my parents before they had immigrated, and our Armenian or American lives here. The experiences may be similar to those immigrants from other countries have had or they may be quite different or somewhat different or even completely different. But it is part of what we were and are.

Armenian history locates what had been a kingdom in space and time, describing what was lost to forced deportations in Western Armenia that became Turkey, leaving only Eastern Armenia to exist as a Soviet Republic until 1991 when it became independent. It is bordered by Russia, Iran, Georgia and Turkey. I realize that in writing about history, politics always enters into the picture somehow, though this writing is not meant to be political but rather an account of our personal situation.

The Rubenian dynasty was the last to rule over the Armenian Kingdom of Cilicia or Little Armenia. The family had married into European nobility, so that the throne had been transferred to the French house of Lusignan of Cyprus. The rule of the last Lusignan king of Cilicia, Leo V, ended in 1375 when the kingdom was overpowered by the Mameluke Sultan of Egypt, and Armenia Major to the north was shortly after overwhelmed by destructive Tartars from Mongolia, led by Tamerlane. A long era of oppression had begun, Armenians a minority in their own country under rule where Armenian history and culture no longer had any great meaning in terms of country.

Armenia was divided by the Turkish Government into six vilayets or provinces. These were Sivas, the westernmost below the Black Sea; Erzeroum to the north near the Russian border; Kharpert (called Harpoot by the American missionaries), at the center; Diarbekir to the south; Van to the east next to the Iranian border; and Bitlis next to Van. Each province had one or two major cities surrounded by hundreds of villages and towns of a few hundred to a few thousand people. These provinces didn't include the semi-autonomous region of Zeitoun, which had held out in a mountainous region for hundreds of years.

The town of Ichmeh was located 10 miles from the city of Kharpert, now called Elazig, with the Euphrates River flowing in between. The 4000-year-old city was surrounded by 365 small villages and was known for Euphrates College, which had been built on the hills of the city by American Protestant missionaries. It had many buildings that were used for elementary school, high school and college. After the tragedy of 1915, college classes were canceled because most of the students had been killed, and the buildings were used to house an orphanage with the missionaries Mary and Henry Riggs in charge of the college.

Ichmeh, built near the base of Mount Mastar on the slope so that the water flowing down the mountain could be tapped, had around 3000 people of which 2000 were Armenians. In the fields of the valley below were farmlands of the townspeople. According to the tradition in that part of the world, the houses were built in blocks attached to each other with the fields beyond, the roofs flat so that they could be shoveled of some rather deep snow in winter.

Many fruits grew in the orchards below the town. The most common of these were apricots and mulberries, the first leaving an influence with the many songs that were written to *dziran*, and the second with the affectionate appellation of the word *toot* used as a synonym for a fool. They were both eaten fresh, or dried or made into syrup.

Kerosene lamps were used for lighting in the houses, though the farmers retired early at night and were up at five o'clock in the morning so that the lack of electricity wasn't a big problem. If one went out at night, it was necessary to carry a kerosene lamp along unpaved roads. Most commonly donkeys were used for traveling or carrying loads, though there were some horses and some oxcarts. Messages were also sent in this manner, often through mountains with many dangers along the way, though local mail delivery was easier.

Telegraph was just beginning to be used in major cities and was mostly for official diplomatic messages to Western countries. There were some telegraph poles in the fields of Ichmeh, children fascinated by their aspect kicking them to hear the unusual sounds they made. In these villages, however, people were isolated from the changes going on in the cities for lack of personal communication and lack of Armenian newspapers that were available in the cities.

No one questioned the traditions except in the late 19th and early 20th centuries when an awakening began. Then only the leaders questioned but had to maintain official silence for the safety of continuing the sort of life of one's ancestors because there was no promise of something better. Some of the more intelligent and ambitious young people of the town would go to the city for higher education or to go to America, always the land of promise.

Families lived in large units, married children with their parents in the ancestral houses built to last hundreds of years. The houses had no yard but had flat roofs to be used for drying food or sleeping in the summer. One common room opened to other rooms, and sometimes the animals were kept on the first floor and the family lived on the second. There was no plumbing, and water was brought from the spring by the women and girls in large earthen jugs. The kitchen, which had the only heat in the house, also had a *tonir*, a kind of covered fireplace in the floor fired with wood pieces for cooking.

A strong sense of sin pervaded the lives of these people headed by a patriarch, the father, and they were hard-working people in business, farming, or trades. An introverted type who liked to read rather than do physical work was considered lazy by their usual standards. Thus they often overlooked creativity, which wasn't a usual part of village life where most people were either unschooled or taught only the elements of reading and mathematics.

There was a strong sense of Armenianism as distinct from any other ethnic group, probably for coherence as a people who were constantly threatened. Families lived for thousands of years in the same village, so that all the people there might be relatives. Metropolitan Armenians looked down upon the peasants as inferior in education and social status, but the exceptional city dweller, as indicated by some of the writers of the period, understood the plight of the villagers and sympathized with them.

Yet the villagers in Eastern Turkey were not as poor as those in other districts. There was usually a school for Armenian boys and by 1913 in some villages also for girls. The Turkish schools were separate, based upon learning the Koran. The custom of haggling or bargaining with the price of any item for sale was prevalent as it still is in the Middle East. By 1913 Armenians showed improvement in all fields of endeavor, but also vast resources were not used by the government in addition to which the transportation system was poor, and nothing was being done about it.

Without any accurate census of population and many people leaving for Europe and America, no accurate population count could be given. The Armenians had many dialects, usually one in each region. For example, the dialect of Kessab wouldn't be understandable to an Armenian who didn't know it, and the dialect of Ichmeh was the Kharpertsi — pertaining to the province of Kharpert — dialect. Now that all the users of most of these dialects have passed away, those speech patterns have become valuable as heirlooms.

The Turks and the Kurds, being Muslim, allowed Armenians no rights in the courts. Though living conditions were unbearable, most Armenians didn't protest, partly due to the impossible conditions of justice and also because they had been trained in docility for centuries. The hopelessness of fighting a physically powerful enemy and the oppression by greater numbers had over the centuries numbed the Armenian consciousness.

Raffi, a famous Armenian novelist of late 19th century, wrote much about village life especially in his novel *The Fool*, translated into English by the missionary Mrs. Jane Wingate. He described sons and lambs to be the most outstanding possessions of the village father. He writes of the landlord breaking an egg over each cow, having the priest read a charm for each, and hanging it around the neck of the cattle, the charm sewn in a piece of blue leather for good luck. Vartan, a character in the novel, comments on villagers thus:

> The villager is a grown-up child. When a child falls and bumps his head against the wall, he cries as long as he feels the pain; when the pain ceases, he forgets all about it as if nothing had happened and begins to love and play once more. It is difficult to deal with such large children . . . Go, tell that villager that the young man who so wisely discoursed to you concerning the individual rights of man, and of what labor is, and how it may be safeguarded, tell him that young man has been imprisoned and possibly he will soon be hanged, and you will hear from all the same remark — "he was crazy."

The remark that the villagers would make about the imprisoned man being crazy doesn't mean crazy in a psychiatric sense of the word, which they didn't comprehend. Rather the word was used in the sense of wildness, rashness, boldness or liberal behavior. The village folk also characteristically placated the rich, the important Armenians or Turks, fawning upon them to win favors which would otherwise be impossible.

Ichmeh was more advanced in the trades than most of the villages. Farming wheat and milling it after it was grown were the most important trades to sustain its people. They were the basis of the economy of the town, and mostly the men and boys did this kind of work, sowing and reaping by hand, while everyone in the family helped in harvesting the wheat. They tied a hand-operated threshing machine to an ox, which pulled the machine around and around in a circular fashion. This was family work, group work, one which expressed the solidarity of the Armenian villagers. The solidarity of the group, especially of the family, has remained a trait of Armenians, especially those who later settled in the Middle East or those in the former Armenian SSR.

The village had two parts, the upper on which the houses and stores were built, and the lower where the fields and vineyards were located. It had a flowing spring rising from the bottom of the church altar, the church built on the source of the spring which flowed into the Euphrates River, for the value of water to the people was equated with the value of the church. The water was essential for the people's physical being, and the church was essential for their spiritual being. There was no lack of water, and each family paid for a general allotment of it. The water was clean and cold and so plentiful that by its force it turned the stones of the 15 flour mills and watered all the gardens and wheat fields.

Shoemaking was the next important trade with 16 shoe stores lined along the main street. Evidently all men in the village were taught how to make the shoes, which were of the Persian type with upturned toes. In addition to these, there was general farming, meat cutting in the butcher store, selling groceries in the general store and selling cloth brought from the city. Men had to have a trade before they were allowed to wed.

The boys learned trades, getting up early each morning and going to church before they went to school. The girls learned housework and helped their mothers, and by 1913 most of them went to school. Important church lessons, intended more for the boys who would be trained to take over church duties, left little time for play. The younger children obeyed their parents and elder brothers and sisters who protected them.

Community activity centered around the Armenian Church, in this case named Soorp Nigoghos (St. Nicholas). The Armenian Church is similar to the Greek Orthodox Church in creed, but the Armenians do not stress doctrine. The music in the service dates back to a time when courtyards of the churches were places where moral and spiritual lessons were taught through drama, such as the literal washing of feet of 12 of the congregation representing the disciples on Thursday of Holy Week just before Easter. Easter was stressed more than Christmas, a characteristic of Eastern Christianity, and resurrection was central in their faith. The fact that Armenians were the first Christian nation from the year 301 A.D. always caused great pride.

Armenians were considered a religious community by the Turkish government, thus the importance of church leaders. Church services started early in the morning with usual daily attendance and on Sunday lasted for hours, since there was no other meeting place except in people's houses. The church had a partition in the middle aisle, and the women and girls sat on one side or in the balcony and the men on the other. Everyone took off their shoes before going into the church and placed them in layered racks. All families had Bibles (called in Armenian "the breath of God") and in between the Old and the New Testaments were several blank pages where dates of births, weddings, and deaths in the family were recorded for lack of government records of these events.

Ichmeh had a Protestant church as well with two services on Sunday. Small elementary schools were sponsored by both the Protestant and the Armenian Apostolic Churches, and one had to go to Kharpert to attend high school. The school sponsored by the Armenian Apostolic Church taught only boys until after the Armenian Protestant Church established a school which taught girls as well as boys, inspiring the other group to emulate them.

Medical treatments were administered by a self-taught village doctor who studied *The Book of Six Thousand*, a large encyclopedia of science, medicine and plants, written in Armenian incorporating the ancient art of herbal treatments probably gleaned from India and China and adapted to the needs of the particular area. These could effect cures, though serious cases were taken to the hospital in the city where medicine was somewhat more advanced. In Ichmeh at the time, the village doctor was my father's uncle Movses, or Mos Amoo, his father's brother.

His daughter Youghaper gave me the information about medicines and treatments she had helped him with such as crushing and powdering herbs from the mountains to make medications. They had used flower of hollyhocks for coughs and its roots to cure vomiting. All flowers were considered to have some medicinal purposes. Abscesses were treated. Malaria was treated by washing the patient in cold spring water. Spearmint was used for colds. Anise tea was used for stomach aches. Violet tea was used for coughs. One who couldn't urinate was treated with a drink made of crushed and cooked honeydew melon seeds. Unprepared herbs helped weakness, and the root of rhubarb was also used for stomach aches. Heart trouble was treated by bleeding, either from the hands or the arms. Mental or emotional problems were ignored for lack of understanding. When death occurred, the body was buried by sundown.

Marriage customs were based on the trust all families had for each other and the assumption that the house would be passed on to their children to create a stable, if not happy, marriage, for families knew each other for generations and wouldn't usually break this tie. They didn't expect romantic love for marriage, and once wed, divorce for couples was almost impossible with the church making the decision. In this sort of atmosphere, attitudes toward sex were puritanical, and shame lay heavily upon anyone's mentality. But in spite of this, occasional love marriages happened.

No real knowledge of contraception existed in the villages, though the process of nursing a child was a contraceptive measure. A midwife delivered babies in the villages, and if the child should be born with a noticeable abnormality, it wasn't brought to life and pronounced stillborn. Families tended to be large with an average of four of five children, but the death rate among infants was very high. The birth of boys was favored over girls because they carried the family name and also the obligation of supporting the older people when they could no longer work.

The grandmother helped the mother with children, and in the absence of a grandmother, a neighbor would help. Taking care of the children was considered women's work generously done by aunts either in the same house or close by. Children were toilet trained early, usually by one year in a rather strict and rigid program.

Respecting the advice of elders had great importance. There were strong bonds of affection between grandparents and grandchildren. Some were more authoritarian than others in trying to impose their will upon the younger members of the family, but no one questioned their will. For example, parents would choose their children's clothing until they were wed.

Godparents, made official in baptismal certificates provided by the church, were expected to take care of the children in case of the death of parents at an early age if there were no grandparents. They also served in an important advisory capacity where death of parents was more common than it is now. These customs and attitudes tended to carry over into the adopted countries of Armenian immigrants.

Most clothing was made in the simple dwellings by the women of the family, and girls were expected to learn the crafts of sewing, knitting and sometimes embroidery at an early age, knitting their own socks by the time they were ten. Since many or most of the families grew cotton, there was a cotton gin in the town that would take out the seeds and leave the cotton to the process of being spun into thread in the home and being woven into muslin. The muslin was used to make sheets for the large household, and wool from the sheep was made into winter underwear, socks, sweaters and shawls. For everyday clothing men wore loose pants with elasticized ankles, called *shalvars*, which were made by the women. Washing clothing, also a woman's job, was done with homemade soap made of natural materials, and boiling underwear and baby clothing sterilized them.

The women would cook in large quantities so that the food would be enough and also be left for other meals. Bread-making was especially difficult and time-consuming, since bread was the basis of every meal. Most of the food was cooked in the pots in the fireplace and in the *tonir*. Enough bread was made to last two or three weeks, and about 200 pounds of flour were used. Storage of food was in fat in the case of meat or drying in the case of fruits and vegetables to be kept in cold storage room. Tea or *tahn* (water-diluted yogurt) were used as drinks; coffee and alcoholic beverages were not commonly used in the villages, with some exceptions.

Belief existed in many superstitions, common among unlearned peoples, the major one being the evil eye. Blue beads were put upon a baby, usually as a bracelet, to keep its influence away, and compliments to a pretty child could bring about evil, which might be attributed to jealousy. Sickness which couldn't be medically diagnosed was often said to be caused by the evil eye, in which case a woman would come into the house, pray over the sick person and put salt upon him or her as a sort of exorcism.

Just a few proverbs will illustrate the wisdom and the shrewdness that guided the Armenians:

> Even the king loses rights where there is nothing.
> When the mind is busy, the eye does not see anything.
> He becomes a false holy man who eats the chickens of the monastery.

He who spits at the wind spits at his own face.
Eat and drink with a friend but do not trade with him.
Pilav is not made by talking.
He who arrives late at the dinner table must clean it.

Leisure time in the villages offered a few customs that were simpler than those of the city, such as visiting people, picnics on monastery grounds, group dancing and homemade toys for children. The most important pastime in the evenings especially during the winter was storytelling after supper. Family and children would gather around a table with a guarded fire underneath and with quilts around their feet. Those who had talent at telling stories might recite the Armenian folk epic of David of Sassoun, telling stories of the kings or folk tales, an oral tradition usually performed by men with memory and wit for improvisation, the narrator tending to personalize the story. The best narrator would be dramatic and create suspense in the telling, for this was entertainment. The realistic tales, as opposed to the wonder tales, expressed the joys, experiences and wit of the Armenian folk in their everyday life and always had a happy ending upholding morale and morality.

The troubadours or traveling singers, called *ashoughs* in Armenian, were an institution in village life and also in city life and composed their own songs and lyrics. They sang for weddings and sometimes also played and sang in the public square, passing around a hat for donations. They would also give concerts in houses for meals and overnight lodging, there being no hotels or restaurants in the villages. The most famous Armenian troubadour was Sayat Nova, who lived from 1719 to 1795 and spent much of his life at the Georgian Court as minstrel under the rule of King Heracles II.

The words of his songs are poetic, spontaneous and emotional, the melody itself giving the songs their distinctive sound, the exotic sad tones of the East with some Western influence. They used the Greek Minor and frequently the vocal wail that is used in the East. The usual subjects were attitudes towards birth, love, death, love of home, field, mountain, sense of brotherhood and of patriotism, and the love songs were romantic rather than sensuous. Following are eight lines from a song entitled "Without

Thee What Are Song and Dance to Me" translated by Zabelle Boyajian:

> Without thee what are riches unto me?
> What worth could I in silks or cashmere see?
> Arrayed in rags and sackcloth I would be
> Wandering around the convents, one by one,
> To meet perchance with someone, who might tell,
> My fair one, how to free me from thy spell;
> For Sayat Nova's torments far excel
> The Seven Wise Men's complaints told one by one!

This very brief description of village life in the Armenian centers of Ottoman Turkey or historic Armenia illustrates the development of the character of my parents and relatives, showing what they lost and also what characteristics they brought with them to America or to any other country. These behaviors, though they were often covered over by negative experiences, helped to develop my personality as I grew up in the wider Armenian community.

The stories and methods of storytelling survived and with them the realistic, practical and shrewd bent of the Armenian temperament as well as its capacity for dreams. My father had an excellent talent for storytelling with incidents from his own life, influencing me to develop my interest in the narrative approach to poetry and in the writing of actual stories such as this one. Everyone who knew him enjoyed his stories as he entertained them and expressed his own personality through them, though his stories about genocidal memories made them sad.

My mother's memory of descriptions from the past was quite good, where my father's seemed more limited. I didn't ask so much about the suffering and loss of parents, relatives and homeland, not wanting to encounter the pain of her memories but rather the freshness of more pleasant details. So I asked about customs, the farming, the food, the lady of the house and the land, in other words, ethnographic facts, which I organized and wrote down on cards as I would a college paper. Then I typed up the notes roughly in prose and found that I didn't have enough material to fill a full-length book as I would have wanted to do. So I shelved the project temporarily.

"Where did you get all that information and how did you know how to write an ethnography?"

"I interviewed my parents. I read some books, taking notes on them and also taking notes on a lecture or two about Armenians and how they lived in the villages of the old country."

"But you must have had some instruction."

"Yes I did. There was some anthropology instruction as part of a psychology course I took. I had to write a long paper as an ethnography of a group of preliterate peoples. I chose the Navajo, the indigenous Native American group centered in the area of Utah and Arizona."

"How many pages was the paper?"

"As I remember it was about 10 pages, and I spent many hours taking the notes on cards and working them into a nonfiction narrative. I typed it all on my old Royal portable typewriter, which required a great deal of strong fingering."

"Did you get a good grade on it?"

"I got an A but don't remember the comments that were made on it. There weren't many. I saved it for a while and then threw it away, thinking it useless. But now I wish I had saved it just for the value of the form. I certainly didn't think I would be writing an ethnography of my own people at a later time."

"The course must have made quite an impression on you."

"It did and I was fascinated by the subject, but I decided not to continue my formal study of it."

"Why?"

"Well, let's say I wasn't encouraged to study the subject of psychology."

"I think you would do rather well with the subject."

"Perhaps at the time..."

"I see. A qualification."

"I'm afraid so."

Underlining Familiarities

During my childhood the surrounding atmosphere of the originally Yankee Watertown tempered the Armenian characteristics of growing up in the Armenian community. Boston and Cambridge left their influences when I was older and trying to reach a higher modality by advancing my education and by employment in the more complicated world of business and of schools. It underlined the stark difference between the old world rural life and a very complex modern American life of city and town, even though at that time I had not researched the rural life and knew it only through the behaviors of the familiar families and by the customs I observed by attending services in St. James Armenian Church.

My curiosity about what was going on around me caused me to listen very closely to conversations even if they were in Armenian because I understood, and I realized how much their speaking in Armenian was a natural and necessary phenomenon. The sounds of this conversation were different from those of Americans because their reasons for being here were different and so were their personalities. I also noticed that no one around me was aware of my listening so closely or of my knowing Armenian so well. Thus events sowed the seed of curiosity that would later grow into a large plant.

My father's stories became legend with his many friends

St. James Armenian Apostolic Church

and his family since they were usually actual events of his life, about the Genocide or work experience in the Star Market with people he worked with or met there. He unraveled details in a very dramatic manner that made the stories irresistibly entertaining and interesting to anyone who would listen, and they all did.

When I was about five years old, I recall listening to the bedtime stories that he would tell me and my sister about the mouse family who had some adventures. I was attracted by this imagination and drama he related to us, and though these stories meant for children didn't continue, my attitude carried on and transferred to the stories I read in books.

I frequented the library from the time I learned to read, which was in first grade. The library was a few blocks away from our house on Mt. Auburn Street, and I used to walk there and back myself when I was quite young because in those days it was considered safe enough for children to walk around during the day. I enjoyed that little bit of freedom and responsibility because otherwise life was strict with discipline and expectations. Some of my favorite stories in those early years were about Dr. Dolittle and animals that lived in a rather human way and communicated in conversations. Was this an early manifestation of escapism or was it simply imagination and the enjoyment of the story? I never quite found the answer to that question.

East Branch of the Watertown Public Library

Another Unlikely Survival

My mother had been one of seven children, her parents being Hovhannes and Toomig Haboian, farmers in Ichmeh. Her father had been in the Turkish army, and just before the deportations went back to his village to reunite with his family and after leaving when the visit was done was never seen again. One day her mother cooked breakfast for the children using the best eggs, knowing it was the end of her life with them and indeed of her life. After the meal, she walked off with two of the younger children and was never heard from again.

At that time my mother had witnessed her pregnant aunt being slashed open by a Turkish soldier with a bayonet, usually fatal. There was no reason for optimism, for this kind of occurrence was common at the time of the deportation and massacres. There were many other instances of horrible tortures and deaths, which are available in many books written by Armenian survivors or their children or grandchildren and by missionaries and government officials, including the American ambassador to Turkey Henry Morgenthau.

In 1915 when the trouble began, a Turkish family headed by a dependable and liked Turkish employee of my mother's father saved her and her sister from deportation by keeping them in the family home they had confiscated, seemingly by an agreement with the Armenian owners. The girls had been treated with so-called respect, though my mother later admitted that the woman hadn't liked her, as they helped with the housework. The usual pattern was that the Turkish family would support them in exchange for work and wait until they were 16 to be of age to marry their sons. In this case the plan didn't materialize because there wasn't enough food for them all with an impending danger of starvation at the time, and so the family turned them out.

Though they had taken the house, the animals and all the belongings, her older sister had the deed to the property. Later when some Armenian boys were trying to escape over the border, she sold the property to give them money. At some point she found my mother beaten unconscious and left to die. The story, as I found out when my mother was 91, was that the Turkish family sent her with a young man (their son?) in a wagon to go some distance to her relative's house. She became nervous as she neared the end of her narrative and couldn't continue, so I surmised from some facts I knew that she had been raped and beaten, then found by her sister and taken to the orphanage at the American missionary school in Euphrates College in the city of Kharpert, where she stayed until 1923 during the time that the miseries of World War I were played out until the armistice of 1918.

Since there was fear of another massacre then, the Swiss missionary and physician Jacob Kuentsler, after serving in the German Mission Hospital in Urfa, gathered the children to take to the surrounding countries where they were placed in orphanages and sent out to work. They began the trek on donkeys and later changed to the faster mules until they reached the Syrian border and went by train to Lebanon. There were a total of 8,000 orphans, mostly Armenian but also including Assyrian, Syrian, Greek and Kurdish children. Searching them out from houses, streets and harems had been a dangerous undertaking, but he had never hesitated to help them.

Dr. Kuentsler served with his wife Elizabeth at his side. Coincidentally, my mother's name was also Elizabeth in English, I suppose the translation of Yeghsa, and my father's mother's name was Elizabeth in English, for her name was also Yeghsa.

"What was your grandmother like?"

"I know her hair was red but maybe not curly. Did you know that I really cared, that I stared at her picture and wished she were with us?"

"What would it have been like to have her with you?"

"She must have been as nice as her sister."

"Too bad you weren't told more."

My mother was placed in the orphanage at Ghazir in Lebanon, 40

Jacob Kuentsler

miles north of Beirut, where she worked as an accountant in a rug factory that had been established in 1923 for the employment of the girls at the institution. The boys lived in a separate institution. These rugs were luxurious Isfahan rugs that were much in demand, and the business prospered. They made a large rug 12 feet x 18 feet patterned with lions, unicorns, monkeys and storks that was presented to President Calvin Coolidge on Christmas day in 1925 in appreciation for U.S. efforts to help relieve the suffering of Genocide survivors. The President loved it and took it home when he left the White House, his mother placing the rug in front of the fireplace.

The President of Lebanon presented the Lebanese Order of Merit decoration to Jacob Kuentsler because of his great work at the orphanage and at the factory. For saving thousands of orphans at the risk of his own life and putting them to constructive work in addition to giving them some education had been a truly a noble undertaking. Subsequently in 1982 the Coolidge family returned the rug to the White House.

Smaller rugs were also manufactured to be presented to those who made large donations to the American Near East Relief for the benefit of the orphans. The money that came to the orphanage was sent to neutral Denmark because it was run by Danes working for the Near East Relief, established in 1915 to help Armenian orphans and now called the Near East Foundation.

As head of that orphanage, Dr. Kuentsler was lovingly called Papa Kuentsler and his wife Mama Kuentsler. Previously it had been run by Miss Maria Jacobsen, a Danish missionary noted for her too-strict discipline, who later established another orphanage for Armenian children in Jbeil, Lebanon, called Birds' Nest. During his early years there, one of the girls at the orphanage died, at which time Dr. Kuentsler took a handful of dirt to throw over the casket and suffered a splinter in his finger. Eventually it gave him blood poisoning in his finger, which the doctors didn't want to cut off until the poisoning went up his arm, necessitating amputation of his arm.

Medicine in those days was primitive as compared to the present, when the approach might have been different. Access to hospitals was limited, even in the city, and whatever hospitals existed were hampered by lack of knowledge and equipment. With no antibiotics in those years, they did the best they could. Dr. Kuentsler headed the orphanage until 1940 and died at Ghazir in 1949.

During her years in Lebanon my mother studied nursing at the American University of Beirut and graduated, realizing that the work was simplified for them because there was such a great need for nurses. She then migrated to a small town called Gardanne near Marseille in France where her sister Khoumar lived with her husband Kevork Hagobian and their six children. While there, she took care of a friend of the family and used her nursing ability in this limited fashion.

After a short stay in France during which time she had a brief but intense correspondence with my father in which they promised each other loyalty and happiness, she met him for the first time after he sailed to France on the ship *Olympic* of the White Star Line. Their wedding ceremony took place at her sister's house in Gardanne without many guests and with Rev. H. N. Ghazarosian, minister of the Armenian Protestant Church of Marseille, officiating. At the simple ceremony, the bride had a wedding veil but not a very special wedding dress, for these people were living very basic lives and had no money for luxuries. They sailed back home on the *Majestic*.

Yeghsa Haboian (top row, fourth from left) and a group of orphans from the Near East Relief orphanage in Ghazir, Lebanon

Living in America

For a while they lived on Compton Street in the South End of Boston near the original location of the Holy Trinity Armenian Church on Shawmut Avenue, a center of Armenian life in that city. They lived in the house with some relatives and with my grandfather until their first child was born and they needed more space. Employment waited as well as an apartment on Dexter Avenue in Watertown, where the family stayed until shortly after I was born. My grandfather had separated from them and lived with his relatives.

"There is always the bad luck and the good luck."

"That's how life is."

"If only the bad luck isn't so bad that one can't recover from it."

"Or if only the good luck arrives in time to cancel out the bad."

"But one has to believe there will be good luck."

"Sometimes one makes one's own good luck."

"The same for bad luck. But one can't always control circumstances. Like being hit by a war or by lightning or even by a car."

"Maybe that's why we pray, not only for thanks but for every day, liking to feel that some power is watching out for us and for our survival and the realization of our hopes and dreams."

"Do you pray in church every Sunday?"

"I honestly can't say that I go to church every Sunday, and I honestly can't say that I pray in church or I don't. I think I more often pray wherever I am when I feel the need or when there is a pressing circumstance. I am likely to pray in the hospital or on the way back from the hospital if I have received some bad news. And I am likely to thank God in my mind for something wonderful that happened because I felt that a wish had been answered by some kind of intercession or coincidence that couldn't be explained."

"You make yourself very clear on the subject of the need for prayer. Have you ever written an article about religion or prayer?"

"No. I can tell you about my feelings on the matter, but that's not my field to write about."

Armenians in America as well as other groups didn't expect much in the year 1930, hardly surviving the difficulties of the Great Depression that had begun on October 29, 1929, when the stock market crashed. After that worldwide economic slump, recovery was very slow. The reason why so many people, including my people, liked Franklin D. Roosevelt so much was that in his first term as president, which began in 1932, he brought about changes to put the unemployed to work and help the ailing economy with his New Deal and instituted the Social Security system.

During that difficult time before marriage, my father was jobless and even dug graves with a shovel for three months as employment, having to almost beg for a chance to show that he could do the work. That was after he was called the "little guy" by the boss who didn't believe he could and initially refused him. However, my father persisted and finally was given the job, which I imagine wasn't very pleasant. But the little guy had a great deal of physical strength which served him well all his life.

Work at the Star Market

During my parents' marriage, the family bore tensions and conflicts, not helped by the fact that there wasn't much money from the hard work my father was doing as a grocer. Life was indeed a struggle, as my father used to say. He had been working in a factory, the Cambridge Rubber Co., and on Saturdays working at the Star Market. Making sneakers in the factory, he earned $22 a week, but the factory was going to close. He then implored Steve Mugar to give him a job in the Star Market.

"You know, you left me twice."

"Steve, he's a married man now."

After that, every time my father was angry about the job, Steve Mugar would say, "Don't forget, you're a married man now." He also suggested the move to Watertown in order to be close to the job, which he started at $18 a week. During the 1940s, his salary there was about $40 a week with no overtime pay or benefits, which was customary in business at the time. He worked a full six-day week about 12 hours a day, and stayed with the job for 14 years.

Also an Armenian immigrant and educated in business at Bentley College, Mr. Mugar hired many Armenian immigrants or their children to work in the original market or the subsequent Star Markets in Newton, Wellesley, Cambridge, etc. His Armenian name was Papken Der Mugardichian, and he had arrived in America in 1906 with his parents at the age of five from the city of Kharpert, the area my parents had come from.

Sarkis Mugar had paid $800 in 1916 and bought the first small store in Watertown Square at 26 Mt. Auburn Street next to the Meat Spot, which he operated as one-man butcher shop. After he was killed in an accident in 1922, Steve worked full time there and went to Bentley in the evenings when it was a two-year college. He then gradually enlarged the business and added to its offerings milk, bread, butter, then vegetables and fruit, working very hard to build up the business. Following his example, all the employees worked hard and were proud of the business.

He called upon his first cousin John Mugar to help with the management of the store after John had finished college brilliantly. The first supermarket they added was the Newtonville Star Market, which introduced the idea of the conveyor belt. This was an original that drew many customers away from all the large grocery stores because of the great convenience of having grocery bags placed in the trunks of cars. Both men were at different times president and chairman of the chain.

The original store in those days was rather plain by today's standards but very well stocked with fruits and vegetables and meat. Lacking checkout counters and carriages, bags of groceries were given at any area and payment taken in that area. In those early years such markets delivered full bags of groceries to homes after the order was placed at the store. Some of the workers tried cheating by sending orders out without paying for them, but there were secret detectives hired to trace those thefts. My father caught five workers stealing in that way.

He learned how to display and sell fruits and vegetables as well as different cuts of meat by working on groceries and displays and how to put certain items on sale to attract people to the store, who once there would buy more. My father and other workers carried the heavy crates, for there was no machinery to help. Neither of my parents complained about the work and long hours they took for granted because there was nothing better available to them in those years.

Comparing the prices to what they are today, a head of lettuce cost about five cents. I have a picture of my father with another worker taken in the old Star Market, the displays of vegetable behind them showing prices for cauliflower at 15 cents a head and tomatoes at 2 pounds for 29 cents. That was in 1934, which some people would call "the good old days," depending on their perspective.

But he was glad to have the opportunity to learn all the tricks of the business world from a brilliant businessman like Steve Mugar, who knew what would bring the customers into the store as far as merchandise, display, methods of payment, sales or anything else was concerned. However, working 62 hours a week for

$48, he became aware of some inequities in amount of pay the workers received. He asked for a raise, which amounted to $2 a week, and since his health was beginning to suffer from lifting heavy crates and doing so much work, he left. The year was 1946.

If what wasn't said had been said, it would have sounded like this:

"Papa works so hard, we have to get him glasses of water when he asks for them."

"He reads the newspaper when he gets home. I suppose he's too tired to talk much."

"Men don't help with the housework."

"Mama works hard too. She did how many hours of washing today, rubbing all the clothes clean by hand, and she put in so many hours of bottling tomatoes yesterday. Now she's getting the food ready with such care, more than some other housewives we know."

"Parents have their own work and don't help children with their homework. I can do that well enough without help anyway."

The changes that led to supermarkets would come about later; incidentally, one of the subsequent supermarkets in this chain was opened in Cambridge about a mile from my father's store, and it was the supermarket I would often frequent, particularly enjoying the conveyor belt there as well as the brightly lit large area with meat packaged in cellophane wrappers, many aisles of dry goods and varied fruits and vegetables displayed attractively. This conveyor belt service lasted until 2002.

In 1964 the Star Market stores were sold to the Jewel Tea Company and then in 2006 were acquired by Shaw's, whose name they now bear. The original store was closed long ago, but most of the other stores still exist under the name of Shaw's or of Star Market. Those near to us are located in Cambridge, Belmont, Allston, Boston, Waltham, Newton and Wellesley.

Home on Kimball Road

We had moved to Kimball Road in East Watertown in 1938. It is located off Mt. Auburn Street, the main street of East Watertown, just across from Bigelow Avenue. I attended the Coolidge School, named after a relative of President Calvin Coolidge, which was two blocks away from our house, and walking there and back was easy. School lasted from 8:00 a.m. until 3:30 p.m. with the break of an hour during which time we walked home to have lunch and walked back.

I remember a few horses and carts carrying produce to the stores in my first year there, but they were very soon replaced by small pickup trucks. Few cars populated the streets, and the trolley ran on its tracks in the middle of Mt. Auburn Street. One could almost feel America's heartbeat in all the hard work that was going on. Sometimes I would go on errands for my mother around the corner at a butcher shop owned by a man named Sam of average looks and with a mustache. Next to it was a five and dime store. Some years later these disappeared into the murky depths of what we call the past, and with more ownership of automobiles we gradually lost the era of walking everywhere.

The street branched off from Mt. Auburn Street across the street from the Town Diner and the banks, which have changed owners a number of times. I watched all this with wide eyes as I sometimes roller skated on the pavement across the street from our house or walked the two blocks to school. For even a small and restricted life has its interesting moments.

We lived on the second floor in a rented house that was next to what had been the Kimball mansion, a large house but not as large as many mansions. It was right next to a back alley where sometimes I saw dogs chasing cats or men urinating or rotting food put out by some of the stores, emitting the stench of garbage that wasn't picked up often enough. Less than a perfect situation, it made my mother very nervous, but she had the tendency to rage anyway.

A view of Coolidge Square at the intersection of Mt. Auburn Street (on the left) and Kimball Road. The first structure on the left is the Town Diner. Many of the stores mentioned in this chapter were across the street from the Diner, including the pharmacy on the corner owned by George and Peggy Srabian. The picture is taken on the sidewalk in front of a convenience store that replaced the Coolidge Theatre.

"Lots of kids cut through our yard to the other street after the movie is over. They get out the back door, which is right across the street."

"Mama always yells at them out of the window."

"Does it do any good?"

"No. The kids call her a witch. I feel so bad."

"For her or for the kids?"

"For her of course. These difficulties make her despair."

"She despairs so easily."

"That's why it's so sad and embarrassing for us."

The house and long front yard were right next to the corner pharmacy belonging to George and Peggy Srabian. I often went to this store to buy the daily *Boston Globe* for three cents, candy bars for a nickel or a dime and comic books for a dime each.

The wonderful part of family life in those early years was that parents could trust the safety of their children to walking around near their area and to school without being afraid that they could be kidnapped or molested. I suppose danger was possible in some areas in large cities or as an unusual happening in the smaller cities and towns. But all was peaceful until about

1990, after which it seemed that parents were always driving their children to school because they couldn't trust prowlers, molesters or drug dealers. Many of us are ashamed that we have come to this.

Soon World War II began. One year a group of soldiers resided in the Coolidge School building for a few weeks before they moved on. They were serious, not jocular, and didn't bother the students or teachers as far as I know; we all understood that the war was bad business necessitating cooperation with decisions that were made by the government. Food rationing of items such as meat, butter and sugar started in 1942 plus a collection of melted fat saved from food that would be used for military purposes.

My parents were very conscientious about those things. I still have the books of partially used coupons my mother had for some reason saved in her box of valuables with her wedding veil, her nursing book and her nursing diploma from the American University of Beirut. She kept that box hidden in the attic of that house and the one we moved to after I graduated from high school. I never knew her to show it to anyone and never knew the contents of it until she was gone.

"Why did she save the coupons? They're not worth anything."

"I heard about the veil, but I never saw it. She'd never really mentioned it."

"She'd never showed the nursing diploma, and I saw the nursing book only after her death."

"What did you do with it?"

"I donated it to a nursing library, the Gertrude Beal Library at The University Hospital that belongs to Boston University."

"Her box was in the attic, and I never liked to climb that narrow stairway that had no railing."

"Maybe she thought I wasn't interested to know about her early days."

"I never really indicated interest until my later years, but if I had been told more I might have responded."

She had never worked in nursing as employment, but she did help my father a bit when he had his own store and of course worked very hard cooking, cleaning, canning and doing many heavy chores. My father used to bring large boxes of tomatoes, which she used to prepare, then cook and put into bottles to be boiled and save for use, a job that required many hours. She also made quince jelly in much the same manner.

A Big Ben clock on the corner of Mt. Auburn Street and Bigelow Avenue chimed loudly every hour on the hour whether it was night or day. Automobiles on the streets were sparse, in the same way that college degrees were. Air conditioning in the houses or in the stores didn't exist then, though there were fans turning. There were no high-rise buildings in the town, and most of the houses were two-family or singles which were either on one level or two. Since it was an old town as American towns go, the houses were older types but were usually in good condition.

We took these facts for granted because we didn't know any others. Of course we had electricity; that was a question my children asked me when I was talking about the old days. Maybe they were joking.

"We didn't have air conditioning though."

"It must have been quite hot. You lived on the second floor didn't you?"

"Yes. But it seems when we were younger the heat didn't affect us as much as it does now."

"We're young and it affects us."

"Because you're used to living with air conditioning."

We lived from one week to another, and fortunately my father didn't become ill and didn't die early. My mother wouldn't have been able to take a job to support her growing children. She was able to continue her working at the slavish washing without a washing machine until later when washing machines became more common and keep up with all the cleaning and cooking she felt had to be done in a very stringent manner. These matters of luck become obvious only in the future when looking back and saying to oneself what if this or that had happened, for they had happened to other families who had gone on welfare or had sent their children out to work to support them.

We subscribed to the *Saturday Evening Post*, and the covers by Norman Rockwell were very suitable to our type of living. They can be seen now in the Norman Rockwell Museum in Stockbridge, Massachusetts — vignettes of people in ordinary situations like buying a chicken or staring at a storefront. Some of the scenes are social commentaries that had great staying power and made the artist very popular. All of my life imitated the *Saturday Evening Post* covers with plainly dressed real people engaged in the mundane activities that constituted the era.

I was an assiduous reader of the comic strips in the *Boston Sunday Globe*, especially of "Li'l Abner" and "Mutt and Jeff." I would sprawl on the living room floor with the papers spread out before me, it being the easiest way to access those pages. Chicken-in-the-pot Sundays and toilets with pull chains with the water-shed above near the ceiling. Roller skating on the sidewalks rather than at a rink. I'm sure they were rinks, but we couldn't afford them and didn't have anyone to take us to them. Actually, the thought never occurred to us, being so far from our experiences.

My mother was a good cook, and my father used to bring us the best of meat, vegetables and fruit from the Star Market. We often had American food such as roast beef, roast pork, roast chicken and charred lamb chops broiled over the coal in the furnace, which my mother stoked a few times a day in winter. We also often had Armenian food such as raw beef or lamb with fine *bulghur* kneaded into what is called *kheyma*, the stuffed grape leaves that are called *sarma*, and stew with green beans cooked with lamb on top of pilaf made of rice or of *bulghur*.

We ate the cracker bread that was made at Euphrates Bakery, located on Dexter Avenue just off Mt. Auburn Street until a fire destroyed it. We couldn't resist the aroma of fresh bread as we entered the bakery to buy some of the bread, which had also formerly been delivered by a man named Peter Kaloustian. This bakery was located a few streets down from Kimball Road where we lived, so that going there was easy enough, and going to the East Branch Library, which I did often, was just as easy.

The Armenian cracker bread (we call it *patz hatz*, which means open bread) was part of our diet. We used to wet it a little bit so that it wouldn't crumble too much and used it to supplement meals. We also had Arnold toast bread and some homemade bread, which required great industry. My mother also sometimes made *pakhlava*, rolling out the near paper-thin dough herself with a stick she kept for the purpose. We all appreciated the cooking and developed a taste for the best food.

Yogurt and Other Allegiances

In our family as well as in most Armenian families, the attitude toward food was generally one of good health and included all the variety we needed in addition to plenty of milk and yogurt, the latter always homemade. No one ever imagined then that yogurt would become a commercial entity and enterprise with flavors, high-fat, low-fat, even frozen. It was simply a staple made in the safety of the family, an Armenian family in America, a tradition I tried and continued until to save time I began buying commercially prepared yogurt.

It was and still is a staple in the Caucasus, the Middle East, Greece, Bulgaria, Romania and Russia. When yogurt was first made commercially here, the first company to make it in my area was Colombo, named for Sarkis and Rose Colombosian, who started the business in 1929 using Rose's traditional Armenian recipe. Sarkis was acquainted with my father and sometimes visited the ADL Club in Watertown where the men would play cards, eat meals and socialize. General Mills bought the company in 1993 and continues to make some of the best yogurt and frozen yogurt.

To be scientific and factual for a moment, consciously switching from the right brain to the left (just remember that left is for logic and right is for creativity): scientific studies of yogurt and its value in immunity and longevity were first done in the early twentieth century by the bacteriologist Elie Metchnikoff, who shared the Nobel Prize in medicine with Paul Ehrlick in 1908. In his studies he found that the lactic acid that causes the fermentation in yogurt acts as an antibiotic in the intestinal tract and tends to aid normal intestinal equilibrium.

Metchnikoff (1845-1916) was a Russian bacteriologist educated at Kharkov, Russia and in Germany and was a professor of zoology at Odessa and an associate of Louis Pasteur. He had started his research after he had become interested in the long lives of Bulgarians who used yogurt in their diets. Yet he thought it was a cure-all and so sacrificed all his money for the cause of scientific investigation, then died at the age of seventy-one. My parents and others followed his belief that yogurt contributes to longevity and ate it every day. Its technical name, by the way, is *lactobacillus bulgaris* and the name of the culture in it is *Streptococcus thermiphilus* or *acidophilus.*

My mother made yogurt every week until she was almost 90, so that plain yogurt has become an important part of my diet. She simply followed the folk wisdom from Armenia and the Caucasian area. I doubt she knew the scientific background that was associated with it.

We used to eat yogurt with pieces of cucumber in it or diluted yogurt mixed with cooked hulled wheat. She even believed in using it as a cream for sunburns, other types of burns or bee stings. She thought that yogurt was the staff of her life, and certainly it may have helped her longevity.

My mother, with many anxieties engendered when she had survived starvation circumstances in her youth and her insecurity in orphanages, would be furious if the food she cooked were rejected or not eaten for reasons of dislike, and she would remind us of all the starving people in the world. But children being children, they will not always eat what is given to them, and complexes being complexes, ethnic children will sometimes reject the food that reminds them of the ethnicity they feel makes them inferior to others in the country whose groups are more dominant in the culture.

However, I never understood why she was angry when I made pudding and put it in the refrigerator, so angry that she yelled at me and threw it on the floor. It may have been the result of her anti-American feelings or frustration with the problems of bringing up children. Or she might have been seeing the dead die again in front of her eyes or the starving still starving. She might have just been taken to an orphanage or just seeing her mother walking away never to return. Why? Why? Why? I was looking for answers where there are no definitive answers and coddling moments out of the past that needed reassurance.

Thus, there was a duality of allegiance at work, even in regard to food, we children were guilty for not obeying in this and other matters. What a strange development that the food

I was fussy about or disliked at that time, including the stuffed cabbage leaves or the raw meat with *bulghur*, have become some of the foods I like the best now and make often for my family, who all love any of the Armenian foods.

Then I was in awe of the work it took to fill those heavy steel barrels with ashes from the burnt coal in the furnace and put them out with such muscular energy. My mother did this as well as helped shovel snow and cut the lawn with a heavy hand mower and dug out dandelions as if they were premonitions of evil. My father did heavy physical work at the Star Market and later at his own store, Huron Spa, so he wasn't always there when the things needed to be done and was very tired in the evening. I had great admiration for the steel muscle, iron will and sheer stubbornness of that generation.

"Home was always very much Armenian, and school was very much American."

"In what way was home Armenian?"

"Well, my parents spoke Armenian to each other and to us, except later my father more often spoke English to me."

"What else?"

"Some of the food was Armenian. I say some because my father liked American food also, especially roast beef or roast chicken."

"Did you observe many Armenian customs?"

"In our house we were not so formal about customs like serving Oriental coffee to every visitor or cooking a meal and taking it to the bereaved. I think my parents didn't know that much about customs either, having lost their Armenian families at the very young age of about nine or ten."

"When did you learn the customs you speak about?"

"On my honeymoon visiting my in-laws in Beirut. They were and still are very conscientious about those customs."

I was one of the next generation and feel that I was fortunate in being able to go through the public school system, which at that time was very good, and to use the public library as much as I did in order to sharpen my reading abilities. This reading ability led to attending classes at Harvard University, my hesitant beginnings at writing, and an eventual job as a journalist-editor. My sister attended Radcliffe College and did well, though she didn't follow through on her interest in writing or with success in her marriage, divorcing after 25 years. Her children Margo and Dana have been friendly with my children when in the Boston area.

Thus I believe that intelligent and objective meditation and reflection on past events in one's life add tranquility and acceptance of difficult circumstances that have been part of that life. Writing about the difficulties means almost reliving them and gaining new meaning from them. In other words, life is more than bread and yogurt.

Lucia Barooshian, seated,
with Helene

Margo Barooshian with her
father Martin

Bob Sarkissian with his cousin
Dana Barooshian (right)

Socializing Here and There

The Armenians were gathered into a close-knit community like other immigrant groups by mutual understanding and by customs and attitudes that differed from those of better-established Americans. The food was the same in all Armenian kitchens, adding a sort of unity to Armenian homes. The music at the picnics, which was the old country village music for dancing, was well appreciated. The music in the Armenian churches celebrated mass with the same liturgical chants and hymns called *sharagans* that were used in Armenian communities anywhere in the world. In spite of political or religious differences and conflicts, these elements along with the common language gave us all a sense of belonging to this group that had such an ancient and proud lineage.

The history of America was markedly different with its Revolution, its Civil War and subsequent adjustments and manufacturing aplomb, the American dream and the unfailing American optimism. The Armenians had an awareness of a long and noble history, of oppression and of great losses, but they were ready to learn optimism as they were surrounded by various people who were just as foreign to them as they were to Americans. Even neighborhoods that were stately and nice left the newcomers feeling alienated or accepted in a limited way.

Their children picked up this feeling of foreignness from their parents or even from remarks other children or teachers inevitably made. The common Armenian inferiority complex arosé from the fact that the parent generation had quite a struggle coming to America with nothing and not enough education to get good jobs, lacking the necessary language skills or clever ways of the dominant groups. Relatively few were able to follow education with which they could succeed in professions, making them more welcome to social groups. The philanthropists of course were welcome anywhere, for with the Armenian work ethic some

individuals overcame all obstacles, especially of Armenians arriving in America with nothing, to become multimillionaires.

People in schools and workplaces often seemed to look
down upon those who spoke the Armenian language or any
foreign language either at home or on the site, and teachers
sometimes wrote notes to parents asking them to speak English to
their children. My parents received such a note when my sister
began going to school. However, it was difficult for most of the
immigrants to speak English all the time since they didn't have
the fluency their children had and also felt like traitors not using
their native languages. It was usual for ethnic families to be bilingual, the children speaking English to the parents who spoke the
language they were accustomed to. The Armenians of that generation felt awkward and untrained except in their own milieu, a
feeling common in immigrants.

We took it for granted that social life, what little there was
in our family, would be with relatives or other Armenian families
we were acquaintance with. Most of them had children about our
age, so we always seemed to have companions when we visited
them. There were the cousins Leon and Joyce close by in the
Kachadorian family, Carol in the Makian family and Jack and
Harold in the Pilibosian family (my father's relatives) as well as
Marion and John in the Haboian family and the Mazadoorians in
New Britain, Connecticut (my mother's relatives). The Kapriel-
ians in New York City were also cousins on my mother's side,
Sara and Walter's mother Shushanig her first cousin. Sara even-
tually married Ralph Anoushian, then the wealthy Dadour
Dadourian when Ralph died. Walter owned an advertising firm.
We liked them all and saw them occasionally as time constraints
and my father's schedule permitted, though we saw more of the
Haboians, who lived in Watertown.

There was another older relative in Whitinsville, Massachusetts, called Youghaper Etoian with her husband Nishan. We
called her *Horkor*, which means father's sister, though she was
actually his first cousin. My grandfather brought her to America
as one of his daughters, both of whom presumably died during
the Genocide. Common practice during that time dictated that
survivors assume the identity of someone who had died in order
to be brought to the United States by a relative, still probably a

common practice among immigrants. The law forbade the practice, but it is too late to haggle over that now.

She had lost her first husband of a love marriage and two small children in the Armenian tragedy and had remarried in America. She was a sweet lady with a marvelous sense of humor and told some funny stories about her adventures in Armenian because she didn't know much English, which she never tried to learn as she never went out to work. Women without much education or use of the English language ran the household and took care of their families in

Youghaper and Nishan Etoian of Whitinsville, Massachusetts

the accepted pattern of their lives. She had had no more children in her long marriage to her kindly second husband. Now I marvel at the courage she had to continue her life happily.

We visited them in Whitinsville often through the years. Armenians being so deeply religions, it seemed appropriate that she and her husband lived on Church Street. Each time we visited, she would quickly go to the store and get the meat necessary to make *kheyma*, the raw meat dish that we liked so much.

"I remember her, Ma."

"You were quite young when you saw her."

"She was very nice and very friendly."

"Extremely nice and pleasant in spite of being of modest means and lacking education or skills."

"Can we go to Whitinsville?"

"Well, we don't know anyone there now. I suppose we could drive through it and visit the park called Purgatory."

"I'd like to."

"I'm surprised that she made such an impression on you."

How well I remember the dialect that came from the area of Kharpert province, a dialect she spoke so authentically. She hadn't learned the more cultured and correct Armenian, but she had spirit. I am not referring to alcoholic spirits here, though she did have a still in her house and used it to make *oghi*, the Armenian equivalent of whiskey for distribution to friends and close relatives. Of the older relatives I remember, only two others spoke that dialect — Haji Amoo Pilibosian (*Haji* refers to one who has made a pilgrimage to Jerusalem, and *Amoo* means uncle) and his wife Haigouhi.

But most of our socializing had to be in and around town due to the difficulties of travel. We had only one car, and that was usually busy. Few people had money then for more than one. In those days there were not as many drivers, for women were not aggressively employed, there were no malls to go to, shopping was accessible by public transportation, and the food stores delivered goods that were ordered.

Our Town, Our Ways

Watertown being historically democratic and humble, the many Armenians who settled there didn't expect anything else. As I would say in later years, "we all ate a piece of humble pie every day, and it kept us strong and healthy." That humility somehow inspired pride in surviving and in accomplishments, for the distinctions in town were more matters of ethnic differences than of class.

The lives of most of the Armenian immigrants denoted hard work and struggle either in factories or in small businesses with a few exceptions. Some of the offspring of the more humble resented being shackled to this humility, resenting it in themselves and in others, and studied hard with ambition to overcome it ormarry rich. But most found contentment in good jobs and happy family life.

In the general aura of the town, people also showed humility that the town had been founded in 1630 by a Puritan group headed by Sir Richard Saltonstall with Rev. George Phillips as one of the original American towns. Saltonstall was a member of the Massachusetts Bay Company, arriving on the *Arbella* with his five children and John Winthrop at Salem in 1629. He returned to England in 1631, still interested in the colonies, after having established the Saltonstall Plantation. From England he helped secure a grant for the settlement of Saybrook at the mouth of the Connecticut River.

Over its many years, Watertown contributed territory to Cambridge (Gerry's Landing), Weston, Waltham, Belmont and Lincoln from what was basically farm land. Its character changed over the years when the original English settlers were the majority and had adapted to the settlement of the Irish, Italian, Greek and Armenian immigrants living alongside some of the original families.

Some outstanding Americans had lived in the town. For instance, Hosmer Street, where I lived for the first five years of my life, was named after the Hosmer family headed by a physician whose daughter Harriet (1830-1908) became a famous sculptor. She had studied in Boston, then in Rome where she was part of a group of women artists, was often a guest of the Brownings in Italy and became the first woman of the 19th century to become a neo-classical sculptor. While living in Rome, she was friendly with Nathaniel Hawthorne, William Makepeace Thackeray, George Eliot and George Sand. Forty museums own her work, among which number *Beatrice Cenci* for the Mercantile Library of St Louis; *Zenobia, Queen of Palmyra, in Chains* in the Metropolitan Museum of Art, New York City; *A Sleeping Faun*; *A Waking Faun*; and a bronze statue of Thomas H. Benton for Lafayette Park, St Louis.

Subsequently, Carole Simmons Oles wrote a book of poems entitled *Waking Stone: Inventions on the Life of Harriet Hosmer*, published by the University of Arizona Press in 2006. The book is a compilation of poems about the life of Harriet Hosmer and her work, especially in Rome, and entails much research into books owned by the Schlesinger Library of Harvard University.

The poem "I Rededicate Watertown's Hosmer School to you, Hatty" mentions Harriet Hosmer's life in the town thus:

> Since you're the one whose children visit at the Met,
> the MFA, the Wadsworth Athenaeum, that church in
>   Rome —
> to name a few.
> Do you demur? Your father and cousin, those
>   good doctors of Watertown, deserved the honor?
> Sorry, I refused to be deterred. . . .
> Let them read old stories, conjure new ones for their age.
> And let them laugh. If someone tells them
> No you may not study that
> Let them rejoice to get expelled three times, like you.

Most likely the house she lived in on Hosmer Street, if she lived there, no longer exists. I didn't follow the story of Ms. Hosmer until much later, when I was looking for mystical connections with the past for lacking them with the present. My parents and sister didn't know about her, nor did they care to.

Relatives and friends we knew were always respectful, and my parents always tried to be helpful. For that generation that had seen so much suffering and trouble had a strain of generosity for others who also might be suffering the same circumstances and also a tremendous interest in continuing communications with relatives, realizing what a valuable commodity they possessed. America in that era didn't seem to have the aggressive individualism and disinterest in relatives that it now has.

My father made friends with everyone he met and could talk confidently with the educated and the less learned. My mother lacked confidence, had very little self esteem and made few friends except for the people my father befriended. For a while she associated with a couple of illiterate Armenian women, and she translated letters for one of them and sewed dresses for another. The latter, an obese woman, repulsed me with her overenthusiastic kisses forced upon me. These women had sons who were a few years older than I, and I sometimes went with my mother to visit the first of them.

When I was about 10 years old, one of the women's sons with whom I had had no conversation or friendship invited me into his bedroom to look at some pictures. I didn't know what to make of the pictures of naked women he was showing me and was frightened when he exposed himself and wanted me to pull down my panties. In the state of child-shock, I ran out of the room to my mother and cried. The women asked me what was wrong, but I couldn't explain for embarrassment and for fear that I would be called stupid or crazy or that the boy would say I was lying. I hadn't particularly liked him and didn't go to that house again, though I suspect my mother had matchmaking in mind.

It was the first time anything like that happened to me, except for some Irish-American friends gathering for a kissing party at their house about a year later. I hadn't suspected such behavior and found it crude and unbecoming, and much later I discovered that the boys-will-be-boys theory was a universal.

To put these incidents into the angle of the 1940s, no television existed for learning as children do these days, even in school, what kind of relationships can exist between a man and a woman. Even movies were conservative. My parents' relationship to each other was rather cold and lacked affection, at least in front of others, and there was no discussion of sex or any subject related to it at home or in the schools as if a deathly embarrassment existed in regard to the subject.

A general puritanical or laid-back mood about public displays of affection or sex even in the movies possessed Armenians. Male dominance was an accepted way of life in that generation in many similar groups. It explained such expectations as getting a glass of water for the father or bringing him his slippers every day. But judgments on this matter were not my specialty, and I am still rather reserved on this subject. However, the generation did what it was taught, and because it had been placed in another environment it wasn't likely to change much unless society in general affected this change in a dramatic way.

When we occasionally went to the movies as a family, my father would walk out of the movie theater if he saw a kissing scene. That was a strong message to young girls growing up, and it could be interpreted in various ways.

"We shouldn't laugh at them. They grew up that way."

"Parents and children have different values."

"I guess it's a generational thing, only more so."

"They have strong beliefs. Maybe that's good."

"I guess Americans are more open."

"But we are Americans of a different kind."

"More like Greeks or Italians maybe."

"In some ways, but always different from anyone else."

"If you look for differences you'll find them, but if you look for similarities you can find those also."

"There is always this feeling of the Armenian character except in school where we were only called Armenians but treated like Americans."

"That's the big question."

"What?"

"What are we? I suppose where we came from will answer that."

"And if it doesn't?"

"We'll just keep exploring meanings."

"The word is ethnic, and some people hate it."

"They may get used to it."

This sort of behavior from those who had seen the worst of what life has to offer and triumphed over it had interest in the values of hard work, dedication to the Armenian cause and to family. They instilled character along with some repression. I felt sad when my mother sometimes, after going to a crowded place, would want to be taken back immediately with a sudden attack of claustrophobia.

But we lived with a life that we considered a gift, though a difficult one. Perhaps it was that difficulty that made us work and study with great zeal to try to accomplish what our parents and ancestors couldn't because of limited resources and conditions.

My Penchant for Movies

I have loved movies and been part of their audience throughout my life, either in theaters or on television, and have found in them an outlet for my emotions by identification with some of the characters in the stories told. Dramatizations of history, such as "Dr. Zhivago," have often intrigued me and made it easier for me to absorb facts, which I never did in reading about places, times, wars, migrations, etc.

Since we lived across the street from the Coolidge Theater, which had movies just about every day, my sister and I would go there many times to see double features with Movietone News and cartoons between the features. The children's price was 10 cents which was then raised to 11 cents, but I was mystified at how that could become a bone of contention between us when she was required to pay the higher price. However, we always went to the movies together in childhood because I think we would have been afraid to go alone or wouldn't have been allowed to.

In those days there were many good movies with impressive actors and actresses and story lines that I could identify with. Among the female actresses I particularly liked Hedy Lamarr and Lana Turner, and among the male actors I always favored Cary Grant, Orson Welles and Marlon Brando. Others I consistently liked were Paul Newman, Tony Curtis, Fred Astaire, Gene Kelly, Cyd Charisse, Bette Davis, Katharine Hepburn and so many many more. For directors, I liked Alfred Hitchcock and his irresistible movies, all of which I have seen at least twice. I always had a great attraction for excellence in acting or in any other field and have been grateful for the rating system. Some people who embodied this excellence have become my role models and given me so much to live up to.

My fascination with movies didn't include the many dramatic war movies, for wishing that there would be no war or violence to haunt us. Those movies were like wolves howling at the door, and the entertaining movies were like graceful giraffes nibbling at the trees of a magic forest. I used to practice playing tennis against the huge brick wall of the theater that faced our house, so that it was a friendly place as many buildings in Watertown and in Boston were. We were used to seeing the brick walls of schools as well as of the buildings in Boston before the new high-rise buildings began to show in about 1960.

Musicals have entertained me, and interpretations of literary masterpieces have inspired me in movies and on television as well with "Masterpiece Theater" and its excellent acting and realistic settings. In my childhood and teen years, movies meant a great deal to me because they spelled out ways of behaving toward others and toward events, depicting values that were sometimes confused in my own family.

I used to identify so much with the heroine in the movie that when the film was over I had to look into the mirror to see if I resembled her in facial features at least. I was probably even influenced by the gestures of these stars and their methods of speech, of walking and even of looking at people, perhaps even of talking, for I never did develop a particularly Boston accent.

The "Lord of the Rings" cycle based on the novel by J. R. R. Tolkien is my most recent favorite, though it is about a war but not a real war to make me feel victimized or guilty. I believe that fantasy stories allow us to act out our emotions and thoughts at a distance and safe remove from the heavy cares that so often besiege our lives. The identification is more indirect and doesn't invite fears and aggression in any way but only lessons from its conflicts and resolutions of them.

"I loved all three movies with their sense of adventure and special-effects as well as excellent acting."

"But it's all fantasy."

"I like fantasy if the story is well made."

"There are some religious implications to fantasy."

"I can't see how there could be objections unless there is a preaching of hate or immorality."

"A marvelous story. I hadn't read the books because of lack of concentration."

"It all comes alive on the screen."

I could go on and on about movies, for they have been a constant in my life to coddle or reassure my moods or to offer me an escape for a short while and to give me hope of seeing other good movies in the future. Poor quality can be a turnoff, and I have tried to choose wisely but regret that at the present time the quality of movies has deteriorated, often leaving me and so many others frustrated with a certain lack in our viewing of films as well as with so much blatant violence and sex.

Television also is part of this need for drama and stories that gave me the opportunity to sympathize with certain characters or to dispel some of my darker emotions.

But I didn't watch television very much until the 1960s and later when with the onset of motherhood I found myself watching "Sesame Street" with my children and enjoying the experience. So began a new era of privileges for younger people when I was evidently reliving my childhood by enjoying some of the lighter experiences and learning available to them.

Now to go back to the past not to pull it out like a weed but to nourish the present. Actually, I revel in some of my past experiences because they point out the perspective and the wisdom that I have gained. It's a way to be young again, if only in reverie. I can actually and see myself roller skating on the sidewalk down Kimball Road and around the corner of Mt. Auburn Street. I can ignore the biting cold and slide down huge piles of snow in the winter until my hands and feet are numb. I can walk to grammar school, to junior high school, or take the streetcar to the high school. I can breathe clean air, free of the fear of crime or terrorists.

Early Influences

The Hagopian family headed by the mother Hranoush, Yenovk Der Hagopian's cousins with whom he was living on Templeton Parkway, were early friends. Yenovk used to sing Armenian songs, which left such a great impression upon me that I was even later attracted to those sounds. Though the music was totally foreign to the mainstream, it was also appreciated by critics of his recording of the songs of the 18th century Armenian troubadour Sayat Nova.

There were four sons in the family, Jirair, Hrair, Dirair, and Norair, who were teenagers at the time, and they had a cousin named Sadie, who lived on Dexter Avenue of Armenian fame. She was about our age, so my sister and I used to look forward to seeing her. She soon moved to California with her family, and I didn't see her again until many years later when my husband Hagop and I visited California and made a point of visiting her and her husband Don Tahmazian and her two children in Kingsburg, California, a suburb of Fresno. This friendly group showed us their orchard to learn how the trees were taken care of and to sample peaches and nectarines freshly picked from the tree.

I appreciated California with its constant warmth, wonderful flowers and fruits, magnificent scenery especially by the ocean, the Redwoods, Yosemite National Park and welcoming people. Later I wrote a few poems about California highlights, included in one of my own unpublished manuscripts called "A New Orchid Myth." One is about Fresno and orchards, another is about Hollywood and movie stars and others are about thoughts on some of its metropolitan areas.

Music in our house in those very early years resounded on a windup Victrola, which would too soon run out of energy and had to be rewound. The very thought of such antique objects got me interested in some collecting of books and letters, and in watching the television program "Antiques Roadshow." I wasn't thinking of antiques then but only of the stopping of the Victrola and winding it up again. The songs on these records were the old-fashioned melodious but sad Armenian songs, setting the mood which agreed with the mindset of my parents, their memories and their backgrounds but not with the mood of us children who were more accustomed to the sounds of American jazz, which my parents thought was crazy.

Was this conservative attitude of Armenians in families and in church the reason that I never took to the popular music of the day, to the wonderful songs sung by Frank Sinatra that were appreciated by other teenage girls to the point of screaming and swooning at his concerts? Was it the reason that I preferred listening to records made by Mario Lanza singing operatic arias? I was thus a square according to my training, wasn't popular, didn't know how to be popular, and cared more about books and classical music.

As the years went on and 33 rpm records led to better phonographs and the recordings included more up-to-date music such as that of Aram Khachaturian, I found Armenian music pleasant and fascinating as part of an identity I hadn't yet realized. The tragic Armenian opera *Anoush* by Armen Tigranian, full of beautiful and poignant arias, was one of my father's favorite recordings. This kind of listening set the foundation for my appreciation of classical music, along with the Bach "Air in G" that was played on a Sunday morning radio program. My lifelong interest in classical music was also influenced by the sounds of the Armenian liturgy when I was attending Sunday school.

Piano lessons followed these early activities, my sister and I often going together on the streetcar to Beech Street in Belmont, where my father's cousin Eliza Kachadorian taught us. She was originally from Troy, New York, and lived with her husband Bill, two children and her mother Flora Makian, who had been widowed early and with her mother-in-law had sewed shirts for the clothing business in Troy. We had taken some trips there by car, but all I can remember is being in a car looking out at a steep incline.

I was favorably disposed to Eliza's mother, who was my father's aunt and my grandmother's sister. My great-aunt had been taken out of the orphanage where she and her sister had been put by her mother, who had remarried and had a new family and thus couldn't take care of the two girls. Subsequently, my great-aunt was brought to America by an Armenian family and married to their son.

My grandmother had died at the age of 25 after the death marches of deported Armenians, so that I never saw her. She had been married after a ruse where she thought she would be marrying my grandfather Dickran's brother Movses but actually wed my grandfather. For they had gone to the orphanage together, but Movses asked for the girl's hand in marriage while my grandfather stayed in the back-ground. During the wedding she was wearing a heavy veil and didn't look up as was the custom. Afterwards, shock and disappointment descended upon her at seeing a man other than the one she had expected, probably because my grandfather had suffered a stroke which left him with a bit of trouble walking and talking. For that reason he did ordinary labor, not being able to do any more complicated work and sometimes had difficulty finding or keeping a job. She did, however, make the best of it and had five children. In the situation these people found themselves in with customs being what they were and with a dire shortage of females for marriage because they had been abducted by Turks and Kurds, women of that era didn't have much to say about the inevitable choices they had to make. Armenian men were all seeking Armenian wives, and there were not many Arme-nian women left to marry them.

Khachadoor's mother Yeghsa

One picture of my grandmother taken in 1906 survived, the only photograph ever taken of her. It was a sepiatone picture of her in a group with her mother, my father and his brother Pilibos as babies, and two children Sarkis and Tateos, who were her mother's stepchildren. My grandmother's image had been taken from it and put into a composite picture with her husband and son and hung in our dining room for many years, the subjects all wearing a serious look. Said to have been a beautiful woman with red hair and blue eyes, she was very plainly, even dressed, and her seriousness seemed more oppressive than that of the others. I used to stare at her image, trying to imagine what she would have been like, trying to feel her living presence and guessing what she would have been like if she had lived. My father had learned when he reached the orphanage in Syria that his mother had reached the city but died shortly after of the effects of starvation and abuse in the form of repeated rape and humiliations.

Of course, we younger people would inevitably make some American friends, who would be judged as Irish or Italian or Greek or Yankee, as the case might be. So there could be some disagreement and even clashes in the matter of dating, since dating for the Armenian group invariably meant likely marriage. The elders wanted their offspring to marry Armenians, and in the early decades from the 1930s through the 1970s many more Armenian-Armenian marriages flourished than at present.

We mingled in school and in the neighborhood, where we had street baseball games because there were so few automobiles driving around. As part of this group, the Murphys next door had a couple of girls our age, Martina and Dinny, out of five children; the Papazians, Louis on the team, lived a few houses up the street; two other Armenian girls, Doris and Florence Mutafian lived nearby; a couple of Irish boys lived up the street; and another Armenian boy joined from the next street, Irma Avenue.

Doris soon died as the result of an accident on the street where she was struck on the head by a hockey puck hit by the boy from Irma Avenue, and the baseball days were over. She had had surgery but developed an infection that couldn't be controlled, for antibiotics were hardly developed in the 1940s. I felt very sad at her funeral and wondered why my parents and sister didn't seem so sad at the death of someone who had been a friend. In this case being made of iron didn't make sense to me, for even that must melt sometimes. Unfortunately, in our family there was little communication of tender emotions, the hug and the kiss seeming nonexistent and sometimes the positive feelings also.

Music has always added a necessary third dimension to my life and been as companionable to me as reading books has been.

It has often dissolved bad mood and cares and brought me inexplicable joy, which was temporary but gave me a glimpse into what the future was going to bring me if I were only patient. Music was my piano lesson. Music, the sad and beautiful hymns of the Armenian service, played at the funeral of my friend Doris. Music, a kind of continuing communication I share with my husband, children and grandchildren. Music, my constant reassurance.

Arshile Gorky in Watertown

Arshile Gorky and Yenovk Der Hagopian were in the same generation as my parents, immigrants from historic Armenia. Yenovk, an amateur artist, gave my father a few of his paintings and in the ensuing years was to be noted for making a model of the historic Armenian city of Van, where he was born. One of these paintings was a still life of fruits that hung on the wall of our kitchen for many years, and another of these paintings was a stylized portrait of my father, who treasured these works of art because he had an enviably close and sincere friendship with the artist.

Yenovk was also a friend of Arshile Gorky, or Vosdanig Manoog Adoian, who subsequently went to New York, became one of America's most famous modern artists noted for his surrealist and abstract expressionist style. Gorky spent four years in Watertown, and they spent much time together drawing, painting and talking. Gorky, called Manoog by his Armenian friends and family, lived in the town from 1921 to 1925. He and Yenovk were both from the city of Van, where they had been boyhood friends and were survivors of the mass deportations and death marches of Armenians.

My father met Gorky at one point and was impressed by his strong personality and his intelligence as well as good English. Although I had no knowl-

1915
Deportation
Painting by Yenovk Der Hagopian

edge of Gorky at that time, I trace my later interest in him and his art to this early influence upon my father.

One of these people who knew of him and of his time in Watertown was the artist Richard Tashjian of the next generation. He told my father about a few of the incidents involving Gorky's Watertown period. My father wrote an Armenian article about these incidents in *Baikar* (Struggle) Armenian daily newspaper, which I rewrote into an English article published in *Ararat* quarterly and then in the book *They Called Me Mustafa: Memoir of an Immigrant* I co-wrote with my father and published from written and oral details he left as well as information in my memory and that of others.

Gorky sometimes set up his easel along the banks of the Charles River. One day a police officer asked him "Where did you come from?" It seemed to be a prejudiced remark, and Gorky replied, "I came from Heaven. Where did you come from?" The officer would have arrested him, but Gorky argued that he was a free man and could go anywhere and paint what he wanted. The officer walked away. That is not to say or imply that the town police were unfair or unkind, but simply that the era of suspicion against immigrants from any country could cause such comments.

He had given a small painting to his landlord, a simple man with no comprehension of art, who had used the painting to cover a hole in the cellar wall. The landlord's son was later dismayed to learn that the piece was worth $300,000 but had been thrown out. Gorky had been working at the Hood Rubber Co. and was fired after a short time of employment because he used to draw on the soles of shoes he was working on. He had tried to pay for a meal at an Armenian coffee house in Boston with a drawing, but the proprietor threw him out in mistrust. In his anger Gorky tore up the drawing.

He was an artist by temperament and personality before he was an artist by profession. Even in his childhood he had been encouraged by his mother to draw and make the most of his obvious talent, and he had the good luck to have a father who could support him while he went to school in Van and in Providence, Rhode Island, where he attended high school. He had obviously been out of his element among a few simple and unsophisticated Armenians in Watertown, who were not representative of Armenian culture as a whole where accomplishments in the visual arts as well as other arts thrived after the first period of migrations.

For in that first immigrant generation of Armenians, relatively few people were able to get a higher education they needed to be doctors and lawyers so that when necessary they could serve their Armenian contemporaries or make valuable contributions to America. In my town these included Dr. Hovhannes Zovickian, lawyer Dickran Boyajian and Professor Elisha Chrakian, who taught at

Arshile Gorky's *Abstraction with a Palette*, c. 1930

Northeastern University for many years and had been an editor of the newspaper I later edited, and his wife, a popular social worker.

Gorky had graduated from the Technical High School in Providence and the New School of Design in Boston, where he was later an assistant instructor. During this time he drew portraits of American presidents in the lobby of the old Majestic Theatre in Boston, painted a beach scene and also left paintings in historic Park Street Church.

After going to New York City, he did a tremendous amount of painting, which brought him recognition that increased after his tragic death. He committed suicide in 1948 after an operation for cancer, a broken painting arm, loss of valuable paintings in a fire and subsequent abandonment by his wife and children. One of the books written about him and his work is entitled *Arshile Gorky Adoian* and was written by his nephew Karlen Mooradian, who was born in Watertown in 1935 and became a professor of journalism at the University of Oklahoma.

This book has become a precious resource for me in providing information that I didn't have when I was growing up or as a young adult and only came to know much later through my involvement in writing, especially in writing about art to trace my father's life and friendships. There are many wonderful reproductions of art work in it and exhaustive facts about Gorky's life that include a description of the tragedies his mother endured before she finally died of starvation in his arms as the result of a death march supervised by Turkish soldiers. Previous to that, she had witnessed Turkish and Kurdish soldiers enter her house and kill her first husband by slitting his throat as she stood beside him.

I am intrigued to look at the book now and see the picture of Gorky at the age of 18 in my town at 86 Dexter Avenue — his sister Akabi's house — the area in the town where most of the Armenians lived in the 1920s to the 1950s, when many of them acquired some wealth and moved to the more affluent towns nearby. But Watertown remained the seat of Armenian character and also enterprise with three Armenian churches — St. James Apostolic Church, St. Stephen's Apostolic Church and Armenian Memorial Church (Congregational) — four newspapers — *The Armenian Mirror-Spectator* and *Armenian Weekly* in English and *Hairenik* and *Baikar* dailies in Armenian — as well as many businesses including those specializing in Armenian and Middle-Eastern food.

The book includes a number of quotations from Gorky's writings about his art. These require interpretation, which Professor Mooradian provides, writing the following:

> Since the artist must work from his reality to achieve universal truth as a primary source, then it becomes obligatory never to do otherwise, lest contemplative imitation results . . . dreams become synonymous with memory of lived events and impressions of real things. And hence his art contains realism in its very abstractness.

These explanations can be difficult for the uninitiated to understand. But the paintings that look out at us from their vantage point of such vivid color and expression speak for themselves.

Gorky wrote about his approach to art, often in Armenian as the language he felt most comfortable with. He was also outspoken and firm about his beliefs as in the following quotation:

> Some people say that art is eternal, that it never changes. Nonsense. Art does change. Man changes. Man changes the

world and in the process himself and his art. That is basic to my outlook. Curved lines define passion, and straight lines structure.

Now I look for a Gorky painting in every art book I come across in bookstores or in museums. In one of these called *The Art Book* published by Phaidon, there is his painting "The Waterfall," described thus:

> Vibrant colors evoke the serenity of bright sunlight and the sound of falling water. The beauty of the work lies in the artist's ability to express an almost spiritual peace through the images of forest and water.

He left a valuable legacy to Armenians, to Americans and to the rest of the world, a legacy of line and color that expresses multitudes of thoughts and emotions, however indirectly. His brilliance, dedication to the arts and of accomplishment from immigrant beginnings inspired many to worship and try to emulate his work. Many books have been written about him, analyzing his life and his work, all praising his tremendous gift to the world while lamenting the loss of such a talent, who exemplified the melding of Armenian royalty through his mother and the Armenian peasantry through his father.

David Marshall Lang describes Gorky's work with appropriate awe as follows in his book *The Armenians: A People in Exile*:

> Gorky's influence on young American artists was and is enormous. He is a great emancipator. He breaks through the rigid structuring of Cubism to a pure poetic imagery, with free-flowing space, constantly moving forms, improvisation and spontaneity. This explosive impetus came partly from his need to express what was Armenian in his own background, the emotional freedom and immemorial splendor of antiquity in the region of Van and of Ararat (the symbol of Armenia). The Armenian past saturated his consciousness, as if the links with his homeland had never been broken.

I was inspired to write a poem about Gorky's work, which was published in *Branches Quarterly* online along with one of Gorky's paintings called *Water of the Flowery Mill*, and later published the poem in my third book of poetry, *History's Twists: The Armenians*.

The first part of the poem reads thus:

ARSHILE GORKY'S LINES

The lines are doing a folk dance
with the flux of paint
divining a picnic,
sharing the tint
while red teems
with a paired delicacy.
A building for large hands,
a circle for detained fame,
a pencil without feint,
a brush that bristled New York,
a palette knife of careful scratch,
a measure of Armenia,
the orange pool of peace,
the height of a communicator,
swim of incalculable gift,
mind bending kind,
words aligning with vision,
abstract expression his session:
all of anguish in a single square.

I continued to write many poems incorporating the experience of art and artists and some about Armenian music, notably the music of Aram Khachaturian and of Alan Hovhaness. And I also tried to digest the coincidence that my son-in-law Gregory Hekimian's aunt-by-marriage is the daughter of one of Gorky's nieces, who also used to live in Watertown.

Suddenly a War

My father's cousin, Peter Makian (Eliza's brother), a buyer for the Star Market, had a television set in those early years before this new medium was widespread. On December 7, 1941, we happened to be visiting and saw an announcement that Pearl Harbor had been invaded and war declared on Japan. I was eight years old and didn't quite comprehend the meaning of this action except that it was very solemn.

"What does this mean?"

"More war."

"Where is Pearl Harbor?"

"Hawaii."

"Why did the Japanese attack American ships?"

"Something to do with their help to China."

"How long has the U.S. Navy been there?"

"For quite a while."

"Is there no end to all this war?"

"Some questions have no answers."

I was suddenly reeling from the effects of this confusing adult world, having hardly heard of the countries involved much less of their problems. A study of history in school hadn't begun or was limited to the American happenings. How was I to know that there had been a World War I, which ended in 1918 and resulted in the founding of the League of Nations? I had never heard my parents talk about these things or politics until after this invasion, or I should say never paid attention if they did. How would I have known about the rise of the Nazi party in Germany, of the rise of Hitler and the subsequent evils of domination, of the rise in the German military and the Nazi invasions of many European countries, finally France and England with an agenda to usurp many countries by force and cruelty, including the extermination of many millions of Jews, the mentally ill, the homosexuals, the infirm? Following the dictates of reason, the United

States and Britain declared war on Japan and after a few days Germany declared war on the United States and Britain.

Sometimes I listened to speeches of President Franklin Delano Roosevelt and President Harry Truman. I always liked to read famous quotes left by these strong presidents, especially by President Roosevelt. I can't say which are my favorites, but a few follow:

> Freedom to learn is the first necessity of guaranteeing that man himself shall be self-reliant enough to be free.
>
> They (who) seek to establish systems of government based on the regimentation of all human beings by a handful of individual rulers . . . call this a new order. It is not new and it is not order.
>
> Be sincere, be brief, be seated. (Advice to his son on how to make a speech.)
>
> There is a mysterious cycle in human events. To some generations much is given. Of other generations much is expected. This generation of Americans has a rendezvous with destiny.

After the death of President Roosevelt, President Truman ended the war with Japan by dropping atomic bombs on Hiroshima and Nagasaki, thus causing a controversy that has been with us ever since. But it did end the war, which had also ended in Europe, and began the period of the Cold War with the Soviet Union to last until 1991.

My father had a friend named Haroutiun Chapanian or Harry, another Armenian immigrant, who had been drafted and seemed glad to be going to the war. I vividly remember him being a dinner guest, where he was talking and smiling happily, talking about getting married before going overseas, and he did. Unfortunately, he was killed in Germany three days before the war was over. The irony and the heartbreak of situations like this affected me, so I was very glad when the war was over in 1945 and we were all able to breathe sighs of relief.

"After so many years we are in Germany."

"It's not the first time."

"The first time I have visited a cemetery for American soldiers. I was impressed that it was so large and well kept."

"I had always wanted to see it."

"I wondered when I was there if my father's friend Harry was buried in that large area. The thought gave me a strange feeling."

"Don't think too much."

There would be peace, but unfortunately it wouldn't last, though the United Nations was established in 1945 in San Francisco with headquarters now in New York City. With the world constantly struggling between good and evil or domination and submission, no peace would last. America has been involved in wars with Korea, Vietnam, Afghanistan and Iraq as well as other skirmishes and dangers. From the vantage point of the present day, the old wondering where it will end and will there be a period of relative tranquility of nations returned to me and naturally to many others. For who is immune to the daily news of what is going on around the world?

Back to the past, since the war wasn't in our country directly, we as children didn't seem obligated to think about the process and what it entailed. We concentrated on school and friendships. There were the casual friends at school I used to visit or walk home from school with — Queenie and Pearl and Joan and a few others whose names I have forgotten. I always thought the kids at school were the nicest with no exceptions that I can think of, but because I wasn't a talkative or a fun person and didn't know how to continue friendships, these relationships were very temporary. However, I would be overjoyed to see any one of them now and occasionally I do casually run into some of them. Others have passed away.

"What is Armenia now?"

"Trying to be a democracy after the collapse of the Soviet Union and its communist system in 1991."

"Is that where Grandma and Grandpa came from?"

"They came from the historic western Armenia, which is now part of Turkey."

"So there are or were two Armenias?"

"There is only one small Armenia now, the eastern part."

"What language do they speak?"

"They speak Eastern Armenian, which sounds quite different from our Western Armenian. Some of the words and usages are different too."

"It must be a difficult language, having an individual alphabet."

"It is if you don't know it."

"I'll have to study it some day."

"Read about the history and the customs. They're informative, and since you're an Armenian in your genetics and intention, they should be especially interesting to you."

"But Grandma, I have so much to do with work and school and study and going to church."

"I know, Honey. Just do the best you can."

"Will you be proud of me anyway?"

"I'll always be proud of my children and my grandchildren."

I didn't read news or editorials for a certain peace of mind with that attitude, but realistically speaking it couldn't last. One has to live in this world and be part of it, and that invariably entails rubbing up against political events, understanding them and being able to talk about them or to write about them intelligently. Then I realized that current events relate to history insofar as past events lay the groundwork for present politics.

"Where were you during the Korean War?"

"In school, I guess. When was it?"

"There was fighting from 1950 to 1953."

"I was just starting in college and not paying attention to current events because I had my own problems."

"You knew about the Cold War?"

"Yes. There were suspicions around."

"Well, the Korean War was brought about by the United States because of the Cold War with the Soviet Union. During the Civil War in Korea, the United States sided with South Korea, which was anti-communist, while the Soviet Union sided with North Korea, which was communist."

"So what happened?"

"Now there are two Koreas, South Korea and North Korea with those respective beliefs."

"I have met veterans from the Korean War."

"You've learned something. I never pretend to know about politics. I would like to learn more, but my mind doesn't absorb that sort of thing easily."

Accepting the world around you personally, socially and even politically is part of growing up. And I did grow up, going through the many stages of life to find its rewards and disappointments. The trick is never to give up on ambitions, even when tempted to.

Pageantry and Customs

The Armenian Church was also part of the picture, which to me was the usual life to be taken for granted, though I later realized that there should be a captivating study of a minor and rather unusual ethnic group comprising the patchwork quilt that was and is America. There have since been many. We girls went to Sunday School at St. James Armenian Church in Watertown and after Sunday School into the church, where I was impressed by the pageantry and the beauty of the music in the minor key. It was a constant reminder of the ancestry and the heredity which would always be part of my life.

My sister's feelings on the matter were not so positive but were more logical and unemotional to an extreme. I was more sensitive and emotional and concentrated on the perception of what was going on around me rather than casually chatting with people. However, we didn't participate in church activities, probably because our parents didn't go to church for their own reasons.

After Sunday School we young people would go across the street into the church sanctuary for part of the service and sit in the first few pews that were reserved for the students. In those years an elderly bishop named Hovsep Garabedian was the priest and sometimes got angry and shouted at the congregation for talking or whispering during the service. Being an old-country man, he understood these old-country people, understood that the simple people from rural areas would learn the rules only after being shouted at.

I watched everything that went on and listened closely, not understanding the symbolism or the ancient Armenian that was used in the service because it wasn't taught in Sunday School at the time, and I didn't make any effort to learn what didn't seem vital in my life. Yet I failed to realize that it was making a vivid impression upon my mentality and my emotions and that later when writing — not knowing then that I would ever be writing —

I often made references to the Armenian Church services and music as part of my root system.

Some years later with a more urbane Armenian community, the symbolism was taught and the liturgy was translated into English though ancient Armenian continued to be used in the church. But by that time I was so taken by raising a family and other obligations that I didn't spend time to learn them, and also I had gone along with my husband to the Armenian Protestant congregation at the Armenian Memorial Church in Watertown.

One day while walking home from school on Mt. Auburn Street I passed by the bishop who was walking in the opposite direction. He lived on Templeton Parkway in the rented room of Mrs. Hranoush Hagopian's apartment, the same apartment that Yenovk Der Hagopian had lived in previously. I must have said hello or nodded, and he acknowledged this with the blessing *"Abriss, Akhchiges"* meaning "May you live, my child." Neither he nor I could have known how prophetic his words would turn out to be. I appreciated the greeting that was made so sincerely and continued walking.

My father didn't go to church though he was a church member. I thought it was because he needed the rest after a week of very hard physical work. But in addition he had become cynical about religion, being a believer in the larger picture but not in the matter of rituals. He had thousands of books, magazines and newspapers and spent much time reading them and doing his own writing in Armenian, much of which was published in the Armenian newspapers.

He had his small office lined with bookcases overflowing with books, mostly in Armenian. Not being able to read or write Armenian, I felt alienated from his work and reading, which he had never tried to explain to me. My lack of knowledge was my own fault because I had rebelled against learning to read the language, another point of shame, from my mother, who didn't make a good teacher. When I was writing poetry later in the modern indirect style, my father admittedly didn't fathom it, his reading of English not that complex, and my mother wasn't much interested in any creative endeavor except cooking. So there was always this wall between us, this lack of comprehension each of the other and of being able to communicate with each other except on a surface level.

My father's writings concerned the sufferings of his generation, and he wrote many poems on or about his early experiences and its effects on him. But he never perceived how his suffering and his expressions of it could affect his children and others. Or perhaps he did and wanted others to read and relive these experiences with him in order to comprehend them. Those in his generation greatly appreciated what he wrote because they had been through similar experiences and couldn't express themselves well enough to write out what they were feeling. This was the burden of history and victimhood and couldn't be reversed.

His poems and stories were direct, simple and lacking in professional standards for the absence of formal education and his limited self-education. He wrote a number of poems for me, for my husband, for my children, for his aunt, for his mother, for his native village, though most of his poems were centered around the Armenian Genocide theme. My husband eventually translated some of them into English. They were sentimental in the old style and often heart-wrenching. He wrote of his mother thus:

> I have brought you, Mother,
> the flowers of my meditations.
> But where shall I place them, dear Mother,
> when the world denied you
> a handful of dirt to at least cover
> your noble being?

We know that many people in the world suffer as much and some perhaps even more, justice sadly lacking. But that doesn't make our suffering any less, and it only makes us want to ameliorate the bad situation that has left Armenians bereft in many ways. But what works best is success in individual lives, prayer and hope for a good future for Armenians as well as other people anywhere. And many Armenians and Armenian organizations have taken up this challenge and endeavor.

Later in life when poetic inspiration overtook my mentality, I found myself writing many poems about my father, my mother, my grandfather and my grandmother. Was this because of an influence from my father or the prevailing interest in searching out roots? A puzzling question.

"Why is it that in some ways we tend to do the things that our parents did but in the more modern setting?"

"Parents have a great influence on their children."

"Even when we consciously deny that influence?"

"Sometimes very definitely. But sometimes through effort we can get away from influences."

"Some people think that being engaged in the same activity as your parents is hereditary. Do you believe in that?"

"Human behavior is much too complicated to say definitely. You have to analyze each individual life to know."

"Not that I worry about it. I'm just fascinated by the subject."

I wrote about the Armenian-American conflicts I experienced and witnessed while growing up because the subject lent itself to analysis and even demanded self-understanding because parents couldn't relate to my world that seemed very different from the one they had known.

This is part of a poem from my book *History's Twists: The Armenians* that is indirectly about my father:

THE STOREKEEPER

Don't be afraid to say
that he was a dried psyche
in a too-quiet town
blowing along the pavement
of his lost ambition
like the autumn leaves.
He wasn't afraid
of the grammar of life
though some of it
was like a loose electric bulb.
He hardly ever wilted
like a pliant plant
and few wished he would.
His spirit has become
a fable for its tabled
quick walks and talks.

I don't usually include the first version of any of my poems, but in this case I will include part of the original poem to illustrate the changes my work has gone through. My own personal criticism of this poem was that it was too direct, too emotional, too old-fashioned in that it was about a relative, and too crammed with meaning to be easily read. In the more modern approach, a poet shouldn't write about relatives because this approach has been overdone. An abridged section of the older version of the poem, which I didn't use, follows:

FATHER

who taught her everything
by not teaching as she worked
at the well of existence;
Father
who came around to emergency
to see his failure
reflected in her plight;
Father
whose life was too thin
with the starvation of success
that impaired his periphery;
Father
who half knew women
by shading his sight
as if the sun were too bright;
Father
who with basic taste spread
jam upon her morning toast;
she found his fate her bait.

My mother's mentality differed in that she didn't go to church because she was uncomfortable in crowds and also had to do the Sunday cooking. This lack of attendance at church wasn't a lack of belief in God or in Christianity for me or for my mother, for God was often with me and I prayed whenever I felt the need for the reassurance and hope it could provide. My mother's belief stayed firmly with the Armenian Church along with the influence of the Protestant hymns that she had been taught in the orphanages, and she always wished to have weddings and funerals at the Armenian Apostolic Church.

"Why and where should you pray?"

"I pray in church every Sunday. That's enough."

"Neither of you can decide for me."

"Your mother doesn't go to church. Is she religious?"

"I've heard her sing a hymn she was taught at the orphanage and also quote a passage or two from the Bible."

"She sounds more like a Protestant than an Apostolic."

"She seemed to be fond of the Armenian Church and devoted to its history and its teachings. Because the Armenian Church and Armenian history are one identity."

"I guess she took the learning of ancestry seriously."

"In some ways."

"And your father?"

"My father questions meanings and beliefs because of turns his life took."

"Going to church might reassure him."

"I guess he doesn't take it that way. But he always kept his membership in the Armenian Church."

"Didn't you say his father was a Protestant?"

"Yes, but he didn't usually go by what his father taught him."

"I guess he wasn't so easy to understand."

"Not always. We have to accept parents as they are."

"We can't change them. I wonder if they can change us."

"Influence, maybe."

For a while the organist in the St. James Armenian Church was the classical composer Alan Hovhaness, a tall, thin and gaunt man with very large hands, who was half Armenian and half Scottish. During the collection in the service he would play one of his own compositions, sounding of modernism and mysticism at once, its lyricism and originality holding my attention, so that later when he achieved fame the music sounded quite familiar and brought back those early moments of Sunday School.

The Christening

The following incident will illustrate the dramas inherent in the practices of the Armenian Church and in the devout nature of some of its people and also some conflicts with the younger generation. We were visiting relatives in New Britain, Connecticut, Nigoghos and Yeghsa Mazadoorian and cousins Charlie and Harry. They showed concern about us, particularly the fact that we girls were 13 and 15 years old and had not been christened in the church. They and my parents arranged for us to be christened in their church, the Armenian Church of the Holy Resurrection, that weekend when Archbishop Tiran Nersoyan from the Armenian Cathedral in New York as head of the Eastern Diocese of the Armenian Church would be visiting. They were willing to be godparents with pride in this grand visit and this final victory in achieving permission for this christening.

Perhaps they felt that they owed my parents a debt of gratitude for having taken them in to live in their apartment for a while after they were first married and had no money. Or perhaps it was the call of kinship, for Nigoghos was my mother's first cousin and from the same village in the old country, and his wife was from another village but quite near theirs. They shared the same kind of upbringing and family background.

They were a very devout family as members of the Armenian Church, where Charlie was a deacon. Though I wasn't a regular churchgoer and not as devout as they were, I felt quite comfortable among them and in later years after an illness visited them for a couple of weeks on the friendship basis. I think his father wished that this relationship would work out in a different way, but it didn't. In the meantime, Harry was married and I didn't see much of him, but later when the rest of the family had died, he took over the family obligations and also showed much interest in my work. Both boys graduated from Yale University.

Back to the past, the archbishop was a conservative and famous theologian, concerned about the effectiveness of the ritual and the amount of water he would have to spill upon us, since immersion was out of the question for older people and used only for babies. Finally after some discussion, it was agreed that we would wear dresses and change them after the christening, expecting them to be quite soaked. It was appropriate for the parents and the godparents to make these decisions, considering our young age. At that time, my sister and I both felt the authority of the Armenian Church upon its flock, not yet understanding that historically it was the accepted way and that traditions continued as they had been. We would have wanted it otherwise.

At the christening, the archbishop asked both of us some questions about God and about the beliefs of the Armenian Church. Evidently because I was a bit taller than my sister, he thought I was the older one and should know the answers. I didn't know the answers, and my sister did. My father explained the situation to him at the picnic after church services while my sister and I chummed around with the cousins on my father's side. For Vartouhi Yessian, wife of Shavarsh, was my father's first cousin and had three children close to our age named Lucy, Mary and Roxie. My grandfather had brought Vartouhi to America as one of his daughters who had been either killed or kidnapped.

The entire situation that weekend was a lesson in Armenian behavior, in human behavior and in the conflicts inherent in the older and younger generations of the Armenian-American community. It was an unforgettable lesson, fraught with meanings that developed into ideas over the years, meanings that writers hunger for. There is an abundant grass of meaning spread over them like a warm blanket that you might say represents custom.

"If I hadn't been christened in the Armenian Church, would I be considered a Christian as part of a Christian community attending services?"

"Why do you ask?"

"I like to be philosophical."

"I suppose you would be an Armenian Christian by inheritance, but not a member of the Armenian Church."

"And if I take this Armenian Church christening to another church, like the Armenian Protestant church which I attend, am I still an Armenian Christian?"

"That may be a matter of whom you ask."

"I guess I should have this discussion with an expert in religion."

"Even they may not agree with each other."

"Religion is a touchy subject to discuss with someone."

"Every denomination seems to have its own ideas and its own ideals."

This christening was an example of traditional Armenian culture as opposed to the more American ways of free choice. Neither side really understood the other, their visions and values being so different. Yet, we had been minors, so should we have had a choice? However, mutual love of family values usually smoothed these differences over. Yes, there were conflicts in growing up bicultural, but we seemed to love our conflicts and cherish them even into adulthood, the writers expounding about them endlessly.

"My father was a farmer with old country inspiration."

"The old pictures were always there on the mantle."

"I didn't know about Armenian culture when I was growing up."

"The kids used to taunt us as foreigners."

"I wished they wouldn't wear those mustaches that looked so different, even though William Saroyan looked impressive with one."

"Their actions and their perceptions were different from those of the others who were established in the country."

Many immigrants seemed to be still living almost completely in the culture they came from, though the men usually adjusted better for spending so much time in the workplace. My mother was one of those who didn't adjust at all to America or to the modern world. It seemed she couldn't relate to people well enough to hold a job and approached all living in a paranoid way, though she did help my father in the store just by sometimes being there to deter possible holdups, of which there were two. But she did know English quite well from the Protestant missionary schools she had been in at the orphanages, though she was slow and careful speaking it; other women who were not in the workplace didn't learn English. Experience taught me that this is a tendency with all new immigrants except those who are fairly well educated, have a more broad-minded attitude or are forced by circumstances to learn.

She had been a trained nurse, but I realized this had been more training than education, for she lacked the broad world view and the reasoning that should go with it. Her isolation by constantly being home or with her peer Armenians and not with the working people in that wide world also kept her view narrower than my father's. He had spent his entire life in the employment world where he made friends and adjusted quite well but kept his Armenian personality.

Now as I look back with a more mature attitude, I see in this situation the meeting of two worlds, of two generations and of varying beliefs, so the conflict though not stated would be inevitable. It was the practice of what seemed like inflexible customs because the Armenian immigrants had a mindset that was impossible to change in their new and strange country and missed what had been so precious to them.

Camp Ararat

Our more familiar picnics were at Camp Ararat in Maynard, Massachusetts. The annual Kharpertsi picnic for people who came from the same area as my parents with their families would attract about 10,000 people with very many cars parked in a rough-shod parking lot. The difficulty was in providing *shish kebab* or *losh kebab* or *kheyma* and drinks for them all as the band happily played Armenian or Turkish tunes brought from the old country on the violin, the clarinet, and the *dumbeg* or Armenian drum. The picnic at Camp Ararat, where there were picnics every Sunday during the summer, gave us an opportunity to see relatives and friends who lived at a distance or continue conversations with people who were not usually around.

"It sure is a crowd."

"The *shish kebab* is ready."

"You kids collect the tonic bottles. And don't break them."

"Can you see who's dancing?"

"The band is resting for a few minutes."

"There are my relatives."

In the later years my father and others used to criticize the band for playing Turkish music or for using Turkish words rather than Armenian words, for there was a natural feeling of enmity due to historic associations. I was part of that criticism. However, the band and many of the people didn't seem to care. Still, years after the picnics were over or were restricted to church yards, I felt nostalgia at hearing some of these tunes, though I still held to my principles that at least the Turkish language should not be used at Armenian picnics or celebrations.

I took these picnics for granted, but now that their time has passed, I miss the sights, sounds and smells of the grounds and the excitement they engendered. I'm sure many people share my sentiments. Since most of the older generation had been orphaned and had endured the same difficulties, they behaved toward one another more like brothers and sisters than friends, so that there was an indefinable feeling of extended family in that crowd. The era was bound to end.

As time progressed toward the 70s and 80s and onward, the world around us became more impersonal and people, especially women, became busier with their careers than they had been. Family life was not to be the same again. That wonderful camp with such a unique atmosphere has now disappeared, and many modern buildings used as condos stand proudly there on the same land where we used to walk around in a sort of hypnosis with the sounds of the music and the buzz of conversations and the aroma of the meat cooking on the grill. The people who live in those condos are unaware of any picnics and Armenian culture that once went on at that site.

High School and Onward

My high school years passed by pleasantly in the college course curriculum after a couple of years of being in the secretarial course by choice at the East Junior High. I had some excellent teachers there: Mr. Adams for geometry, Mr. McCurdy for biology, and Miss Appel for English in the public school system that had garnered praise and respect. There were regular morning exercises in all homerooms before classes began — a short reading from the Bible, which was usually done by one of the students by turns, and then a salute to the flag when the salute read "one nation indivisible" rather than "one nation under God."

Having a healthy liking for school and for studying, my marks were good enough for acceptance into the National Honor Society and the Cum Laude Society. The class consisted of about 300 students. But I was left to wonder why my parents and my sister weren't quite thrilled but only compared my accomplishment to my sister's as valedictorian of her class.

Being shy and introverted, I was liked but not part of a group. Throughout my life I had quite a few acquaintances and a few casual friends, but no deep and lasting friendships. I was really embarrassed to ask friends to come to my house and converse or to go somewhere, for I felt I couldn't be myself there because of the stress of outspoken criticisms I had been subjected to. My mother always considered me rather incapable of either taking care of myself or doing housework, though she had to believe in my schoolwork because it was good. The attitude somehow transferred to the others, and it seemed that they didn't really believe in me.

Actually I lacked an adequate identity as an Armenian or as an American, perhaps even as a person. My Armenian name was Hasmig, and the teachers couldn't pronounce it quite right so it became Hosmig. Among my relatives I was comfortable with my Armenian name because it fit the circumstances, but in school it was too different and reminded me constantly of the conflict of the two cultures I was caught between. Sometimes the students teased, though the teachers were always quite respectful and showed liking except for Miss Libby in seventh grade. That year I had long periods of nausea and loss of appetite, and I was often absent though I was able to make up the work. But she showed no sympathy, and my mother had to intercede and fortunately defended me. I passed into the next grade and usually did quite well in school.

My physician had said these spells of nausea and vomiting with some weakness were brought on by nerves. However, the medicine given to calm nervous stomach didn't help much, and eventually I had my appendix taken out though there was no emergency. The surgery at Mount Auburn Hospital was my first admission there, and I was awake and unafraid during the procedure with spinal injection, though I did cry because of the pain when in a room. Better after that, I had a later vomiting spell and another doctor gave me an injection of B vitamins, which immediately stopped the problem.

Then soon I freed myself from the limited help I got from my mother for my tendency to constipation. She usually had given me a teaspoon of mineral oil and often mother-administered enemas, perhaps a carryover from the village, the orphanage or early nurse's training. I knew instinctively that this wasn't genteel and later found the more helpful bran cereals. But who was I to demand genteel anyway?

My name didn't in itself cause my complex but was simply a symbol of it. Conflicts of values and of expectations assailed me with a very strict mentality as opposed to the free individualism of the American world I wanted to be part of, or realistically speaking, had to be a part of. I worried that if I should have a date with a boy, I wouldn't be able to face the situation of introducing him to my family. He might not be acceptable to them, for I witnessed that situation when my sister had a non-Armenian date and my father wouldn't speak to him when he arrived at the house.

Worry about the name was taken care of easily enough after a few years when I added the American name Helene to the Armenian name Hasmig. That was also a symbolic gesture designed to make me feel less self-conscious and more part of the wider world of going to school and working. It gave me that kind of freedom for a while but also led to confusion of the two names after I was wed, for then I had a foot in each world by using Hasmig for Armenians and Helene for Americans or Armenian-Americans. Some thought it was Helen and even tried to teach me the correct pronunciation of my name according to the French or the Greek pronunciation.

Many features redeemed my everyday existence like going to school or to the library, like walking along the peaceful streets, like going to differing stores, like listening to the radio to find out what the Green Hornet was doing or how Superman was flying through the air and apprehending criminals. I relished the approach of every September when I could go shopping for saddle shoes and white Bobby sox that I would be wearing all the school year along with blouses and plaid skirts made of wool, not a uniform but the kind of clothing generally worn by the girls.

I didn't like talking about politics or reading about it then, though the others in my family seemed always to be talking about such subjects. It all sounded to me like so much arguing and disagreement. Later I realized the use of it and also the disappointments of it but never became fully a political person or even a history person. I liked my history dramatized as in movies, relating its facts like a story with real or imagined characters.

Meanwhile in high school, in addition to studying I spent my spare time reading literary novels like Dostoyevsky's *The Brothers Karamazov* and made lists of words I didn't know, after which I looked up these words in the dictionary and wrote down the definitions, typed them all and memorized the lists. What may have been work and drudgery for some people was fun for me, and my favorite project in English class had been memorizing 350 lines of poetry in order to get an A. My favorite project in biology class had been the writing of a research paper on the subject of dinosaurs and drawing a few pictures of them on the paper. My favorite and perhaps only hobby was reading books which stirred my mind and imagination. I wrote a couple of poems on simple subjects that were published in the high school publication and did adequately well in math but had to work hard at it with only the feeling of necessity, eventually glad that I did the studying.

"What was that poem about?"

"Which poem?"

"The one you said was in the high school publication."

"What does it matter?"

"It could show what your interests are."

"It was about my small garden."

"You said some of your ancestors were farmers?"

"Yes, on my mother's side. So what?"

"What did you plant?"

"Flowers."

"You love flowers?"

"I guess everybody does."

"You love the soil?"

"I found a certain satisfaction in working with it."

"You love your parents?"

"Yes, but I guess I took them too much for granted until later when I realized how much they had been through and how much they sacrificed and worked for their children to be allowed to have the best possible life."

"There's your garden."

"Where?"

"In your mentality and in your ancestry."

"Isn't it natural for many people to love the soil?"

"Yes, and many people have ancestors who worked with the soil."

"You mean my liking to work with the soil is an influence from my ancestors."

"It's a kind of conditioning of mentality over the centuries."

"You give me a great deal to ponder."

For seniors we had Freak Day on April 1, a day of fun when I pretended to be Little Red Riding Hood and made a sign that read, "Who's afraid of the big bad wolf?" I also had a small red cape, and a smiling picture survives from that day. The quote though, in retrospect, does seem to indicate that there was something to be afraid of. It was something that was within me — the moods, the fears, regardless of who or what helped cause them.

I liked my fellow students and most of my teachers and developed a crush on one boy in 10th grade and on another in 11th and 12th grades but never had an outside-of-school relationship with them. But it did make school very pleasant to be in, and I looked forward to being there every day. The era being

Freak Day, Watertown High School, April 1, 1951
Helene at the far right

the 1940s, we began the day with the 23rd Psalm or other Bible reading, then saluted the flag. There was never any complaint about that, and throughout the years I often invoked the 23rd Psalm from the Old Testament in my mind, hoping that the prophecies of it were working or might work if I wished hard enough.

Sadly, I missed my high school proms because no one asked me, and once someone refused me. Any way you look at it, it was a matter of lack of self-confidence, which compounded itself. As my father once said, "She's a little bit shy, but she'll be all right." Yet, missing the high school prom did leave a void, which some-how wanted to be filled as necessary for social self-confidence.

"Was it really necessary?"

"It was a matter of self esteem."

"But you did alright without it."

"I really began to hate myself."

"Why?"

"Because I couldn't do what the others did. I couldn't make social connections as they did. A person needs that."

"So you had a vengeance against yourself?"

During my last two years, I worked part-time as a page at the East Branch Library on Mt. Auburn Street, checking out books and sometimes repairing them in that small, cozy building. I loved working there, being surrounded by books, which I would dip into and swim in the words when no one was watching. The friendly librarian Miss Harney taught me my job as well as supervised me. Mrs. Elfick, a charming woman, was the librarian for the children's room down a winding staircase to the noise of the children. Sometimes I worked upstairs and sometimes downstairs, liking both atmospheres.

In that era, checking out books was done with a stamp attached to a pencil. One would stamp the date, and the other would write the number of the library card on the card in the front page of the book for identification purposes, then file it. Of course, there were no computers then, and no one could visualize computerization. I often took a few minutes while working to peruse the books that were returned in order to get an idea what they were about and which ones were most desirable to read. When I found a book that really impressed me, I checked it out.

Elissa and Edith were my friends in high school, but they were more friends with each other than with me. The classes with their challenges and the atmosphere of just being young kept me going, and I wasn't likely to get involved in groups or athletics. Now I very much wish I had gotten involved, if I had been able to, even with people in the church where continuing relationships would have been more likely. But my life was apart and I was apart from the crowd and from the family, not knowing why or how and not knowing what another life would be like.

I was disappointed the job had to end at my graduation in 1951, for being only a high school part-time job. Then we moved into a two-family house on Poplar Street as owners of a house for the first time. It had its own gratifications without any threat of possible evictions, though we had had none of that. That summer I went to downtown Boston to a job typing letters in the office of a furniture store, where I also got training on an early telephone switchboard.

"Did you like that job?"

"It was boring, typing the same letter over and over again for a full day week after week. But it was only for a short while."

"It kept you busy."

"It was full time, and it was the first job I had in Boston or any place not in my town or in my father's store."

"Did you like working full time?"

"Yes, because it kept me busy. Otherwise it would have been a very long summer. In those days I could easily work full-time hours, but in the later years after I had more responsibilities and after I had been through illnesses, I could manage only part-time hours."

"Did that bother you?"

"No, I loved working part-time hours because I was very comfortable with that arrangement. I was lucky I was allowed that in some jobs."

"So there was good luck and bad luck in anything you did."

"For the most part, yes."

Huron Spa and Poplar Street

Huron Spa, the convenience store my father had bought in 1946 with money his aunt gladly lent him after he left the Star Market, provided some part-time hours for me and did well, giving us the dignity of being owners of the business. In my early teen years I used to take the bus to Huron Avenue in Cambridge near Harvard Square on Sunday mornings so I could be there for the after-church rush to help my father with so many customers. A pleasant neighborhood on the street that was parallel to the magnificent and wealthy Brattle Street, which still wears history on its shoulders from Colonial days when it was called Tory Row, Huron Avenue was more modest and average in scope but teeming with fascinating life.

My father had bought a car to facilitate going two miles to the store and returning for lunch before continuing to work until late evening. Automobiles were scarce at the time, so he bought a used 1936 Pontiac, a big black car, which he nicknamed Bozo with his on-and-off sense of humor.

The experience of owning a store was a pleasant one, except for people who were out to make trouble. He put to good use what he had learned of the grocery business at Star Market and often put milk and cigarettes on sale to attract customers who would buy more than that. He bought the store from Frank Boghosian, with whom he worked for a short while. Frank was doing $650 worth of business a week, enough to support one family, and within a few months my father raised the income to $1000 a week and then

Khachadoor's aunt Flora Makian

$1200. Later it was $1600 a week, and he offered to buy Frank's share. Frank retired, and my father took my uncle to be his partner in the store. Though his approach to business and to people was rather different, Mesrob was a diligent and dependable worker and a partner for the 22 years they owned the store.

They worked 16 hours a day, sometimes alternating hours, seven days a week at Archie's, the name coined by the customers. My father put more light into the store and bought electric cases for display of frozen vegetables and meat, ice cream and tonic. He remembered what he had learned, "Let the customers see the goods." They made sure the goods were fresh and attractive and well displayed and kept quite a lot of milk because it brought customers into the store to buy other items. They dealt exclusively with Hood Milk Company for milk and ice cream, and by selling many cold cuts, ice cream and popsicles for the children and with a full candy case, they soon tripled the business.

Rationing of sugar and butter started during World War II continued. He went to the wholesale markets in Boston at four o'clock in the mornings to stand in line and get those items with a coupon book to be ready to open the store at six o'clock. Sometimes a vendor would bring those items into the store, my father insisting that they must sell them so as not to disappoint the customers.

Shortly after he had opened the store, Steve Mugar dropped in one day to congratulate him. "I knew you had it in you. I heard all about it. You're doing a good business here." My father was happy about that. A few years later in 1953, the Star Market on Mt. Auburn Street in Cambridge, right over the Watertown line, opened. The company had bought the building that had housed The Big Bear, a large department store, and moved into the large store located about a mile from Huron Spa.

By contrast to all this tumult in the business world, I stood off in the corner trying to do my conscientious best and have some good memories of the store. There I learned to use the old clunker of a cash register and give change accurately in addition to seeing how a business is run efficiently and with the required speed. I also learned that the customer is always right for the sake of the business and that one must accommodate various needs and personalities. I wasn't bored there, though the work wasn't suitable for me. There was much to see of customers and business transactions and just the variety of items being sold, and I felt warm and safe being there and working with my father.

As a young adult going to college, I also worked in the store part-time selling penny candy and waiting on some customers and cherished the malted milk balls that sweetened my hours. The cats that were part of the store and the kittens that I fed milk with a doll's little bottle are unforgettable. There was the large gray cat named Chi-chi, who had some interesting antics such as getting drunk on the smell of spearmint chewing gum and clawing or licking the cardboard box which had held the packs of gum.

I also witnessed many difficulties such as emergencies at night when my father was called because his store was on fire and also the result of a couple of holdups, in one of which he had been beaten on the head. The other holdup was at the point of a gun. My uncle had suggested to my father in Armenian that it wasn't real and that he could forcibly take it away from the man. My father warned him not try.

Neither will I forget a story he told me the day after he had gone together into a department store to get something that we needed, for no cute story ever went untold. When we were in the store, my father saw one of his acquaintances and greeted him briefly. The next day the man came into his store and asked him, "Who was that chick you were with?" I had never thought of myself as a chick and found the implication quite amusing, because though he liked to talk to women, he would never go around with a chick, the implication being a morally loose young woman. He wasn't that type.

For the 22 years that he owned the store, he never had a vacation and was barely able to take a few days off if he became ill, which he rarely was, from the difficult but proud work which was more profitable than he or my uncle had hoped for during their trying years of working for other groceries. They both did their best not to get sick and fortunately enjoyed good health. My father developed soreness in his legs from so much standing and walking, so they both decided to retire, my uncle soon developing serious health problems.

It had been important to own the store rather than simply work in one, for the pride of ownership was a matter of class distinctions, and we all had some reminders of differences in financial and social strata. Nevertheless, attitudes of being lower in rank to those who were wealthier or more educated persisted and still do, distinctions remaining as always in human nature. Some people had extraordinary luck or with effort and business sense could surmount the obstacles that were usual to immigrants.

Toward Professionalism

I was tremendously gratified by my studies, and an examination I took in high school showed that my scientific interest was very high and my literary interest was less. But life showed me another direction that propelled me to decisions that would provide appropriate fruitions. My interest in literature, writing and journalism was budding and eventually outshone my scientific interest, though I always read in some areas of science meant for the layperson.

We went shopping for clothes and shoes at Filene's, Jordan's, Conrad's, Woolworth's in Harvard Square and in Watertown Square or other small stores that were convenient for us. Soon my sister and I got to know the Museum of Fine Arts in Boston and the Peabody Museum in Harvard Square, visiting the glass flowers at the latter. This probably influenced my lifelong interest in art and museums, but my true fascination began with the art courses I took at Harvard.

After I was 16, I would go shopping at Touraine's in Harvard Square in Cambridge for some lovely dresses. By that time I didn't hesitate to go by myself on the streetcar that ran on tracks to Harvard Square or even to Boston by changing and taking the MBTA train to Park Street. Once when I was in high school and I had gone shopping at Jordan Marsh in Boston, I returned to find my wallet missing. I thought I had probably left it on the counter somewhere, but perhaps my naive pocket had been picked for a $40 loss and a difficult lesson learned. Now Jordan Marsh and Filene's have evaporated into history and Macy's has taken their places.

From then on, I was fascinated by the aura of Harvard Square and was destined to attend evening classes for a number of years at Harvard Extension School, part of the Division of Continuing Education, after I had attended the Katharine Gibbs School in Boston for secretaries and had worked as a secretary at the National Research Corporation for a year in 1952-1953.

Secretarial work wasn't at all fulfilling for the mentality I definitely had, and the inability to make close friends as well as the family conflicts of the years crowded in on me. I began to have difficulty relating to people and talking to them, especially men, whom I would approach trembling with fear.

I had chosen the secretarial field and won a scholarship for $150, because I lacked ambition to go to college though my marks in school were very good. Ranked sixth in a class of 300 students at graduation, I just missed the top five, but I was glad because it would have meant making a speech, and I was terrified of public speaking. Neither my parents nor my sister had ever discussed the possibilities of work experience for me or attendance at a college, and I had been afraid to initiate such a discussion. The new mentality of women striking out on their own and aggressively getting their education and even demanding careers lacked full focus and hadn't yet reached me. And the symbolic title Ms. had not yet been invented.

"Do you believe in destiny?"

"My life seems to work out that way."

"Maybe you can change that."

"How?"

"By trying to be your own person and making your own decisions."

"That's not as easy as it sounds."

"It takes a lot of trying."

"And some luck."

"Do you make your own luck or do other people make it for you?"

"I'll have to think about that."

My sister had won that advantage because she verbally fought for it, my mother thinking that a college education was wasted on a woman, though she had had that opportunity through the orphanage in Lebanon. My father was reluctant to spend the money but relented because my sister won a partial scholarship and worked for the rest of the tuition, which was then $600 per year for commuters. I suppose I was intimidated by these attitudes and also the prevailing thought at the time that a college education wasn't absolutely necessary to pursue a career.

Miss Parker, my guidance counselor in high school, had told me that intellectually I could do anything I wanted to do and had suggested the Harvard Extension School as a good possibility for one who felt she couldn't afford the high costs. This program of study sponsored by the Lowell Institute offered courses given by professors from Harvard or other colleges in late afternoon or evening for $5 a course.

"It's a good program, and I hope you will consider it. School doesn't have to end when you get a job."

"She was a nice woman and cared to think of my ability."

"Many of the other kids went on to college."

"But you went to Gibbs."

"It was only for one year and strictly secretarial."

"How did you feel about it?"

"I felt let down because I was in a group I felt I didn't belong to."

At work as a secretary while I was taking the first two of my many courses in the evening, I typed technical reports without any interest in them. My boss, Mr. Vaughn, was usually busy with the process of making frozen Minute Maid orange juice but did buy me a new electric typewriter to make my work easier. Some of the other secretaries in the company resented my acquisition and also the fact of my having lunch with a black employee because she demonstrated more friendliness to me than they did. A lesson in the outside world of employment and employees.

Sometime during that year I had to have my tonsils out because the infection in my throat kept recurring and giving me a fever, penicillin only a temporary help. My appointment with Waltham Hospital fell on a Sunday afternoon, and somehow my father and I arrived there slightly late, so that the hospital denied me as a patient. Then Dr. Pericles Canzanelli, my primary care physician, arranged with Dr. Gettes, a surgeon, to take out my tonsils at home under local anesthesia.

During that surgery I sat in a chair in the bedroom, and after a couple of injections into my throat the surgeon proceeded to clip out my tonsils and part of my uvula. I won't say it was completely painless, and I won't say it wasn't frightening, but I bore up very well, the only difficulty being that there could possibly have been a hemorrhage that no one could treat there. However, not knowing about this possibility, I wasn't afraid.

"Grandma, tell me about the time you had your tonsils out."

"Well, I was just sitting in the chair. I didn't know what it would be like."

"I'd be terrified."

"I didn't know what to expect."

"Weren't you shocked by the operation?"

"I suppose that in my silent way I was. I cried after the doctors had left."

"That's quite a story. You should write about it."

"Maybe I will someday."

At the company Christmas party I had an alcoholic drink to give me the courage to face the group, but having never been versed in drink philosophy, I didn't stop with one and ended up having about six, after which I kept falling on the floor. I had never drunk alcohol until that point, had never had any warnings about it and lacked awareness of what it could do in making one's mind completely fuzzy and nerves completely unreal. Someone drove me home then, not realizing that my emotions had been running on low.

When I went back to work, I found myself being teased and took it as ridicule, mortified by the incident. I spoke to the sympathetic personnel director but couldn't face the others and left the job without telling my boss, for I didn't know the right thing to do or to be able to do it. I was sinking emotionally and there didn't seem to be much I or the people around me could do to help or didn't try to help and either taunted or misanalyzed.

"Are you sure you want to leave?"

"I can't stay here anymore."

"Do you panic? Are you depressed?"

"I guess so."

"Why don't you talk to your clergyman?"

"I can't talk to him or my parents."

"Your family doctor perhaps."

"I mentioned that I was nervous."

"I guess he didn't understand."

"No one does."

"I understand that you are suffering."

"I still don't feel well."

It was time to start another chapter of my life, not realizing what it would entail and where it would take me. Certain unusual events turned me around, in the long run for good and for the joy of living.

As a young girl of that era, my primary goal was to find a good husband and perhaps get some sort of education. It didn't have to be much, and I never aspired to be wealthy nor have I ever been. Fortunately, I have always been provided for by a hard-working father and a hard-working husband as well as my part-time jobs. But I have always had a sense of incompletion, of not accomplishing enough, by not having worked years at a full-time job that was fulfilling.

The Difficult Years

Depression set in and gradually worsened without my family being aware of its problems. In the meantime, my sister had graduated from Radcliffe College with honors, but our lives and our attitudes went in different directions. I soon left with a severe claustrophobia and temporarily stayed with my aunt and uncle until I moved on.

Alienation and loneliness even when with people took over my personality, and I accepted the harsh reality that something had to be done. I reached out for help that was offered to me, first by my aunt who invited me to stay with her and my uncle and cousins at least temporarily. Then someone at work recommended a psychotherapist. I desperately reached out for that help, completely uninformed about mental illness or people who were treating it. I had no idea about differences in treatment or even what I was suffering from, and neither did my parents or relatives.

I hesitate to write much about the next three or four years during the time of psychotherapy with Dr. Goodhue Livingston, and my behavior gradually got more and more out of my control. I was briefly a student at Boston University and stayed in a dormitory. The teachers were good, and an English teacher was quite sympathetic after I had panicked at an attempt to read a paper in front of the class. It pains me to remember all that happened during this time, though I have had to in order to make sense of some people's attitudes towards me and to clarify the story to myself and others who have wondered about me and my past. Only someone who has been through a similar experience can really understand the why and wherefore of it. People who work with this sort of illness and study all the ramifications are or should be the exception.

Later I realized my great mistake in accepting therapy for that condition from a psychologist. He couldn't prescribe medication, even though I was in severe emotional pain. I still think about the advice I didn't really understand at the time. For when talking about and facing for the first time all the negative emotions I had been repressing, I found it was just too much for me without medication or more extreme care. I tried to justify this situation by telling myself that perhaps he didn't realize how serious my condition was. But then, perhaps he did.

The sessions had begun with me lying on a couch and not being able to see him. Since I appeared to be so terrified, he allowed me to talk to him sitting up. I had felt that he was considerate, and he had always spoken to me with great patience and kindness. I was doing much writing and he had greatly encouraged me with it.

"He said I had to learn how to hate."

"What did he mean by that?"

"I don't know, and later I figured that I had to learn how to get angry so that I could defend myself even verbally. I always used to cringe within myself, not being able to feel any fury, not able to verbalize any feeling of disagreement or anger."

"Why was that?"

"I didn't know. It seems I grew up with fear."

"Memories of hearing fights and many disagreements. Memories of seeing physical attacks. I hated conflict of any kind."

"Your fear doesn't seem as serious as some I've heard about."

"But scary nonetheless."

"Especially for a child."

What I saw of other patients in the state hospital in Mattapan, where all of the very serious cases were together on common ground, gave me the shock of my life. Dr. Livingston took me there one day when I couldn't face the outside world anymore, falling on the floor and refusing to get up until the police came because he had called them and told them I was suicidal. My two weeks in that hospital turned out to be kind of shock therapy, though I felt that I didn't belong there. The other patients were obviously very serious cases, most of whom were completely out of touch with reality and either walking around dazed or strangely dressed or saying strange things like "the Nazis have been resurrected" or trying to beat each other. They were all roaming in one hallway, and someone came into my room to stare at me while I was sleeping.

I found one girl who had recovered from a nervous breakdown and was to be released soon, so I was able to talk to her. After some testing like a Rorschach test but no treatment, I was discharged because I promised my therapist I would try hard to get along in that painful world from which I was estranged. Since I had been a voluntary patient, there was to be no record of admission.

At that time I had been working part-time as a bus girl in a Viennese restaurant called the Window Shop located on Brattle Street near the Brattle Theatre in Harvard Square. It was originally established by the wife of Professor Howard Mumford Jones of Harvard University to give employment to Jews who had been brought from Germany to America during World War II, and it was a thriving business. It is now the Blacksmith House, named after the blacksmith shop from Cambridge history. They served some high-quality food there like *wiener schnitzel* and *sauerbraten* as well as the Viennese coffee with whipped cream. My employment lasted only three months, for I accidentally broke two coffee pots in the dining room and sprained my wrist carrying the heavy dishes. I was awarded $150 for that and used it toward my expenses.

I lived on Pemberton Street in North Cambridge for a while until for some reason I had to terminate that and moved to Scott Street near Kirkland Street in Harvard Square. These were rooms rented to students or working people by families or individuals, sometimes with kitchen privileges and sometimes not. I don't remember the amount of the rent, but it may have been about $10 or $20 a week, which is certainly not expensive by today's standards. My memory is hazy about the motivation for these moves, and subsequently there was another move to Irving Street. They could all be traced to simply illness and claustrophobia.

Some people I knew were amused by these unexplained moves.

"My organization can't keep up with your different addresses."

"I called in to give the new addresses."

"We like to keep our list up to date, but . . . why do you move around so much?"

"I don't know."

"What does that mean, a smart girl like you doesn't know?"

"I'll try to keep you up to date. Goodbye."

In that state of desperation, I tried to socialize even though I was terrified to go into a crowd of people. Being quite attractive, I soon found someone who was interested in dating me, a foreign graduate student at Harvard Law School. We had both frequented the International Student Center on Garden Street nearby, where I met him. He later became an ambassador to the United Nations.

I deny trying to climb the social ladder with my bottom-of-the-barrel mentality because I didn't know who he was or where he was headed but only that he was friendly and nice to me. We went to a nightclub called The Cave somewhere in Boston, where we had a couple of drinks and talked. I can't imagine what we talked about, but we did talk in a cordial manner. Another time he took me to Harkness Commons, the restaurant at the law school, for lunch. I found it a pleasant place, and I enjoyed his company.

I was 20 years old at the time and very naive about involvements with men. My parents had never told me much about situations that could arise and be so complicated as to be insoluble. My therapist didn't tell me much in detail, nor did he warn me that this could have negative effects and what they would be.

My new relationship was the only real friendship I had at that time, though my behavior wasn't exemplary and his wasn't understanding after the first bout of sympathy. I kept calling him, wanting to be with him as long as he was willing to be sympathetic, not out of a physical attraction but rather out of a desperate emotional pain, like an alcoholic needing a drink. But that stopped when at his suggestion I went out with someone he knew and had suggested for dating after making it clear that our relationship would not lead to marriage. I found I could not cope with this situation or with any dating situation, and my consciousness began to dim considerably. My unsuccessful attempts at sociability only left me feeling more isolated and alone.

How can I possibly duplicate the conversations I had with him when I hardly remember much of what I told him?

"Dr. Livingston is my therapist, and we've talked about everything in my life. I was briefly hospitalized. I feel so alone and lost."

He once took my picture in front of Widener Library, and I was smiling. So I must have gained some comfort from this relationship, at least at the beginning.

"I think I have a split personality."

"Your personality isn't split. It's shattered."

Despite his friendliness, he could be quite blunt.

This all happened shortly after Dr. Livingston had left town suddenly under duress. Since I had depended on him for any analysis of my condition, I was stunned and felt my brain turning around backwards in my head. He had been sympathetic and had explained reasons for my misery, so that I didn't know what to do.

I had no answers to the questions then of how I would face my parents if they knew that I had a boyfriend who was a Muslim, hardly different for them than a Turk. I couldn't visualize that situation until later when I realized the need to be silent about those things.

"I didn't like him when I met him."

"He didn't like you either."

"Do the parents and therapists ever get along?"

"I suppose when matters are serious, there is stress."

"Shouldn't therapist know how to handle this?"

Self-hatred. Paranoid darkness everywhere. I knew nothing anymore. I didn't return to my friend's company out of fear and even worse confusion. The rest was a jumble and a nightmare.

With the different values of a moderate Islam, he thus became a personal disaster for me with my Armenian-American upbringing, which was completely different from his background. Fragmented memory. Lack of controls or caring or understanding, as if in a strange dream where there are no feelings and the world has become a dark place.

The other side of the matter was the cultural difference between Middle Eastern Muslims and Americans, in this case especially on the question of women. The famous American freedom meant something different to some of the foreign students or even to some Americans in the matter of dating young women, resulting in irresponsibility on the part of the men and often naïveté on the part of the young women who didn't know how to act with a man on a date.

For Muslims in their own countries there was no dating. There was only prostitution on one side and young women who were introduced by families as suitable for marriage on the other, the latter expected to be virgins. Any young woman from a good family or a wife who was suspected of being friendly, even moderately friendly and in some conversation with a man without the husband present, could meet with severe consequences. The most extreme of these consequences would be death at the hands of the family or stoning of women even suspected of dishonorable behavior. The latter kinds of punishment most often belong to extremists such as those in the Taliban that we have recently heard about.

Women were not yet part of the student body at Harvard except in the evening division, the summer school or certain graduate schools. Yet students in Cambridge were more adventurous than the people of Watertown. I have no idea how many were desperately ill as I was and had lost the sense of what was right or wrong. In other words, the meaning of right as opposed to wrong or good as opposed to bad didn't register in my mind as part of a certain emotional blindness caused by the illness.

I surmised even then that I would be lucky to find anyone who understood the illness. Of course, psychiatrists did understand mental and emotional problems but not in the more accurate way they do now with alternate treatments directly in touch with cognition rather than severe remarks or treatments.

Dating behavior was thus often quite problematic. Colleges also were likely to expel women students who were inclined to flirt with professors, at least if there were evidence of this in her collegial behavior. I was so naive I didn't even realize they had these rules and that certain things that I was writing for classes, such as writing classes, put me under some suspicion.

"You said you have a therapist?"

"I do."

"Do you discuss these matters with him?"

"Of course. That's what therapy is for."

"He wasn't very effective, was he?"

"I don't know."

"Over the years, have you thought over the situation with that therapist?"

"Very much in trying to make sense of it all."

"Did everything make sense finally?"

"Yes, after talking to many doctors and finding the most of them didn't try to pursue the matter either because of lack of knowledge or caring."

What's Right, What's Wrong

From that time to the time I was taken to a psychiatrist — a step suggested to my father by Dr. Livingston's partner Dr. Sigmund Gruber — I must have done and said some outlandish things as I descended into a numb world where I seemed to be someone else whom I didn't know. After seeing the Harvard psychiatrist Dr. Graham Blaine to whom I was sent to after my erratic behavior toward a professor, all awareness seemed to leave me. I have no memory of what I said to him or any of the things I did in regard to the professor except that I was making unnecessary phone calls, but it must have offended him greatly because he shouted at me to get out. As the dimness became worse, I stayed in the room I had rented without going out.

My father found me that way on one of his routine visits, and I vaguely remember him driving me to the office of a psychiatrist who was recommended by Dr. Canzanelli. Fortunately, he had been forced to be that much aware of what I was going through, though he knew that there was such a thing as nervous breakdown. All hurt feelings aside, I was fortunate that these people at Harvard had made it necessary for me to get appropriate help. I didn't blame the university for my illness, which existed and became worse. If I hadn't had more help, the situation would have been dire indeed.

It took me a long time to face the fact that the psychotherapist had led me to doing some things that were not suitable for my condition. Perhaps it was because my condition became worse after he left in such abrupt circumstances and I simply couldn't face the conflict of realizing those two years had been all wrong by my own choosing and cooperation. Ignorance indeed. My parents hadn't realized the seriousness of my problems until I left home, though my mother in anger had once said, "You had a nervous breakdown long ago." I suppose my father was at work so much and had been so busy that he didn't pay attention, though he knew my mother was often prone to verbal abuse, and my sister followed that type of behavior. There are always excuses for whatever we do or don't do.

Lacking adequate explanation, some people overreacted with interpretations that were not told to me because it was assumed I knew. But I thought they knew what I had been through and could fathom my plight. To be fair I would have to say that the people I was dealing with in school were conservative and didn't know much about Armenians and the similarities or differences in values. It was a time of a strict moral code when permissiveness was just slightly taking hold, often resulting in a perplexity of ideals.

"It ended in another hospitalization."

"Only for two weeks. After the shock treatments, I felt like my old self but very insecure and with quite an amnesia."

"Did anyone understand how you felt?"

"No, and no one asked me."

"Not a psychiatrist either?"

"No, and he didn't think much of the amnesia, hinting the reasons for it were emotional rather than caused by the shock treatments."

"I had to find my own answers on what had happened and why and where I was going. I felt safe only if I followed orders and did what I was told. I stayed with my parents again, and even with their lack of perception of what I had been through, I felt safe. That sick behavior was the very antithesis of poetry or of any kind of art, which demands mental and emotional focus and complete attention with good judgment."

"You didn't feel that the trouble could happen again?"

"I didn't feel that I could do those things again. It was really a split in personality. I was confused by it all."

There were a few other questionable situations with regard to the psychology department at Harvard University while I was a student there. I had been cautioned by my psychiatrist after electric shock therapy not to take psychology courses, probably because the subject matter might upset me or perhaps because there had already been an incident in a psychology course that had brought me to his office. It was in regard to Prof. Roger Brown's interpretation of the confused values of prose manuscript I had showed him while taking his course Psychology of Speech and Communication. I was judged guilty of some unacceptable and unexplained behavior, and I was forbidden to see him. I guess he thought I understood what he meant by this action.

Only recently, many mental blocks later and after his death and the death of a couple of the others who reacted with some panic, have I been exonerated from the "misunderstanding." I can only guess that either he thought I was pursuing him for sexual reasons, which would be strange behavior because he was gay, or that my writing about the mental institution I had been in was misread and considered "crossing the line" into the exclusivity of his subject matter. Or was it a rumor that I must have had an affair with Dr. Livingston or that I made up the bit about the hospital? I wouldn't have cared except that the accusation was spread around, and I often seemed to be under the same suspicion long after it happened and was thus denied opportunities. But now it makes more sense because I can think about it all with clarity, and I have forgiven the past and also myself. I expect the people I deal with to do as much.

The shock therapy was about 80 percent effective, for me the difference between night and day or unconsciousness and consciousness of behavior. I rested for a few months before I went back to school. The advice was to face it. Yet with an amnesia of at least a year of my experience, and with difficulty communicating and as much difficulty in facing the fact that I had been totally not myself for awhile, I had the burden of trying to figure it all out in my own mind, which no one could read.

With sudden shame and mortification, I had destroyed the manuscript that initiated some worry. I wanted to reorient others who had observed my behavior and the marked changes in it without knowing why, but I didn't know how. Unfortunately, I hadn't realized then that some people at the university would have been willing to defend me from serious accusations which carried over into my later life. But not really knowing what happened or why, what would I say to anyone?

"I threw the manuscript into the fire and watched it burn."

"Did it all burn?"

"Yes."

"Do you remember what it said or how many pages it was?"

"I can only guess it must have been around 50 pages. It never reached publication though I did send it out once. I did submit it to my writing class with novelist John Hawkes at the time."

"What did he have to say about it?"

"He had written comments that I should continue to write about the Armenian family. The mark I got might have been a C."

"Was there any other subject in it?"

"Yes. There was something about my therapy with Dr. Livingston and also a long section about some of the things that happened in the state hospital."

"Did he comment on that?"

"No."

"How did you take that?"

"That he wasn't enthusiastic about the subject or about what I did with the subject. Because I had said it was written in the style of stream of consciousness, he disagreed and wrote in his comments that the style I was trying to imitate consisted of one long unbroken sentence or a number of them and not the short choppy sentences that I had used."

"Did you agree with that?"

"I really had no choice. He was the teacher and I was a student."

"But if you had been asked, would you have disagreed?"

"I suppose I would have said writing in short sentences is the way my particular consciousness ran on as representing my thoughts. Are there different ways to represent this process? I mean, does my stream of consciousness have to be the same as someone else's, say of James Joyce whose work we had studied for its stream of consciousness effects?"

"I don't know that much about literature."

"Do you know free association?"

"Saying the first thing that comes to mind."

"Well, stream of consciousness is similar in that it's the constant stream of thoughts coming into recognition without being thought over or done over in the rush of words you put down on paper."

"That's good to know, especially in reading literature or even in the psychoanalytic process."

"That's how it came about, I guess."

"I don't know if I could read your work and give you an opinion."

"I wish you could. I trust your opinion. I wish more people would be interested in this sort of thing so that we could have some literary discussion outside of courses."

"What did you do with the manuscript?"

"Facing this situation of waking up and finding that I had done some things that were considered hostile or strange was too much for me. I found the manuscript then, and also found that I was terrified to read it, to find out what that period of my life was about. You understand that it was very painful. So I threw it into the fire in the fireplace."

"Why did you burn the manuscript?"

"After the shock treatments I was suddenly aware that there were frightening meanings in what I had been writing. Maybe it wasn't so bad, but I was terribly mortified and not able to think about it or talk about it then. Nobody encouraged me to, and my psychiatrist let the matter ride. So in burning the manuscript, I thought I could destroy that part of my life as if it never existed, and I expected that it would work, that other people would also forget that certain things had happened and not be suspicious of any of my subsequent behavior. I didn't acknowledge anything that happened during the time or talk about it or defend myself. I do wish now that someone in school had summoned me in a kindly and understanding way and asked me to explain, though I might not have been able to."

"The psychiatrist didn't encourage you to talk about the pain of it?"

"Not at all. Maybe he didn't know about it. But I thought he must have known."

When I went back to school, a couple of people I had been friendly with approached me, but I looked at them as if they were strangers. I just didn't remember them. And for a short while, I was stammering quite a bit while speaking. A couple years later I did remember Donald Marston, the assistant in my American literature course, because I had been so fascinated by him.

The subject matter of psychology didn't upset me because I took a few courses on the topic. The tendency of the professors to experiment or humiliate, thinking they were helping, did.

Knowing of my interest, my psychiatrist had recommended that I see this professor, Dr. George Goethals, to ask about possible graduate study. I made an appointment, and managed to talk to him in my confused way. Later when I was in class minding my own business, this same professor while looking at me uttered a number of innuendos, then glared at me and said, "Get out if you don't like it." I'm not even sure what he meant by what I didn't like because I did like the subject matter of the course but found the innuendos embarrassing. I had no interest in his attitude and status, and I actually thought he was trying to humiliate me. The others in the class were wondering what was going on.

"Weren't you embarrassed?"

"I didn't have much of a feeling or reaction because I was taking tranquilizers, and the shock treatments for my condition had castrated me of certain emotions. Or maybe I didn't have them anyway."

"Could you feel happy?"

"I didn't feel any strong emotions. Sometimes I thought I was half dead."

"But you were able to study well and enjoy the courses."

"Yes, that was all I had to enjoy then. I continued to meet men but lacked conversational ability and maybe even seemed boring. Maybe they thought I didn't show any interest, and when they took me back to Watertown after an evening and saw that I was living with my parents, they seemed discouraged to pursue the matter."

"In other words, they weren't serious about marriage."

"They weren't even serious about friendship."

"Did you meet some men you liked?"

"Liked in a very platonic way. As I say, I felt castrated, physically and psychologically. This applies also to creative writing, and I didn't want to do any, had no motivation and no dream, no inspiration. But I did write papers in school very well and wrote all the exams without hesitation. They were all essay exams and fortunately they were only and one and a half hours. In the summers the exams lasted three hours, and I had more trouble there with such lengthy concentration."

"Are you saying that you put love and creative inspiration in the same category?"

"Now I know they seem to relate to each other. I didn't know it or much of anything at the time except what I learned in school and that I wanted to continue learning until I got to that degree. It was my third try, having failed twice before when I was ill. That seemed to make me more determined."

I stayed and finished the term, learning about the Navajo ways of life and writing an ethnography about them, which I used as a model for an article in this book, the brief ethnography of village Armenians. Then I never took another psychology course though I was fascinated by the subject.

From his class I had learned that one has to be psychologically naked to love, though I think his personal vision was something else, and that psychiatrists were often working in the dark for lack of experience with patients and knowledge about them. Fortunately, there have been tremendous changes in the fields of psychology and psychiatry since.

"I met many young men, but only one developed into a relationship. When I mentioned to one brief acquaintance that I was writing poetry, he declared that I was one of those crazy people."

"Was he a student?"

"Yes, I think a graduate student, probably at Harvard because this was in Harvard Square even though others also congregated at the International Student Center."

"Did you see him again?"

"No, and I didn't want to."

"What did others say?"

"Some were considerate and gentlemanly. Others were not. Most of them were students."

"Were they all foreign students?"

"Mostly."

"Did you like any of them?"

"Some in a casual way. But they were the ones who didn't come back."

"Did you get called names?"

"Sometimes, though not often. One guy called me Marilyn Monroe in a teasing or taunting way. He wanted to kiss me, but I pushed him off."

"You didn't like him?"

"At first I liked him, but after he called me that, I was offended and decided I didn't like him. He wasn't from Harvard but from another school of theology. I don't remember where."

"Why were you offended to be called Marilyn Monroe? She was very beautiful."

"She was a sex symbol and beautiful for that. I wasn't in any way trying to be like her. Besides, I never had the significant cleavage she had and never tried to flaunt my sexuality. If I were like her, it would only be in basic insecurity. I think I did right in some instances, except for making social mistakes, but there were so many considerations. Damn all these differences, though they can be wonderful as well as troublesome."

Youth and beauty can be a dangerous combination; brain-work triumphs in the end. Why should I not admit it? I was 25 years old, 120 pounds with dark hair and large innocent looking brown eyes. Subsequently I did my own readings in the subject of psychology and learned a great deal about how men and women react to each other and which behaviors are good and which are a bad, not necessarily in the sense of morality but in the sense of happiness and good health. I always accepted the fact that morality, if not too strict for the circumstances, was a good thing.

Some of my remembrances, the few which are negative, are not meant to be a condemnation of the University, for I have felt and still feel it has been a great, interesting and continuing part of my life. They are only a revelation of some of the unfortunate things that happened there. Obviously these things wouldn't have affected me so much if I had been a healthier and happier person with a great deal of moral support behind me.

These being evening courses, students tended to drop out toward the end of the courses if they felt they were not interested or they didn't need that particular study. Except for the time I was ill, I never dropped out of the courses I was taking, for the pursuit of a degree meant so much to me that I would have declared "live or die, I'll get that degree."

I realized all that deserved praise and began to revel in the intellect that I had worked for. I realized that without this experience of disciplining my mind, I would have been quite a different person and certainly not a writer. Most likely I would have married, had children and perhaps done some office work.

Why was that not enough for me? Having been trained for answers, I have no answer except that fate was somehow working on my side in and around experiences of the next few years.

The negative experiences were pulling me one way and the positive experiences were pulling me another way until I could reach a final equilibrium. Actually, I was pleased with my courses and professors who seemed to respect my presence, but when I was depressed I couldn't really enjoy any of my studies, but I continued with them as much as I could.

It took a few years and much effort to bring about a final resolution to these difficulties. Now in a high-flying euphoric mode, I can look back and relive with enjoyment what I didn't enjoy then. I can throw the misconceptions away and begin the adventure again with gratitude for the privilege of having been able to attend this university.

"Were you ever afraid that this nervous condition would descend upon you again?"

"In those early years, yes. I was most afraid of that in my last couple of years as a student and in my first couple of years of marriage."

"Did you have any depression after you were married?"

"In earlier years I did have some slight depression and once in a while a dip into a bad negative mood that lasted only a couple of days. But as I described in an upcoming chapter, I got over those tendencies at about the time I turn 50 and was better able to cope with life's vagaries."

It takes time for painful memories to fade away gradually, but they do when one is dedicated to achieving the positive in life in a process that's not quite like magic.

American Literature

I would go to Harvard Square by bus and ascend to the street from the substation. Crossing the street, I would enter at the Harvard Yard through one of the entrances of the iron gate that seemed to have something serious to say. Walking through the yard, I could hear Bach concerti spilling from the open windows. My previous life paled before such an atmosphere.

In those days male students wore suits and ties to classes, and women either at Radcliffe or at the evening school wore dresses and skirts and blouses with stockings and dressy shoes. The cafeteria style Bickford's, located near the entrance to the station next to the Cambridge Savings Bank, achieved popularity with a plain type of hamburger for $.25. Nearby across the street stood the five and dime store Woolworth's for the small refinements. Next to it stood Bailey's, which served excellent ice cream Sundays with chocolate sauce dribbling over the cup. Across the street the Wursthaus served the best pastrami sandwiches. The Harvard Coop for books, stationery and clothing occupied the opposite corner of that large intersection.

My favorite of all the courses I took at Harvard was American Literature from 1890 to 1920 taught by Howard Mumford Jones, who was head of the American Academy of Arts and Sciences for 20 years and won a Pulitzer Prize in 1965 for general non-fiction with an analysis of the state of American literature in the book *O Strange New World*. His erudition was remarkable, and he had even

Prof. Howard Mumford Jones

learned Italian so that he could read the poetry of Dante in the original language. One of his favorite poems was "The Raven" by Edgar Allan Poe, and one of his favorite novels was *Uncle Tom's Cabin* by Harriet Beecher Stowe.

Not realizing a mutual interest, I had written a short report of that book on cards that we were expected to hand in after reading some of the books on the reading list. I didn't know then that the professor and his assistant were judging me as a person and as a potential writer by my reports on those cards and that I needn't have felt embarrassed at having characterized the style of Henry James as "stuffy and dull" because I had been asked for my opinion.

The names of some of these books indicated the depths of their subject matter: *Fantastics and Other Fancies* by Lafcadio Hearn, *Through Nature to God* by John Fiske, *The Tragic Muse* by Henry James — "The author is unmistakably an Englishman. He is witty and clever. His language and style are impeccable and aristocratic." — *Ethan Frome* by Edith Wharton, *The Call of the Wild* by Jack London — "Who else except in children's stories has written a book from a dog's point of view?" — *Up from Slavery* by Booker T. Washington, *A Lost Lady* by Willa Cather, *Pragmatism* by William James, *A Masque of Mercy* by Robert Frost, *The People, Yes* by Carl Sandburg. With these and the lectures, no wonder I was suddenly in a different world.

Though some of the cards are in the form of notes and not completely written out, the following on the book *Fantastics and Other Fancies* by Lafcadio Hearn shows the form of my completed small review:

> These weird little stories are beautiful and poetic with themes of love and death that recur in various forms. I particularly like the psychologically interesting aspects of the Fantastics as reflections of an unusual mind and personality. Phantoms of an elusive love, gravestones in the moonlight, storms — these in "The Name on the Stone" weave the spell of a nightmare with a sort of horrible beauty. The Fantastics remind me of German expressionist painting or even surrealism in the fantasies of the subconscious. I can almost hear modern music (Stravinsky, etc.) when I read these stories. In "Hereditary Memories," however, I completely disagree

with his idea that impressions made upon the father will be transmitted through the brain of the child, unless he meant impression through discussion rather than physiological impression. But on the whole, Hearn fascinates me.

Having written a few poems at the time, some of which were published in a newspaper, I wrote to Mr. Jones asking his opinion of the poem that I sent to him. It would embarrass me too much to reproduce that poem here, for it was a rhyming poem based on 19th-century style. The idea of sending out letters to literary people for comment came from Dr. Livingston to teach me aggression and to get me some connections in the field. I received encouraging remarks from some people, but the letter I received from Mr. Jones almost immediately was my first lesson in the importance of style and of self-discipline in this field. It is dated April 2, 1955, and is reproduced below.

Dear Miss Pilibosian:

There are fashions in all the arts, including poetry, and whatever one thinks of these fashions, they condition the tastes and beliefs of readers and editors. I fear your poetic mode is not sufficiently modern for the times. Your vocabulary is, so to speak, an inheritance from the later 19th century, and your poetic mode comes largely from that period. You are trying, I think, to paint watercolors after the manner of the Boston Art Club at a period when the fierce and satiric energy of somebody like Jack Levine dominates taste. For that reason, except as a private diversion, which is in itself not a bad thing, I think you had better face the fact that the kind of poetry you send me, whatever its excellences in itself, is — how shall I say it? — too old-fashioned for 1955.

I took the criticism quite seriously and really tried to improve my style, not submitting any more poems to him frankly because I was afraid to. Wondering what the Boston Art Club was and who Jack Levine was, I bowed my head in concentration and continued the course with reading the novels from the lists and reporting on them. My reports were evidently getting a perusal because they were quite individualistic. It may have been a good thing because I did get an A in the course.

Then I read a few books of poetry, one on the imagists, another by Robert Frost and *The People, Yes* by Carl Sandburg. The review of the last follows, showing how I could get carried away:

> Original, different, interesting. Sandburg, instead of gentle rhyming word-strokes, uses slashing, slangy-tangy strokes. It is good reading and complete explosion of the old poetic forms. Where will it lead? Where are we going on our fascinating flights? We are flying about trying to hold to one place — the United States — the people, yes. Sandburg's socialism shows to remarkably good advantage. He writes for the people in their daily or nightly languages. He amuses them with his clever epigrams. He carves stairs in a wall of stone so they can clamber up or down instead of slipping, sliding, or falling. It is a solid, roughly gentle poetry.

The review of *Some Imagist Poets, 1917* reads thus:

> I was very much impressed with Amy Lowell's contribution to this anthology. It is a Japanese or Chinese poetry and like these has a distinctive appeal. It is wise and profound, pretty and wonderful. It seems to combine these opposites into a wholesome sweetness, the same sort of flavor of some Japanese personalities I have known.
>
> The rest of the poetry was quite good. Being interested in writing poetry myself, I have recently acquired a hunger for poetry anthologies. It is a wonderful, satisfying, hobby. I think that sort of expression of one's personality should be valued and encouraged, and the more one likes to write poetry, the more one likes to read it. Then a deep appreciation for art, writing, and different personalities develops, an attitude necessary in a healthy society.

And the review of *A Masque of Mercy* by Robert Frost reads thus:

> Great, deep, clever. Subtle meanings, plays on words, Biblical and political references make it explosive reading with pregnant meaning. For example, "the curse of modern lenience was the discovery of fire insurance from which the modern state is springing." So original and completely modern, this poetry captures the 20th century mind-flavor. The 18th century seems pretty but flat.

I reproduce the text of another card on *The Red Badge of Courage* by Stephen Crane because it is appropriate to read during wartime, since it deals with the psychological experience of a soldier in war.

> This is an excellent novel. The psychological penetration into the mind of Henry Fleming in his first battle experience is true greatness of fiction writing. He begins to feel battle a monster; he cannot escape from the "iron laws of tradition;" he tries to read the answer to the Question in dead eyes; he feels guilty about not being wounded; he steals the "quiver of war desire;" he wants to run and fighting in anger and confusion, emerges a hero. This is the eternal philosophy of any young soldier.
>
> Crane does an excellent job of capturing the speech, the personalities, and the feelings of these soldiers without any false descriptions. I felt almost a spectator while reading his descriptions of battle, wounds and death and found myself in tears. A book that can move one's emotions so is truly great. I also like his phrases such as war, the "blood-swollen God," which suggest a poetic imagery and add more depth and appeal.

And why not read about *The Sea Wolf* by Jack London?

> London creates the almost unbelievable character of Wolf Larsen through the observation of Humphry van Weyden. Larsen's barbaric ruthlessness, his materialist philosophy of the "eternity of pigishness, and "might is right," his explanation of life as hopeless ferment and immortality as eternal movelessness — these show the great characterization in a tone of deterministic pessimism. The story is of course beautifully written, but appeals to me more as a great example of the negation of the purpose of life, the negation of happiness, optimism, and human decency. This negation is certainly in a large part of life. The story leaves me with an awesome feeling. The world is so full of strange phenomena, yet nothing in the world is strange to nature.

The last report I shall reproduce here is on the book *Up from Slavery* by Booker T. Washington:

> Washington's optimism and kindness in the face of extremely disadvantageous circumstances has furthered my

admiration and sympathy for his race. Washington has a very appealing style. He is understanding and objective enough to be impartial and yet subjective enough to give his genuine feelings. I particularly like his explanation of the effects of slavery on the whites, who regarded work as degrading, and the effects of freedom on the slaves, adding the responsibility of being free in a straightforward and penetrating analysis of this situation. There was no bitterness against masters if the slaves were treated decently, and most were but lived in poor conditions. Washington's father was white, not married to his mother. He was convinced that greatness will be recognized in spite of race or creed. He had to struggle for education, working and going to night school and later taught at Tuskegee Institute and did public speaking.

In this *Guide to American Literature*, there were many lists of books under a heading about literature, criticism, poetry or of the novel with social and historical background provided and commentary on the influences. The commentary called "Poetry and Criticism: Latest Phase," explains the type of criticism that was employed for poetry written in those decades:

> Literary criticism in America seems to be still under the influence of the "New Criticism," no later school having arisen to challenge its supremacy. However, volumes in which American literature is made to relate more closely to American cultural history than the New Criticism allows have appeared.
>
> The movement in poetry, however, has been a movement away from the elliptic verse of T. S. Eliot and his contemporaries. Under the influence of Auden, Spender and other British poets, verse has been restored to the duty of immediate communication in terms of living language and now tends to avoid the studied difficulties of the previous generation, to get out of libraries with occult references to all kinds of anthropological and literary lore and to get into the life of the world, thus reverting to the practice of the Poetic Renaissance that public communication is part of the duty of art.
>
> Both movements are too new for final judgment.

Some of the books in this list were written by W. H. Auden, John Ciardi, Richard Eberhard, Randall Jarrell and Robert Lowell.

Finally, even though my reports were overdone and immature, I'm glad I saved those cards, copies of which I handed in to the professor, written about books I read from his noted booklist of valuable and classic works of American fiction, poetry and philosophy. The year was 1952-1953, and the *Guide* was the first edition of his booklist, which had many subsequent editions. Reading the cards takes me back to those days, to the room in Emerson Hall with its squeaking floors and dim lights which didn't in themselves lend the enthusiasm that an innate love of literature did. However, I have realized the sincere concern and even affection behind the seemingly stern words of his letter.

"He had a somewhat gruff and nervous manner, but when he started to lecture about literature there was so much kindness and depth in his words that one could feel the love that went into his work. The compassion he had toward the writers and their characters came through."

"Did he ever say anything offensive?"

"Not really. I heard that he had said he didn't like teaching in the evening division. The reason not definite, it might have been that people sometimes walked into class after the lecture had begun. Of course, there might have been other reasons."

"Was this a popular course?"

"Yes, and everyone was quite taken by the charming assistant who sometimes lectured."

"I'm sure they liked the books also."

"Yes, or they wouldn't be there."

"Usually many people drop out of the evening courses unless they are quite popular. Was there much attrition in that class?"

"I don't think so, but my remembrance of that point is not too clear."

Now I still remember everything connected with the course — the buildings, the voices, some comments, the assistant who impressed me tremendously, the brilliant judgments of Mr. Jones — as if it all happened yesterday. His most famous quotation that survives in information about him is this:

Ours is the age which is proud of machines that think and suspicious of men who try to.

His invaluable *Guide to American Literature and its Backgrounds since 1890* was the height of erudition in the subject of American literature, and I did my best to keep up with its subjects and its standards. It covered many subjects, such as The Genteel Tradition, The Regional and Local, Historical Romance, Travel, The Literature of Entertainment, The Literature of Childhood, Humor, The West, The Application of Evolutionary Theory, social reform, political reform and valuations of American culture with a sizable reading list for each heading. I still keep this worn little volume without its cover.

No one else except Mr. Jones and Donald Marston had previously read these cards, which I never showed to anyone and hid away like a personal treasure. When I threw my notes away finally after years of feeling that I should keep them though hardly able to decipher them, I couldn't throw these away but wondered who else would ever be interested in reading them.

In the same year I was taking another course called Democratic Theory and its Critics with Professor Louis Hartz. I learned about various approaches to government and governing a country, democracy being the preferred method of rule, beginning with the mentality of the individual thinking and manner of behavior in which people treat others with differing beliefs and backgrounds. The democratic individual tolerates and attempts to understand others, conversely expecting the same treatment from others.

We read *The Communist Manifesto* by Karl Marx for comparison, the system of communism being the opposite of the democracy we know. All of the assigned readings broadened my base of comprehension of history and current events, which hardly existed up to that time.

Modern Poetry

In the summer of 1955 I studied literature at Harvard Summer School, this time in a course given by Paul Engle from the University of Iowa called British and American Poetry of the Twentieth Century. The lectures were given in a hall in Lamont Library, a pleasant daily study, and my absorption grew with each passing week.

Paul Engle was director of the Iowa Writers' Workshop from 1941 to 1965. He increased enrollment there and oversaw students of future fame such as Philip Levine, Donald Justice and Robert Bly. It provided a model for hundreds of all the writing programs that followed, and Prof. Engle raised millions of dollars for it. In 1967 he and his second wife founded the International Writing Program, which later became the most important center of the study of poetry in the entire world with many international authors invited to Iowa City. He was nominated in 1976 for a Nobel Peace Prize for this work. As a novelist, a critic and a poet he was best known for his first book of poems *Worn Earth*, which won the Yale Series of Younger Poets, and for his second book of poems of *American Song*, which received rave reviews in the *New York Times*.

Prof. Engle spoke convincingly as a poet, critic and exceptional teacher and was vital in the field. I felt comfortable and very willing to listen in his class, liking his Western down-to-earth sophistication, friendliness and democratic attitude.

The text of the course was entitled *Reading Modern Poetry*, compiled with an introduction and some analysis provided by Paul Engle and others in the modern poetry field who were qualified and extremely competent in literary analysis. The book, which I greatly enjoyed, is a first edition in hardcover edited by John Gerber and published in 1955 by Scott, Foresman and Company. It was evidently compiled by Paul Engle, who also provided the Preface with W. C., initials of the teacher, mystery writer and prize-winning poet Warren Carrier, who wrote some of the

Professor Paul Engle and students

criticism in this volume. Subsequent paperback editions are still selling on amazon.com.

In addition to all I learned in that course, I would have to remember the famous stanza by the outstanding poet and professor Archibald McLeish: "A poem must not be mean/but be." In accordance with the purpose of this text, the stanza is explicated in the book by Paul Engle as follows:

> He did not intend to argue that a poem must not have meaning, but rather that the poem must be, in all its images, its rhythm, its tone of innate or pure emotion, its use of concrete details, the thing which it wishes to communicate. Phrased differently, one might say that all the parts of a poem added together equal the meaning, which may never be stated at all. This is another reason for the difficulty of modern poetry and this means the reader must work hard. Why shouldn't he? The poet did . . . the insights into his own life which the reader can get from discovering another man's vision of life will give him a heightened awareness of

his own human existence in a way that no formally organized field of study can give him.

And Prof. Engle provided this comment on the form of modern poetry:

> Much modern poetry is the succession of details with no obvious links between them, like a sequence of stills taken from a film. The reader is asked to fill in the lines with a story from his own mind. The poet's job is to make the details so hard and sharp, so dramatic, so rich in hints, that they express more than a plain statement. This is nothing new in poetry . . .

The analysis goes on and on, for I still have the book and often read from the poetry in its pages. At the time it drew me into a maze of wonder and a method of self-expression that I was later to follow, sometimes using writing in prose for practical reasons of communication and sometimes using writing in verse as a more private and subjective communication. The course taught me how to practice the art of words that were used with highly controlled emotion to elicit a new awareness and emotion from the reader.

Appropriately, the presentation of poems begins with Robert Frost's "Stopping by Woods on a Snowy Evening." Commentary on this poem is made by John Holmes from his important book *Preface to Poetry*. John Holmes was a poet, critic and teacher at Boston Adult Education Center and at Tufts University and had authored a number of books of poetry. I began taking a workshop with him in Boston in 1956 but didn't continue beyond the first meeting because I had so many studies at the Harvard University Extension School.

Anne Sexton, about my age and attractive, also attended that workshop, evidently at the beginning of her studies in poetry. No one could have predicted then that she would soon become a famous poet after studying with Robert Lowell, win a Pulitzer Prize and leave an influence, especially on women and the confessional school of poetry. I had no idea about her or her mental and emotional problems, and of course she had no idea about mine. We were both inexperienced in poetry and from totally different backgrounds, she of Yankee upbringing of Mayflower ancestry and I of lower-middle-class Watertown breeding.

Digressions aside, John Holmes' commentary on Frost's poem is highly detailed and technical, culminating in a summary of meaning in the last paragraph:

> It can be thought of as a picture: the whites, grays, and blacks of the masses and areas of lake, field, and woods, with the tiny figure of the man in the sleigh and the horse. And it can be thought of as a statement of man's everlasting responsibility to man; though the dark and nothingness tempt him to surrender, he will not give in . . . built on the image of the pull of wildness and lawlessness against man's conscious will and the promises he has made to be kept.

The book then goes into the work of James Joyce, A. E. Housman and Carl Sandburg, amply represented with an analysis by Paul Engle of the poem "To the Ghost of John Milton," beginning thus:

> This poem, like all of Sandburg's, is written in free verse, which does not mean that it is free from any rhythm, but that it has been freed from the fixed regular meters of traditional poetry. Sandburg's poems have a strong rhythmic cadence, like a man speaking in a measured way, but they certainly are in revolt against all those patterns of strong and weak syllables which make up the "feet" of meters with Latin names.

My favorite of Carl Sandburg's poems presented is "Good Morning, America," a long poem that endeavors to capture the characteristics of Americans and their culture. An excerpt from that poem appears below as Sandburg writes in his easygoing style:

> Aye, behold the proverbs of the people:
> The big word is Service.
> Service — first, last and always.
> Business is business.
> What you don't know won't hurt you.
> Courtesy pays.
> Fair enough.
> The voice with a smile.
> Say it with flowers.

Let one hand wash the other.
The customer is always right . . .
God reigns and the government at Washington lives.
Let it go at that.

One of my favorite poems for rhyme and rhythm is "General William Booth Enters into Heaven" by Vachel Lindsay with its wonderful alliterations and couplings of word sounds that seem so natural and unaffected. Powerful in its subject matter and evocations of lepers and drug fiends and slums, it tries to bring these into the paths of belief. About salvation of the soul, its rhythms are influenced by the worshipful singing of Southern blacks in their churches as follows:

Jesus came from out the court-house door,
Stretched his hands above the passing poor.
Booth saw not, but led to his queer ones there
Round and round the mighty court-house square.
Then, in an instant all that blear review
Marched on spotless, clad in raiment new.
The lame were straightened, withered limbs uncurled
And blind eyes opened on a new, sweet world.

The book offers explication of a poem by Thomas Hardy by C. Day Lewis, who later became quite a familiar name as Poet Laureate of Britain. The poem "To an Unborn Pauper Child" is difficult to read without some analysis. The poems of Emily Dickinson are also represented and explained by R. P. Blackmur, who comes to the conclusion that her work was good but not great because she had not learned to control objective expression though she had the themes and the insight necessary for great poetry.

Robert Penn Warren is another of the analysts who became a very famous poet, novelist and Pulitzer Prize winner, and Cleanth Brooks, literary critic and professor, provides some analysis of Warren's poem "Bearded Oaks." Robert Mayo provides analysis of the poems of E. E. Cummings (spelled the traditional way), whose most colorful and original poem in my opinion is entitled "what if a much of a which of a wind." But the poem that needs the most explication is T. S. Eliot's "The Love Song of J. Alfred Prufrock," for which Paul Engle provides seven pages in a step-by-step analysis that is impossible to compress into two lines or even two paragraphs.

I enthusiastically wrote comments from the lectures on the pages of the book in ink, never to be erased as they were never erased from my mind. I liberally underlined the commentaries with red pen, so that when I read the book a number of times I could concentrate on what were the most important ideas. Of course, Paul Engle's poetry was also represented in this collection but not analyzed, perhaps because his work didn't need as much analysis as some of the others. This is an excerpt from his poem entitled "Cuban Voyage":

> Land where the sugar cane took shallow root,
> Land fat with the carrion-eating flower:
> Unreal to a pale and northern man the roar
> Of burro, parrot, boy in the hot noon hour,
> Wanting his winter night, birdless and mute.
>
> A naked, asking land for one who wore
> Grief around him like a growing skin,
> Too much, too urgent life for one to change
> Who still can feel the live blood leaping in
> The bold brain, calling still: More, give me more.

A few women poets are also represented in the book, few because they were not many famous women poets at that time. Those whose poems are included are Elinor Wylie, Edna St. Vincent Millay, Elizabeth Bishop, Marianne Moore and Marguerite Young. Marianne Moore's work was and is still among my favorites in modern poetry, her description of poetry including the line "imaginary gardens with real toads in them" thrilling me every time I read the poem.

Another poet whose works I greatly admire from my study of this book is Gerard Manley Hopkins. I love his poem called "Pied Beauty" for its worship of nature as well as its alliteration and imagery. Here are the first few lines:

> Glory be to God for dappled things —
> For skies of couple-colour as a brinded cow;
> For rose-moles all in stipple upon trout that swim;
> Fresh-firecoal chestnut-falls; finches' wings;
> Landscape plotted and pieced — fold, fallow, and plough.

During that summer, I visited Paul Engle's office briefly to show him one of my poems and ask his opinion of it. I can't quite remember which poem it was, but my poems of that time were all rather old-fashioned in concept and some of them unbearably cynical because of my depressed state of mind. The poem reproduced below will do to give the reader an idea of my initial style.

MOONLIGHT

The moonlit air spills mesh unseen
As cobweb dust to crown a queen
Whose eyes look, bared; no film can hide
The curious moons that trickle tide
And sketch their outlines multiform,
But through the mesh there is a norm . . .
Dust that sprinkles artist's dew
Loves to mesh a queen, all new
From toes that dance a mile unseen,
From fingers fondling airy sheen,
From smile that makes beholder feel
His nervous outline really real.

"It is rather traditional, but don't change it." Those were the exact words this pleasant gentleman said to me in that brief encounter in his office. It would have been nice to be able to work with him, but my life didn't work out that way, for I would have had to go to the workshop in Iowa and leave my family. Because of my emotional problems, I was rooted and dependent and couldn't leave or spare the money for such an adventure.

The course ended as pleasantly as it began with a good grade in that warm and balmy summer in the Harvard Yard, which was different from the often cold and calculating real world with warm areas if one could find them.

Reconciling with Family

After psychiatric shock treatments, I suddenly came out of a dim and nightmarish existence into which I had briefly fallen. As I returned home, I realized that I needed help from my parents and I began to feel the guilt, shame and awareness of the realities around me I had lost for a while. But I had a large amnesia, not remembering until much later the things that happened in school that had trapped me into trouble.

As I was resting and recovering, I made my first and only visual art work, a drawing of circles and triangles on drawing paper into a slow, careful and colored abstract pattern. I was very pleased with the finished product, though my parents didn't react to it, and I hung it up on the wall of my bedroom. It hung there for a while, but a few years after I had married and moved out, I noticed it had disappeared. I didn't ask why or how because I knew it had been considered useless and thrown away. If I had the picture now, and I wish I did, I would name it *Balance* for the new sense of emotional balance I had found in the days when I drew it and colored it in with pencils so carefully. How could anyone know how much it meant to me or how much creativity was working through me?

What was this thing called art anyway that it could mesmerize my thoughts so and elicit strong emotions as much as or more than a scene of magnificent nature could? It was an entry into an imaginary world as much as in the courses in novels and poetry had been, but even more for the vivid colors and shapes and the variety of the works. Bright and striking scenes flashed onto a screen for an immediate reaction of liking or disliking and for gradual appreciation and analysis.

In the ensuing years, I would visit many art museums in the cities of America and abroad and also write quite a number of columns about art works, artists and the process of art as creativity. And creativity itself would become the main focus of my life besides my family.

Also in the future I recalled that isolated artwork I had produced and the wonderful feeling of accomplishment it gave me. I was frustrated that it had been thrown out and that I had not thought of taking a photograph of it so that I would at least have its picture. But in my mind I remembered it rather well and from that memory wrote the following poem that was published in *The North American Review* of November/December, 2000, and is included in my book manuscript "A New Orchid Myth."

TEEN-TALK EXCHANGE

took Taralee to the drawing board
pretending to be desk.
She abstracted shapes
from theorems of geometry,
held the compass point firm
and turned it like a pirouette,
its trance of triangle
touching at a sharp point
then bouncing toward a rectangle
leaning upon the balance
of a diagonal. Add thirst of line.
Then coloring in was less a fuss,
the third dimension,
the light effects of life,
the ginger stain,
the strawberry rain,
the privilege of trees,
transgressions of berries,
blood of dandelion stems,
legendary encyclopedia of plants,
red ants transporting crumbs,
Armenian blue beads or *gabouyd hloun*
for luck of color or lack of chance,
circumstances allowing for birds
with prancing feathers —
parrots, peacocks, love birds —
the soft eyes of deer,
mathematical monkeys jumping at trees,
fish exchanging gills like a hobby,
exotic flowers bowing to girls,
magnanimous tomatoes juiced,

oranges diced with skin,
even the slithering of snakes
through the yellowed grass,
the romance of cherry blossoms in spring,
a fling of ripened cherries
along with apples, pears, apricots
and the science of brochures
adding or subtracting every feature.

She framed the drawing with self-expression
and hung it in her room.

By writing about it, I almost had my drawing back again but in a more complicated and more stylish form. It expressed balance through poetic metaphors that pleased me as well as readers. It gave me the deep satisfaction not only of telling a story but also of the connecting with a past moment and correcting the error of the destruction of the piece. I began to explore the possibility of many other such connections and corrections and wrote as if my life depended on it, though it really didn't. But my sense of hope and inspiration did as I continued along that road.

Summer School Again

I had taken Mr. Jones' course in two parts, the first in the evening school in 1954-1955 and the other a few years later in 1958 at Harvard Summer School. Donald Marston happened to be the assistant in both, and we had had some conversations after he recognized me and asked me to come to his office. The last time I had met him was at the conclusion of the first part of the course a few years before, after which I had written to him asking for a meeting to discuss the poetry I was writing, so we met over coffee at a restaurant in Harvard Square. What I remember from our talk was his remark, "you can write to me if you have the time and the inclination." This remark, like a promise, has never left me, and I sometimes feel that in writing all this poetry and prose, I am still writing to him and trying to explain what I couldn't explain then.

In this second part of the course, he initiated the greeting at seeing me in lecture room of Allston Burr Hall, asking to know what was going on. I believe I had written him another letter when I was confused, though I don't remember what it said. I don't blame him for asking, now that I remember more of what was going on, but at that time I had no recall. How would he know that?

However, I couldn't resist visiting him in his office, but once there I was so taken by his charm and good looks plus my fear or guilt that I couldn't talk much. He didn't seem to mind and did most of the talking. I was recovering and in psychiatry, and I hoped he had the compassion to deal with the marked changes in my behavior from one year to the next, a hostile or confused and cynical person in writing or speaking and the other person quiet, demure and well-behaved.

Always kind and friendly to me, he was conversational when I went to his office a few times, though sometimes I suspected that he was ridiculing me in encouraging me to send out poems to some important magazines. I knew I wasn't ready for this. He

Caricature of Howard Mumford Jones

told me some things about literature and about Mr. Jones, including the fact that his wife Bessie Jones was a Zionist. It didn't ring a bell with me, but later I began to feel that there was some political intrigue I didn't understand when psychology professors seemed angry at me after my social problems of a few years back had been taken care of and completely reversed as if they had never existed.

No one had questioned me on the matter or asked me where I had been for six months when I was absent from school and suddenly reappeared without any explanation. But I felt that I owed them an explanation, which I wouldn't be able to verbalize until much later after I had worked out my problems and had the chance to put all the pieces together because no one else had. Anything that complicated takes years to remaster.

I concentrated on what was being said in the lectures on American literature and on returning the gaze when Mr. Marston seemed to be looking at me so much. I remember specifically that Mr. Jones expressed annoyance at graphic sexual references that appeared in books and even in children's books. We could conclude from this either that he was straight-laced or that he was sensible and acknowledged that going too far with literature in this way was a ploy to get bigger sales and didn't have much literary value.

Donald Marston gave only a few of the lectures in the course, and I cherished every word he said. This summer of my emotions was matched by the magnificence of the weather and the atmosphere. The only way I felt that I could express my appreciation to him was to give him something to keep if he wanted to.

I gave him a copy of a very small mimeographed booklet of poems called *Voices* put out by some of the students in the

Summer School. It was edited by Ralph Hickok and Claude McNeal with a line of gratitude to Dr. Jules Chametzky of Boston University for helpful advice and honest criticism. It was the first magazine to publish any of my poems. The only remarkable thing about this little booklet was that I kept it all those years since 1958, so it became a bit of history. Two of my poems were published in it: "Dream of the Table" and "Tempest." The first of these reads in part as follows:

> A black top flashes scenes.
> A plant sprays leaves
> To lap the Os of air;
> A map lies under
> To hold the letters there.
>
> Chess men tumble
> In an intellectual trial
> Of white versus black;
> Freud offers a solution
> Of sense-smiling grays;
> The boy checks red and black,
> Judging in a compromise.

Looking back with an analyst's perception, there could have been something in the writing after this section that left some suspicions or that played in with the suspicions of the psychologists. For I had written "TIME and LIFE lie juxtaposed/ in friendly sunning/ on ATLANTIC shores." The way things were at that time, we were all prone to some Freudian interpretations, which in the long run were not at all true.

For Freudian theory expresses a general pessimism about human nature and human intentions. Freud interpreted symbols and anyone's use of language in a negative way, ascribing sexual motivations to many communications in an across-the-board fashion. He had laid out a structure with which to interpret the human mind with its feelings and behaviors. That structure remaining in place, later his disciple C. G. Jung turned Freudian theory around and made it more positive, seeing symbols as part of any individual's personal thoughts and feelings without suspecting any generalized sexual undertones.

So it could seem there were double meanings here, referring to the prominent magazines mentioned as casual allusions.

Of course I didn't know at the time that Mr. Jones was connected with *The Atlantic* monthly and had been one of its prominent contributors, nor that he had as one of his other assistants at about the same time a young man named Peter Davison who soon became the poetry editor of the important magazine. It was one of my most naive gaffes, which I didn't figure out until after I was a convert to the theories of C. G. Jung.

Of course I had to reveal my interest in Donald Marston to my psychiatrist, Dr. Arthur Berk, who didn't think much of this relationship that seemed to excite and inspire me, never encouraged me in my efforts at writing and didn't seem to want to hear about my writings at all. But I was still trying to find my way in oral and written communications and in personality. I didn't really know myself. I knew my past when I never had any trouble with anyone, but that agonized girl who was angry at others and with herself was a complete stranger to me and always remained so.

Dr. Berk was very conservative and old-fashioned in approach and never spoke to me much about what I had done and how I felt, seeming interested only in strict discipline without trying to find out the circumstances of my previous behavior. I was in my last year of school before graduation.

But after this disappointment that the relationship with Donald Marston and even with the whole field of writing went nowhere but nonexistence, I relapsed somewhat, and Dr. Berk threatened me with hospitalization and more shock treatments. His most unforgettable words to me were these: "You have to suffer to get well." I felt I had suffered enough and resisted only by remaining silent and soon left his care, still very insecure and somewhat confused and depressed. Perhaps I should have stayed. Perhaps he was only throwing out barbs and trying to get me to fight back. But I always had comparison to Dr. Livingston in my mind, for he explained a great deal to me and always talked to me in a friendly manner, though it didn't work well because of lack of medication and also the stunning revelation of his sudden departure and the reason for it. I never discussed him with my psychiatrist, who never asked about that situation.

In these illnesses the crucial element is a matter of degree and not of kind, though the kind does or should determine the type of treatment. Dr. Berk made clear to me from the beginning this was a case of paranoid schizophrenia on the basis of brief oral and written tests. That condition is said to be incurable and has components I didn't show such as hallucinations, self-neglect, delusions, — my recitation of things that actually happened wasn't accepted as truth — no extremely bizarre behavior, no laughing for no reason. Simply extreme depression, hopelessness, lack of self-esteem with a brief psychotic break during all of which I was able to study and learn, though I couldn't stay at jobs.

Carl Gustave Jung

However, from what I have read of bipolar schizophrenia and from following my moods throughout the years I have no doubt that there was a bipolar component, and I doubt there was schizophrenia at all. Having researched my family background a bit, I found that at least one relative was treated for bipolar disorder, which for people who don't know is a mood disorder and is also called manic-depressive. It is thought to be hereditary.

Now there are better diagnoses and treatments for this condition, and it does not indicate the end of any chances in life for one who has it. I have also researched the condition somewhat, because not being a professional in the field, I don't need to go into great detail. But I was pleased to find that the condition is diagnosed in stages of slight cases to somewhat more severe cases to severe cases, all of which are considered treatable with hope that in middle age the condition will almost disappear. Medicines for this are much advanced from the previous shock treatments and lithium that had been used, and therapy is based on love and acceptance.

As a result of this reading, I found that an outstanding psychiatrist who is responsible for much of the research and practice in this new approach to bipolar disorder is named Hagop Souren

Akiskal. An Armenian born in Syria, he received his M.D. degree at the American University of Beirut in 1969. He is now a professor of psychiatry at the University of California in San Diego and is said to be "today's leading conceptual thinker in the area of bipolar subtyping." Much honored for work on temperament and bipolar spectrum disorders, he is also a researcher, writer and editor of academic journals. Poet was also mentioned in an article about his credentials. His theories and his approach would certainly be welcome here not only by me but also by the many other people who were negatively affected by my lack of adequate care and the very negative prognosis that had been given.

Now diagnosis takes years of getting to know the patient. Breakdown was certainly bad enough and since it was caught almost immediately and treated, I felt insecure but largely cured with gradual improvement over the years. Now I would ask, what illness?

Dr. Berk and I didn't communicate well in therapy, and I must have been trying to hide my wound. For he didn't listen to my conflicts with my parents and only wanted me to accept everything they said to me or decided for me. I never argued anyway, even when he wouldn't accept my complaint about the psychology professor who was harassing me in school and dismissed it by telling me the professor was trying to help me.

In retrospect, I think he was using the theories of Sigmund Freud, now outdated because they led to extreme discouragement and because women have taken charge of their lives and of their behaviors. Criticisms of Freudian theory and adjustments to it include the following paragraph from New Foundations, an Action Focus for Education on the Professions at newfoundations.com/woman/freud.html, which gives a summary of Freud's attitude toward women:

> Supported by his loving wife and six children, Freud ruled his house in the manner of a Hebrew patriarch. He was firmly convinced that woman is a castrated male who is cognizant of her castration and of her inferiority to man, and that her rebelling against "this unpleasant condition" causes the conflict between the sexes. Despite this "insight," however, Freud, by his own admission, remained forever puzzled by the female psyche.

Another summary about Freud's attitude toward poets and artists by Norman N. Holland, professor emeritus at the University of Florida:

> Freud's remarks about writers and artists reveal a deep ambivalence. He admired their powers as seers, their ability to see quickly and intuitively human psychology that he had to work laboriously toward. Yet he compared them unfavorably to scientists like himself, because they were given over, not to reality, but to the pleasure principle. They were venally motivated, oversexed, and analogous to daydreaming children, primitives, and madmen. His attitude toward Shakespeare, making him into either a degraded or a superhuman figure, serves as a paradigm for his admiration and jealousy . . . Freud envied writers and artists because of his need to know; his driving curiosity about sex; his need to feel that mental powers could alter the physical world; his need to outdo fathers; and his need to see, sight being identified in his mind with mental and sexual power . . .

I always knew that positive gets more results than negative, but now I am able to perceive more specifics in regard to the psychology of this situation. I learned about the theories of Jung by my own reading and not through any course.

About financial considerations, I felt that I could no longer ask my father to pay the $25 a visit twice a week, for he had no health insurance and no wealth. At that time $25 an hour was a fair amount of money to pay for anything. He never discussed my treatment with me in the same way that he never really discussed any important subject of my life except my marriage, and that never in much detail.

My mother had her own interpretations but fortunately we never got into any discussion of school or of treatment, except that she did make a remark once accusing me of having an affair with my psychiatrist. I didn't even reply to this impossibility, for the doctor was 70 years old and I was only 25, and I had no romantic inclinations for anyone then and if I had they would have been for the assistant in my literature course. It was in my mind as an emotion but I couldn't form the words to say I wouldn't be a receptacle for masculine smut.

For a long time I resented Dr. Berk's seeming lack of interest in what would make me feel secure and happy, but now I realize that if it hadn't been for his original intercession I would have had a terrible fate. He didn't hesitate to remind me of this fact or to threaten me with further hospitalization and shock treatments if I lost my cool and began to act undisciplined. The worst of it occurred one Sunday when I had sunk into a terrible despair that could have been suicidal. I telephoned him at his home for the first and last time.

"I feel terrible. I can't stand it."

"Don't bother me on Sunday."

I had to swallow my agony. I had been taking tranquilizers for a couple years, but at that point the medication had been stopped. No medicine and no reassuring words, though they were needed desperately. But he justified my suffering by saying that it was good for me, though I never understood how. I have no doubt there was a mutual lack of perception with the early more primitive psychiatric approach to patients.

I left his care after I graduated and agreed to be wed to someone my parents favored from the same kind of family background because they knew he would be dependable and consistent. His name is Hagop Sarkissian, a friendly and personable young man who had the ambition to get married. He also had accepted my background hospitalization.

Full recovery was a constant conflict for me that I had to resolve somehow, so I took to reading all I could about how mental patients had found their cures when they had found themselves. I continued to improve over ensuing years, but whether this happened spontaneously and from my own efforts or from the unquestioned discipline of the psychiatrist defies my ability to judge. The reason for this is that I am simply the obtuse narrator here looking for the "ineffable wee bit" Professor Aiken talked about in his course Philosophy of Art as being the quality that will put a work of art and a work of life along with the best.

But evidently I am a rather complex person to be able to analyze my own illness and carry through with improvements upon it. For I found my answers spontaneously with my meanderings into the subject and with the wonderful care and encouragement of some physicians as well as my small family.

Philosophy and Art

Reference to my Harvard courses would be remiss without the mention of perhaps one of the greatest lecturers in the subject of philosophy, Henry Aiken, who always attracted a large turnout for his lectures. With little if any attrition at the end of the course, everyone sat in fascination as he expounded on the questions "what is right" or "what is beauty." The lectures differed from what people usually expect of readings in philosophy — that they would be dry, dull and difficult.

I took two of his courses, the first in the year 1952-53 called Major Traditions in Western Ethics, reading works of Plato, Aristotle, the Book of Job from the Bible and others. I learned that Plato of ancient Greece with Aristotle and Socrates left a legacy of philosophy in government and ethics so important and so magnificent that Western civilization was based upon what they taught.

Socrates (b. 469 B.C.) was the teacher and Aristotle was the student in the academy Plato established. In addition to providing the philosophical foundations of Western culture, Plato was also a mathematician and writer of philosophical dialogues whose academy in Athens was the first institution of higher learning in the Western world. Plato had been a student of Socrates and was influenced by his teachings and his unjust death by being forced to drink poison after a trial for defending the concept of justice during a period of political unrest.

Socrates left much wisdom, preserved in the form of quotes, for the Socratic Method of teaching was one of philosophical dialogue with his students. One of these quotes from Plato's *Dialogues, Apology* reads thus:

> The unexamined life is not worth living.

The quote refers to self-examination by introspection and also to judgment by others. Below is another quote provided by Plato in *The Death of Socrates*.

> I do nothing but go about persuading you all, old and young alike, not to take thought for your persons or your properties, but and chiefly to care about the greatest improvement of the soul. I tell you that virtue is not given by money, but that from virtue comes money and every other good of man, public as well as private. This is my teaching, and if this is the doctrine which corrupts the youth, I am a mischievous person.

Plato (b. 424 B.C.) wrote dialogues, one of the most famous of which was entitled *The Republic*, his most mature work that contains his entire philosophy. It consists of 10 books entirely describing the concept of justice. Socrates is the narrator, and the book describes the ideal state with its fortunes and misfortunes.

Aristotle (b. 384 B.C.) wrote the *Nicomachean Ethics* and the *Eudemian Ethics*, describing and arriving at conclusions for the human good. He identifies the human good and happiness with virtue, an idea with which we generally agree. Following are three of his quotes:

> A flatterer is a friend who is your inferior, or pretends to be so.
> A friend is a second self.
> All human actions have one or more of these seven causes: chance, nature, compulsion, habit, reason, passion, and desire.

It is amazing that so much brilliance and deep thought existed at that time and in that place — ancient Greece in the city of Athens, not only in philosophy but other fields of thought as well. Not the least of their considerations was the definition of "what is truth" as a philosophical theory that had not been debated before.

Other philosophers such as John Dewey and Immanuel Kant left works relating to the same question, which I studied and pondered as Professor Aiken lectured on the subject that was his forte. He conveyed the idea that truth is a much more complicated construct than one who is not versed in its history can imagine, and these theories have developed from ancient times to modern to include correspondence theory, language theory and mathematical theory. In essence what I learned was how to search for the truth in any given situation. That's what the Harvard motto Veritas stands for.

Accordingly, I have witnessed many stages of truth throughout my life — partial truths, delusional truths, accurate truths that have been ripped from their moorings, logical truths that have been waiting for water just as a drying plant would, pretending truths, American truths, Armenian truths, international truths, childish truths, adult truths and so many more. But to be absolutely sure, the real truth lies in the thinking and in the searching that makes it worth the effort.

Another course I took with Henry Aiken was Philosophy of Art, in which he provided the analysis of what art consists of in terms of its meaning and beauty, its inspiration and desirability. I remember so well the question "what is beauty," though I haven't saved any notes on the subject nor do I remember the readings, though I think Aristotle was one of the authors. For this question also has had many ramifications throughout history and philosophy, its spiritual meanings being perhaps as important. However, I have so much internalized the material that I am able to write many poems on art works and the process of art.

A number of art courses I took were given in the basement lecture room of Fogg Museum, where many perfectly photographed slides of world-class works of art accompanied lectures. Ongoing analysis drew me into the subject that stayed with me and led me to peruse many art books and view many paintings in many museums, thus leading me to influence others to like art and to frequent exhibitions.

One of these courses was entitled Masterpieces of European Painting given by associate Professor George Levitine of Boston University, who also gave another course I took called French Sculpture of the Medieval Period. Another art course was entitled Ancient and Medieval Architecture given by Assistant Professor Albert Bush-Brown of Massachusetts Institute of Technology. Yes, architecture constructs art works and provides us with a great deal of inspiration and enjoyment in our activities. In addition, I took a course called Art of the 17th and 18th Centuries given by Professor Leonard Opdyke as well as a course called Introduction to the Art of the Middle Ages given by Professor Joachim Gaehde.

We glimpsed not only the Mona Lisa, the most famous of paintings which I later saw in person at the Louvre, but also the paintings of Francisco Goya, of Pierre Renoir, of Paul Klee, of

Jean-Honoré Fragonard, of Eugene Delacroix, of Salvatore Dali and of the irrepressible Pablo Picasso. I loved the variety of seeing one painting after another in different styles and of different periods with the little bit of the history of the era in the description that went with each work. I had developed a third eye for perception of the visual and of its meaning.

One of the students in the class was Alan Rohan Crite, who had distinguished himself as an African-American artist after his graduation from the Museum School in Boston in the 1930's. He was born in 1910 and had won a scholarship to that school. He distributed postcards of his artwork then to some people in the class. I was pleased to have them but unfortunately have lost them.

I shan't leave out the unforgettable Candide, who lived in the "best of all possible worlds" no matter what difficulties or reversals happened to him. He is the main character in Voltaire's 1759 literary work, a French satire by the Enlightenment philosopher in which he uses the naive Candide to poke fun at religion and theologians, governments and armies, philosophies and philosophers. Since I was quite naive myself, sometimes I felt like a female Candide going about exploring the wide world of school and work.

A recitation here of a few of the chapter headings gives the idea of the satire in this immortal work:

> Chapter 1 - How Candide Was Brought Up in a Magnificent Castle and How He Was Driven Thence
> Chapter 2 - What Befell Candide among the Bulgarians
> Chapter 3 - How Candide Escaped from the Bulgarians and What Befell Him Afterward
> Chapter 4 - How Candide Found His Old Master Pangloss Again and What Happened to Him
> Chapter 5 - A Tempest, a Shipwreck, an Earthquake, and What Else Befell Dr. Pangloss, Candide, and James, the Anabaptist
> Chapter 6 - How the Portuguese Made a Superb Auto-De-Fe to Prevent Any Future Earthquakes, and How Candide Underwent Public Flagellation

In addition to the courses mentioned above, two professors from Harvard University taught the art of comedy in literature. Professor William Van Lennep lectured on Comedy in the

Thater, including the plays of Molière and Aristophanes. Professor Wilbur Frohock lectured on Uses of the Comic, in which class students read the hilarious *Gargantua and Pantagruel* by Rabelais as well as other works that provided laughter.

With the addition of many other courses in subjects such as psychology, biology, botany, economics, I received a well-rounded liberal arts education. The era of specialization had not yet entered the educational picture, but subsequently more mathematics requirements were added as well as many more specialized subjects so that for a while liberal arts in college education was on the wane or opaqued. Recently there has been some talk that it will return for the necessity of understanding various subjects and also of relating to different cultures and peoples as a result of globalization, international trade and of war with Iraq and Afghanistan.

During the years that I was a student, I worked part time at various jobs, most of them lasting a few months. I worked some afternoons at my father's store for about two years waiting on customers or just waiting around for customers to enter the store. Then my father looked for someone who could do heavier work, so he hired successive male college students. My mother would help him some evenings mostly by just being there to deter possible holdups, and my aunt helped my uncle in the same way.

In my final college year I worked mornings at the Boston University Faculty Club on Bay State Road in Boston for Mrs. Grady, a personable woman who ran the restaurant in the club. I learned how to operate the mimeograph machine, and thus ran off the mimeographed menu for each day and did some typing on one of the old and heavy typewriters. The people I worked with consisted of waiters, cooks, professors and other college personnel as well as Mrs. Grady's daughter — all friendly and helpful. The food was probably good, but I don't remember ever having had a meal there, though I probably did.

I left that job after I graduated and became engaged, for I was to be married in September. Mrs. Grady requested that I stay longer or to return after my honeymoon, but I knew that it would be a matter of months of travel by ship with stops at a few ports and countries. However, I did appreciate the compliment.

Commencement at Last

The commencement ceremony in Tercentenary Theater at The Yard impressed me with its ceremonies. As graduates of University Extension, five of us that year led the parade of students down the aisle towards the front near the podium, and I had been chosen to be class marshall, probably because I was the youngest. I was also the most nervous, though no one could really see into my inner turmoil and absolute fear of the unknown future. I had had reason for pessimism and was trying not to give in to it.

Two of the honored guests at the graduation of 1960 left an indelible impression on everyone. One was John F. Kennedy, who was then a Massachusetts senator a few months before being elected president. The other was His Holiness Vasken I, Catholicos of All Armenians, the first Armenian Catholicos to visit America. Consciously or unconsciously, the day was as great as the people there in attendance and at the podium.

The following discussion approximates the one I had with a friend who had recently graduated with a doctorate in physics.

"You went to Harvard. You should be able to solve this difficult math problem."

"I didn't take mathematics there."

"Why not?"

"It wasn't an absolute requirement. I took biology and botany for a science requirement, but no math."

"Didn't you feel that something was missing in your education?"

"No, and I don't miss it now. I was never a math person."

"What kind of person are you?"

"I am a literary person who is interested in philosophy and loves art."

"Do you feel that your education was complete?"

"I certainly do. And it was well rounded as far as my interests were concerned."

"You don't give much importance to math."

"Quite the contrary. I have the greatest respect for people who can do higher math and for the wonderful projects they complete with it. For either men or women who are interested in math and science, I say more power to them and good luck. The only experience I had with math was in high school where I took first-year algebra and geometry. I had a difficult time with geometry and spent many hours thinking out theorems. Each time I did this I was stretching my mind to the limit, and I'm glad I learned how because after that I stretched my mind around the ideas of philosophy, psychology and poetry. The same principle applies."

The name of the degree was Adjunct in Arts in Humanities (bachelor equivalent) from Harvard University, but the sheepskin was presented by Dean Phelps in his office. I emphasize sheepskin because in those days the diplomas were printed on actual sheepskin and signed personally by President Nathan Pusey. For some years now diplomas have been printed on high-quality bond paper with the signature of the president of the university also printed.

After the ceremonies when I was tired of standing or walking and still in my graduation attire, I took off my shoes and sat down on the grass in the corner of the Yard. I didn't think much of it, but evidently President Pusey did because as he walked down the path with John F. Kennedy, he threw me a disapproving look. But my feet really had bothered me a great deal in those high heels, so that in the future I gave up wearing them. I remember that incident with a tinge of irony, thinking that it was really nothing compared to what President Pusey would encounter in the years to come — the incident in 1971 of students riotously taking over University Hall in protest to the Vietnam War and being forcibly taken to jail by outside police called in to deal with the situation. And in April of 1972, a similar takeover of Massachusetts Hall, which included the office of President, was another such chaotic move in the student unrest.

Reginald Phelps was Dean of the Harvard Extension School. The course offerings were very good but sparse as compared to the more sophisticated and generous program of studies that later thrived under Dean Michael Shinagel. The price tag also changed.

HARVARD UNIVERSITY

ADMINISTRATIVE BOARD FOR UNIVERSITY EXTENSION

REGINALD H. PHELPS, DEAN

11 WELD HALL
CAMBRIDGE 38, MASSACHUSETTS

May 11, 1959

TO WHOM IT MAY CONCERN:

The degree of Adjunct in Arts is given for courses taken under the Commission on Extension Courses in classrooms located around Greater Boston. The instruction is given by members of the teaching staffs of the cooperating institutions and the work is under the Chairman of the Commission, who is the Director of University Extension at Harvard University. We do not accept any work done by correspondence, unless it was taken during service in the Armed Forces and approved by the proper authorities here. Thirty-four half-courses are required for the degree. This is equivalent to the amount of work required for the Bachelor's degree in many colleges. It differs somewhat from the Harvard A.B. at present, which requires sixteen and one-half full courses, and, in many fields, tutorial work and General Final examinations.

The degree of Adjunct in Arts admits to our Graduate School of Arts and Sciences the same as a Bachelor of Arts degree from any accredited university. Admission in every case depends, of course, on the quality of the record of the student. The degree has been taken in the past by men and women usually beyond college age, who wish to take for credit our late afternoon or evening courses. We do not accept for candidacy for this degree students who have left Harvard or any other institutions with poor standing or deficient records.

Reginald H. Phelps
Chairman of the Commission and
Director of University Extension,
Harvard University

Derek Bok was subsequently president of the University from 1971 to 1991. I admired him greatly for his dignity, his consideration of the students and of the entire field of teaching and his compassion. Now we have entered another era with Drew Faust, the first woman president of Harvard University, who seems to be following his lead.

Having the degree was one thing, proving that I had it was another. For through the years of working as an editor and interacting with people as a writer, I have been asked many times where I obtained my degree. I always responded Harvard Uni-

Helene receiving her diploma from Dean Reginald H. Phelps

versity in 1960, much to the amazement of the questioner, and stated that I didn't graduate from Radcliffe, that women were always students at the evening school, that my degree wasn't an associate degree but a bachelor equivalent. I still wonder how many of them really believed me, though I have kept all my certificates and my diploma as proof.

"Who bothered you and why?"

"A few people seemed quite angry with me. I didn't know why."

"Do you have any guesses?"

"Rumors about political alignments, which I didn't have, or for something I did or was suspected of doing."

"What were you suspected of doing?"

"It all had to do with that attempt at writing a novel. There was one scene that contained an indirect allusion to sex but really wasn't under the circumstances. There was a scene at Dr. Livingston's office where I fell on the floor deliberately in despair, nothing erotic."

"So would they link you with him?"

"They seem to link me with somebody."

"Why were you on the floor?"

"I didn't want to leave because I was so depressed I didn't know what I would do. I was afraid. He said I was suicidal."

"So how could they read sex into that?"

"One of the mysteries of human nature."

Poetry enters into the picture, for I began writing poetry and some prose when I was about 19 or 20, perhaps following my father's penchant for writing poetry in Armenian for the Armenian press.

"When I look back at these poems that were published then, I feel embarrassed at the negativism of them."

"But the editor published them."

"I guess he believed in me. Then once I returned to his office after not having dropped in for a while and he wondered why I hadn't come along sooner."

"And you wondered why he had wondered."

"Yes, I did."

"Was he a young man and was married?"

"He was older than I but not married."

"Maybe that explains it."

My early work was immature, and being embarrassed about it, I soon destroyed most of the work I had done or simply didn't reveal the early poems that I had written and pasted into a scrapbook I tried to keep away from dust. After that I did no serious writing for a while with the exception of exams and papers in school.

A Permanent Marriage

On September 17 of 1960 Hagop and I were married three years after he had immigrated to America from the thriving Armenian community in Lebanon. My sister was against this marriage because of general prejudice at the time to marrying someone from "across," meaning across the ocean in the Middle East. This attitude was a standard at the time when there were so few Armenians from that part of the world here except for the early immigrants of the 1920s who were the parent generation with children, some of whom were rebelling against Armenian values or trying to work themselves into the more sophisticated American values. But my parents heartily endorsed the marriage, my father having arranged the meeting with Hagop.

My father also made arrangements for the wedding at the Holy Trinity Armenian Church on Shawmut Avenue in Boston, which moved to Cambridge the following year. We were married by Reverend Fr. Papken Maksoudian, who as a layperson had employed Hagop in Beirut as a typesetter when he was the manager of a printing establishment. His son, Father Krikor Maksoudian, not yet an ordained priest, sang a marvelous baritone solo at the wedding ceremony.

We had a small, cozy wedding reception in the Skyview Room of the Smith House on Memorial Drive in Cambridge, for I hadn't wanted a large wedding, and Hagop's tastes were just as simple. There were about 60 relatives and friends in attendance, including all the people who worked at the Baikar Press, publisher of the English-language and Armenian-language newspapers my husband worked for as Linotype operator. No music played, but instead a series of speeches by the editors of newspapers filled the room — Antranig Antreassian in Armenian, Bob Vahan in English and also by our best man Hratch Berberian, a violinist who later became a professor of music at the University of South Dakota. His father, the well-known composer Hampartzoum Berberian, a survivor of the Genocide, knew my father previously from an orphanage in Syria. For me it was a reassuring simplicity with pictures at the wedding taken by a friend with a camera and a few posed pictures at the studio. Hagop's family was in Beirut and couldn't attend.

My father and my husband became good friends, and throughout our marriage Hagop got along very well with my parents. I felt that this was a distinct advantage for all of us and a good example for my children as well. We had decided from the beginning of a short courtship that we would honeymoon with a trip to the Middle East to visit his family. I had no idea how long, complicated and interesting the trip would be as we set off to travel on a shoestring, for neither of us had much money saved. The guests, however, were very obliging in giving money gifts.

Our first visit to Europe and then Lebanon took place in 1960 and began on September 22 when we went to New York City to board the steamship RMS *Queen Mary*. The places we visited — Paris to and from, Germany to and from, Venice, Pompeii, the outskirts of Beirut, Rhodes, Athens, Syracuse, and the endless tossing Atlantic Ocean — were spectacular, especially for me since I had only seen my hometown and environs.

Apparently most Americans wanted to travel to Paris as did people from the multiple countries of the many-sided world. So our few days there were a magical sphere of contentment as we perused the French on monuments, trying to digest the history beginning with the Arch of Triumph, especially history that existed before America as a country was conceived.

The Eiffel Tower and the boulevards astounded me with their majesty and expanse. The tower stands 984 feet high, but we didn't climb to the top because of our mutual fear of heights. Our visit to the Paris Opera, where we saw the *Swan Lake* ballet by Tchaikovsky, enthralled me in spite of my embarrassment at wearing informal clothing and walking shoes while others dressed formally.

Another highlight of our tour was a visit to the Notre Dame Cathedral on the banks of the river Seine. It was as large as the Gothic cathedrals should be with its lovely glass rose window reflecting color in sunlight. Its age spoke as loud as words, and history seemed to echo from its every corner.

Helene and Hagop's wedding picture

Additionally, we walked through the Bois de Boulogne, a renowned park, and visited the Palais de Chaillot across from the Eiffel Tower. Adolf Hitler had been pictured there during his tour of the vanquished city in 1940. Obviously, much had changed. We passed through Montmartre, famous for its colony of artists, and attended a show at the Follies Bergère, noted for its elegant performances by topless young women.

I more than Hagop had an interest in the French food — rabbit and beef tongue cooked in delicious sauces as well as other delicacies. We just picked out a restaurant that looked inviting and very clean from the outside and entered with a sense of adventure. I even tried snails and found them quite tasty. I had always liked food adventures from the time back in Boston that I had tried Chinese food, duck and pizza and liked them.

The Louvre drew us on with its miles of paintings in galleries. I was particularly enthralled to see the Mona Lisa in person, not that she looked any different than in photographs of the painting. But the actual work close up held a different mystique; just being close enough to scrutinize it left me with bragging rights.

On the way to Lebanon we also stopped at Alexandria, Egypt, for two days going in October and two days on the way back in January. I saw a sudden disorientation of people rushing around, heard the loud speaking and watched the magic acts on the wharf. In the middle of winter the weather was hot, the sun threatening a sunburn. The atmosphere differed completely from the atmosphere in Europe.

We took a ride on a horse and buggy to Farouk's Palace, which had been turned into a Museum. I found myself equally interested in the Museum and in the driver who was dressed in a long nightgown-like shift and stayed in the carriage to take a nap while we toured the museum. We also saw the Roman catacombs there as well as the Little Sphinx and had *shish kebab* at a restaurant, giving what was left to the driver, who blessed us many times over.

On the second stay of two days on the way back, we took a taxi driven by a man wearing a business suit, thus more efficient but

Farouk's palace

not as colorful. It was the first time I saw women who were dressed in black from head to toe, some of them carrying baskets of goods on their heads while walking home from stores. I found Beirut more cosmopolitan with European and American influences.

Once there, we stayed with Hagop's family and explored that beautiful terrain. Even with its differing value system, I was fascinated with the country of Lebanon, with its sea and mountainous scenery, with the ruins of Baalbek as the ancient Roman Heliopolis was called, the marketplace downtown, the mood of the country and of course with the many people I met there. The country of Lebanon is in the Middle East between Israel and Syria. Beirut, as a Mediterranean port city with mountains rising abruptly and near, is very hot and humid for six months out of the year.

As the capital of Lebanon, it boasts a population of about two million and is its largest seaport, the economic center of the country with many banks and businesses, and the center of culture there with universities, press, theater, night life and activities. It was first mentioned in history in an ancient Egyptian text and has been in existence ever since. For one interested in ancient metropolitan centers, Tripoli, Sidon and Tyre are the country's secondary cities. The people of Lebanon live mostly in cities, and there is a delicate balance between the Christian group and the Muslim group because representation in Parliament depends upon religious affiliation. It had been and was when we were there a mostly Christian country. Now perhaps the balance has changed, but there has been no census since 1932.

Lebanon had a thriving Armenian community with newspapers, businesses, private schools, and churches, all with the expectation of Armenian language and traditional ways. Their school system especially and also the mostly Armenian-Armenian marriages kept them in the constant use of the Armenian language for socialization with their peers. Our visit was well before the Civil War no one could then envision, and many Armenians left after heavy losses during and after those difficult years.

Some basic differences in our families were quite acceptable to all of us. My in-laws belonged to the Armenian Protestant denomination, which had broken off from the mother church in the 19th century with the influence of the American Protestant missionaries in what is now Turkey. They called it the Levant or the Bible lands.

My father-in-law Ohannes or Hovhannes was a trained minister and had converted to the Armenian Protestant Church from the Armenian Apostolic, becoming a teacher after being educated in the American Protestant missionary St. Paul's College in Tarsus, Turkey, and graduating from the Near East School of Theology in Beirut. He had been born in the old Armenian village of Kessab, Syria. Leaving the village to pursue his education, he found at his return that most of his relatives had been killed during the Armenian Genocide.

When I first entered the house and was introduced to the family, he greeted me with the words "I'm going to speak to you in English so you will feel at home." His English was excellent, and he was pleasantly considerate. He always seemed eager for me to ask a question on the subject of history or geography so that he could bring a book or a map to explain some things about the subjects.

My mother-in-law Haigouhi, 18 years younger than her husband, was a very devout woman who read from the Bible every morning before she started her work. She was from the city of Osmanieh (near Adana and Aintab) and had lost her father during the massacres of 1909 in the vilayet of Adana when she was a toddler, and her mother in 1918 in Aleppo from disease. Aram was the eldest brother, Alice the eldest and Mary the youngest child.

There had been mixtures of Protestant and Apostolic in my father's family, his father having been Protestant, and there was also this mixture in my mother's family. My mother herself was strongly Protestant because she had been in a Protestant orphanages. My father in his reasoning seemed to have Protestant inclinations in that he didn't believe in the rituals of the Armenian Church. But in his heart he appeared to be Apostolic and was a member of the Armenian Church though not an attendee except when necessary.

When he had been forced to live among the Kurds, he had accepted Islam at the point of a knife, and the experience seemed to leave a lifelong questioning in his mind on the subject of

Hagop's parents dancing for the first time
at a New Year's Eve party

religion. No one who knew what he had been through with the trauma of many beatings, threats and attempts on his life could blame him for his doubts, though some kind of reassurance would have been good for him. He read much on the subject of comparative religion, giving it a great deal of thought but not really arriving at a conclusion for his own peace of mind.

In Beirut, we also had the chance to see the old custom of bride-seeking as our family and the family of my husband's friend Hovhannes Norendzayan went to visit the family of his prospective bride, Anahid Tahmazian. In these cases the bride appeared only to serve coffee around to the company. An engagement soon followed, as both families found such a union acceptable. This charming incident was the first and last time I witnessed the tradition. I later became interested in learning about and writing about the old customs, especially in the historic villages of my ancestors.

I greatly enjoyed visiting a cave called Jeita near Beirut with its fascinating and colorful mineral forms. I was taken there by my aunt's niece Alice Khanigian, who lived just a block away from my in-laws' house. It was the first time I had met her and her family and found them quite hospitable, as most of the people I met there were. She took me to the cave without Hagop because that day he was out on an errand somewhere. The guide paddled us in a small boat on the lake in the mountain and told us to be very quiet.

I had never imagined such wonders as the colorful crystals and rocky growths that existed there, so unlike anything I had seen. A green Christmas-tree like growth with white sparkles on it. Small rust-colored out-croppings looking like a model of a city. Mineral growths of white, blue, pink. Nature's imaginings.

Scene from the grotto of Jeita

On the way home from the Middle East we stopped again in Paris for a couple of days during which time we met with Hagop's friend Shahé Oughourlian, whom he had not seen for many years. They had studied violin together at the Conservatory in Beirut, Hagop having left that study because he had been compelled to work full time and over-time at his trade in order to support the rest of his family.

We saw several other European countries. Our visit to Venice in Italy included a stop at the Armenian Catholic Monastery (the Mekhitarist Order) on the island of San Lazarro, where a portrait of the poet Lord Byron has hung since his study of the Armenian language there. This institution has been one of the world's centers of Armenian culture since 1717, when the ruling council of Venice gave the island, a former leper colony whose patron saint was St. Lazarus, to a group of Armenian monks who had escaped from Turkish persecution five years earlier and placed themselves under the protection of the Pope.

We took a gondola ride there and back, after having an audience with the Abbot Monsignor Srabion Wolohojian, whose brother Mugerdich Wolohojian we knew from Watertown. A friendly and humble man, he left us proud and happy to have met him and to have toured their printing establishment. Their typesetters were all Italians who had been trained to set type in

Armenian without knowing the language, and they have produced many fine books over the years.

Coincidentally just as we were leaving, an acquaintance from Boston, the lawyer Dickran Boyajian, arrived on the island. Mrs. Haigouhi Boghosian, who had been Hagop's landlady in Cambridge, was one of his clients and had encouraged my husband to get to know Archie's daughter. To see someone from Watertown when traveling abroad was a greater pleasure than meeting that person at home. Suddenly I began to appreciate what I left behind and felt that I wouldn't take it for granted again. For if familiarity breeds contempt, then unfamiliarity breeds nostalgia for that which was too familiar.

Abbot Monsignor
Srabion Wolohojian

San Marco Square houses the ornate St. Mark's Basilica, many pigeons, and a vast area which could accommodate thousands of people. The Ducal Palace on one side of the square is a study in history and in art. In the Palace stands a huge room with magnificent paintings displayed on a ceiling so high I became claustrophobic looking up at it and quickly left the building. It was awe working on me.

A visit to the excavated city of Pompeii near the volcano Mt. Vesuvius was a must-see. The city, along with Herculaneum, had been

Helene in St. Mark's Square

Pompeii — Strada Dell' Avondanza

buried under 60 feet of ash from the eruption of Mt. Vesuvius in 79 A.D., was rediscovered in 1748 and restored. We walked through its streets and viewed the Roman houses, baths, bakeries and the statues of people and of a dog made by the volcanic ash. Some of the intact artwork on the walls and on the floors of mosaic informed us along with the damaged houses and stores of the kind of life these people had lived in that ancient era.

We didn't have as much experience with the food in Italy as we did in France. We had an unremarkable spaghetti at a small restaurant in Venice. I used to insist on stopping at bakeries for sampling at the sight of tempting desserts, for in those days I didn't need to watch my weight as carefully as I must now and could walk miles without any problem. I was always somewhat addicted to sweets.

In Germany we stopped at the small cities of Freiburg, Giessen and later Homburg because Hagop's brother Hovsep, a pediatrician, and his wife Mechtild lived there. We saw the Black Forest from the top of a very high mountain and visited the old castles and churches and as well as art museums. We stayed longer there than we had in the cities of other countries and were part of the daily life of the town, even going into stores to buy items while trying to make ourselves understood to the people who spoke only German. But with the few words of German we knew, we managed to communicate what we wanted to buy. On a holiday, a storekeeper surprised me by offering me a small glass of the alcoholic drink *schnapps*.

"I was wicked after that party though."

"Why?"

"When we walked out to the street on our way to our room, I sang 'God Bless America'."

"Tsk, tsk. In Germany!"

"Well, I was half drunk."

"You didn't mean to be rude?"

"No. I know they are sensitive on the matter of World War II and who won or lost."

"It was very late. No one heard you anyway."

"Only my conscience."

"Don't worry about it."

"I won't."

Several odd incidents happened to us in our travels, for both of us were just learning to be less naive by succumbing to mistakes. The first ship we crossed the Atlantic on was a huge ship and the ocean rocked it enormously, so that my husband was often not feeling well. On the *Esperia* crossing the Mediterranean going toward Lebanon, I became seasick. Later on the way back to Europe on the same ship, we found we had been assigned to

Mechtild and Dr. Hovsep Sarkissian

different cabins, this on our extended honeymoon of six months. It didn't occur to us to fight for our rights, the recognition that we should be together, and we continued the entire voyage on the Mediterranean separated except during the day.

Additionally, Hagop was traveling on a Lebanese passport while I was using my American passport, which didn't need visas for entry and reentry into European countries. When we left Germany to reenter France to visit my aunt, we were stopped by the officials at the railroad station who said that he couldn't travel but that I could. We saved that trip and waited for our return by way of the Mediterranean to board another ship called the *United States*, Hagop then well armed with the proper visa from the French embassy in Beirut.

Hagop and Helene at the Corniche in Beirut

Meeting My Aunt

My aunt in France had lived simply and even on the edge of poverty, especially during the years of World War II and the Nazi occupation of France when we used to package our used clothing and often send these packages to them. Her husband had worked in the mines, and I remember hearing that he had gone blind. No one in my family ever mentioned to me what his age was when he died, but he didn't live to be really old.

It was an unusual delight to see these people I had heard about all those years and thought I would never see. After we found their house on a humble street and announced our presence, a small white-haired woman who bore a resemblance to my mother came to the door with smiles and greetings. Others in the house were Joseph, the only son of six children, and Suzanne, the youngest daughter, their married sisters visiting us in Gardanne or we returning the visit to Lyon and St. Etienne. They were the Hagobian family.

"Hello, Joseph.”

"You look like Suzanne."

"France is a different judgment for me."

"How do they judge us or our country?"

"The residents of Paris were more severe. I remember that woman guarding the public bathroom who shouted at me when I didn't have enough change and didn't believe my husband was waiting for me."

Hagop as usual was my interpreter because his Armenian is so excellent, mine being stronger in understanding than in speaking. The Armenian-French family spoke French and fluent Armenian but didn't embarrass me by asking why my spoken Armenian was inadequate. I have wondered many times in these years what I would have done without my husband's help on many such occasions.

We took an automobile ride through Cézanne territory (Paul Cézanne, the famous French artist who painted in that area

Left to right, Khoumar Hagobian, Helene, cousins Joseph, Suzanne, Lucienne and the latter's husband Antranig der Ghazarian, in Gardanne

and set the foundation for the transition from 19th-century Impressionism to 20th-century Cubism) in Aix-en-Provence and the wonderful meals of chicken and rabbit my aunt cooked from the live animals we occasionally saw in the house, a no-frills and no bathroom dwelling. That situation was taken care of some years later when the town developed a sewage system. I don't even need to close my eyes to see their house and a small open food stalls near it where fruits and vegetables were sold and the carcasses of rabbits were hung.

My aunt had been a heroine during World War II, when lack of food forced her to go out into the forest and kill a deer with her bare hands to bring back meat to feed her husband and children. She was and always had been a tough woman who had seen much, suffered much and was able to fight to survive. She showed no traces that we could see of cynicism and bitterness but seemed quite happy with her surroundings and with her children.

"She looks like my mother and my uncle."

"They were very nice to us."

"No reason not to be."

"At times like this I wish I were fluent in a number of languages, but languages are not my strong point."

"How did you like meeting your cousins?"

"A new experience and in this instance a good one. Of course I care and always will care, but distance and busy life tend to separate people."

"They seem more interesting when they are at a distance and there has been a long separation."

"Maybe."

A continued correspondence was impossible, however, because they didn't understand or read English, and I didn't understand or read much French, though I had taken a few courses in French in high school and one in college. My written Armenian was nonexistent, and perhaps theirs was also. In addition, we were all firmly entrenched in our own lives and ways of living, busy with all we had to do and aware of our responsibilities to family, friends and jobs. Zevarte, the oldest of the cousins, visited my parents some years later with her husband Nishan Aydabirian for a delightful but brief memory with pictures to prove that we were all younger then.

The meeting made me doubly aware of caring about Europe and its way of life. Of course, experiencing the fascination of visiting Paris greatly helped me to visualize what the country was about and what its people were like. Certainly what my cousins were like, always having wondered about similarities and differences in the way they were brought up in France versus the way I was brought up and also the similarities and differences in personality and temperament as compared to my mother and my uncle.

"I could see physical resemblances, but my aunt seemed more prematurely aged."

"She has had a hard life."

"She has seen at close hand two wars, starvation, the cruelty of Turks and of Nazis and has brought up six children on the edge of poverty."

"I'm so glad I met her."

I also had cousins in Armenia, in Turkey, and in South America as well as in other parts of the United States such as

California and Michigan. They were more distant cousins, and I only met one of them from Turkey and another from California. Hagop had cousins in Lebanon, and Syria, in Australia and in Canada. I met most of them and enjoyed the meetings, finding that the Middle Eastern culture as practiced by Armenians was more than specific food dishes and more than the Armenian language. Their attitudes differed from mine in many ways, and some of them who were better educated or had been exposed to my culture understood my customs better than others did.

But I was still repressed on these tours and didn't react with as much joy and emotion as I should have and did later at remembering these places and writing about them. My husband thought I lacked much interest, but really I was impressed but not able to feel the thrill of emotions that he did. Who would not be impressed at entering a Crusader's castle and looking out of one of its narrow windows? Or ascending to the top of a mountain and gazing at the deep blue of the Mediterranean? Or seeing the ancient ruins of the temple of Baalbek shining like pinkish marble imploring the sun? Or meeting an aunt and first cousins for the first time?

Living in Cambridge

When we came home to America, my parents had rented an apartment on the first floor of Mrs. Boghosian's house for us at 461 Huron Avenue in Cambridge. It was close to my father's store, which I was able to visit often. However, six months after we had resumed our life there, Hagop received word that his father had passed away. He was 71 years old and had been suffering with a heart condition for a long time. Hagop and I were both very sad, and he always felt guilty about having left his parents.

After returning from the first trip, I took a job as a full-time searcher in Harry Elkins Widener Memorial Library of Harvard University. It was named after a graduate and book collector who died with the sinking of the *Titanic* and was built shortly after his death by his mother, dedicated in 1914, and subsequently became the largest university library in the world. The catalog room I worked in was on the first floor; as of this writing in 2008, the room has been changed with the extensive renovation and modernization of this library to serve other purposes.

As a searcher I would select a book from a given few and search through the card catalog, which was extensive and filled the entire room, to find the card that described that book and put the two together in a neat pile. This went on all day and could have been monotonous except that I took small breaks to read snatches of the books and to peer at the vivid photographs of art. I left that job after a year when I became pregnant and was quite ill for three or four months.

In the middle of pregnancy when I felt better, I managed to pick up another part-time temporary job for two months in the basement of the Memorial Hall working at typing letters in Swedish for the recently appointed Nobel Prize in Medicine winner Dr. Georg von Bekesy. I didn't work with him directly but for his secretary, though I did see the great man, and hated myself for being too shy to go up to him and shake his hand in congratulations, but no one seemed to mind.

"Don't you feel embarrassed going out to work in that condition?"

"Not embarrassed but a little scared."

"As long as you can manage."

"Well, I did have a problem bending over to pick up something I had dropped, and the young girl who worked with me was unsympathetic. Evidently, she had never been pregnant."

"It looks that way."

"Now with winter and snow on the way, it's time to quit. I don't want to risk a fall."

"It seems safer, since you have to walk a way over snowy sidewalks to get there."

We lived in Cambridge for the first five years of our marriage. Then on April 30, 1962, our daughter Sharon Anoush was born at Waltham Hospital, now an extension of Boston's famous Children's Hospital. It was a Monday morning, and I had gone to the hospital at about 2 a.m. for this great adventure. She was healthy though jaundiced and had to stay in the hospital a few extra days. Then she went about the business of living, and I for a while was mothering and cleaning and cooking. A new tenderness entered my life with the birth of the child. Self-development and maturity began for me and gradually came into fruition as the child brought a new joy to my parents also as well as to all our close relatives.

The Cardiac Arrest

One event illustrates the point that experience teaches as nothing else can. It happened before I started working at the newspaper and before the birth of my second child, but its psychological implications continued to influence me for the rest of my life. The following is a less than graphic description of that event.

It was a year and a half since I had given birth to my first child, and I was disappointed that I should have the major health problem of gallbladder disease, which had not yet become an emergency. My stomach ached every day, and I couldn't digest food well and occasionally vomited. My general practitioner at the time, Achot Khoubesserian, had given me some pills to lessen the ache, a temporary measure. There was no recourse except gallbladder surgery after medication and an extremely restricted diet of mostly canned fruit and cottage cheese.

As I heard some good things about him, I chose the prominent Armenian surgeon Dr. Karl Kasparian, since that was what Armenians usually did. I was convinced without anyone telling me that some of my physical problems were caused by my dark moods, and I had felt isolated. Yet no one around me seemed to understand, and I was avoiding the psychiatrist who did because of his negative approach.

While in surgery having my gallbladder removed in October of 1963 at Mount Auburn Hospital in Cambridge, I suffered a cardiac arrest on the operating table, necessitating resuscitation by emergency surgery. This was different from the external resuscitation we think of these days that is fairly common and often successful. Because the initial external attempt failed, my rib cage was opened and my heart manipulated as the doctors put forth their best efforts. This was done quickly by Dr. Harken and his team, though it took some minutes, during which time brain damage had already begun. Then I was kept unconscious for four days on a respirator for fear that my heart would stop again. But it didn't.

In those days any successful resuscitation was rare, for lacking the refinements of treatment we have now. Cardiac arrest was considered clinical death, whereas now brain death is considered clinical death. If necessary, surgery had to be done immediately in order to be effective, and few surgeons were versed in the necessary techniques and follow-up care that this required. For that reason there were many specialists present during and after the surgery, giving me the best care possible.

Dr. Harken and his crew administered multiple electric shocks after the chest cavity was opened and soon administered urea and cortisone to my brain to reduce a slight brain damage that had occurred, probably under the direction of the neurologist who was present. I never did ascertain how they administered those chemicals, but I thought they must have somehow injected them through my scalp. For in the back of my head there was a small area they called an abrasion where hair never grew again.

I remember waking up, not realizing how long I had been unconscious, not knowing what had happened except that it had been very serious, knowing only that I was attached to an intravenous tube, an oxygen mask, and a number of other devices. Stiff on my back and unable to move because of pain alleviated somewhat by injections, I tried to ask what happened. Evidently my attempt was hardly audible. I remember that during my three-week stay in the hospital one of the nurses had asked me if I knew of any reason why this sort of thing should have happened. Had I had a serious illness like rheumatic fever? But I was too weak to answer or even to think clearly. I had been successfully treated, but I wasn't able to think past the pain and clearly about what had happened or being reunited with family and taking care of myself and my child of one-and-a-half years again.

It took me many years to fully decipher this experience with no memory of the four unconscious days; no one really told me in detail what had happened, and no one knew exactly why except to theorize that it was the anesthesia cyclopropane with atropine that was used but is no longer in use. So that my question why and theirs ran along the same track. The nurse who had inquired may have been influenced by the doctors who had inquired, as no doubt they did.

The entire hospital was obviously shocked by this event, and many of the employees came to glance at me after a few days when I was out of a private room, coming into the room one by one and taking a look at what they considered a miracle. Dr. Blumen told me that none of their resuscitated patients had done so well and attributed that fact to my youth. I was 30 at the time. My husband, my father and my sister came to see me one by one, for visitors were allowed only for brief periods. My mother came in to see me once and hurt me as badly as she had ever done by laughing at the sight of me in this unfortunate condition.

Now I realize that perhaps the reason it took me so long to be able to produce clear writing on the subject was that it was so difficult to face the emotions that were tangled with the events of those days coupled with the fact that though a slight brain damage had been reversed, it evidently slowed the process of thinking a bit. Or was it psychological damage? There was so much significance to weigh. Then I went through some years of facing lack of sympathy from some people who didn't know my problems and some who did.

Dr. Dwight Emary Harken was one of the greats in the field of thoracic surgery. I knew nothing about him at that time and was surprised that he wasn't mentioned by the doctors who had attended to me. I had a memory of that name and also a mention of it by a nurse's aide. Later I always had an intuitive feeling that he had some idea of why this happened and wanted to hear more about it from me. But I am sorry that I didn't know the extent of what had gone on in surgery or the details until some years later when I applied to get the report. I had asked some questions to a few of other doctors,

Dwight Emary Harken, M.D.

but they hadn't been adequately answered, leading me to a great deal of soul-searching and thought later when realization set it.

It was luck, good luck and bad luck all mixed up into one incident. It had happened while my husband was at work, and an emergency call brought him in to the hospital where Dr. Kasparian, the operating surgeon, had talked to him with my blood on his hospital attire. It was a shock to Hagop and everyone, though he reported that my family was rather cool about it. It was difficult for me to realize the effect this situation had on anyone, except over a period of time, and it was impossible for any of them to conceive of what I was going through.

Of course the people who worked with Hagop all knew what had happened, and Father Papken Maksoudian came in to pray over me for my recovery after it was sure I would recover. My sister came in from New York and talked to me for an hour when I didn't have the strength to talk or even to listen.

I was in the hospital for three weeks with continuous morphine to ease the extreme pain of this double surgery. For those three weeks I was surrounded by the compassion and care of many doctors and nurses, including private nurses for the first week during which time I was fed intravenously.

The doctors who visited daily were Dr. Kasparian, who had done the original gallbladder surgery, Dr. Louis Blumen and Dr. Richard Gibson, who were Dr. Harken's assistants. I am sure Dr. Harken not only directed some of the proceedings but also spoke to me in those four days that are blacked out of memory. The report states that he and his assistants watched me carefully when I was in the Recovery Room. What had they said to me or to each other? Did I say anything to them when I woke up briefly as was stated in the report? What did I say? Did I comprehend what they were saying to each other in discussing what might have happened and why? Is that why I somehow instinctively felt that I knew but only had to find the proof and a way to communicate it to myself and to them? It was a custom of the time that doctors not tell patients much about their surgeries.

On one of the first few days that I remember, a doctor with attractive gray wavy hair was at my bedside looking into my eyes with a small flashlight. Perhaps it was Dr. Harken or it could have been Dr. Donald Osterberg, the neurologist present at the operation. I don't remember seeing Dr. Thomas Burnap, the anesthesiologist at the operation.

I noticed then that Dr. Kasparian didn't speak to the other two doctors, and they didn't speak to him even though they examined me at the same time. Dr. Blumen showed great concern and caring about how I was responding. On his daily visits he watched me carefully for any signs of discomfort and often instructed the nurse to give me morphine or oxygen. Dr. Gibson only watched what he was doing and listened. Dr. Kasparian was friendly, as affectionate as he was puzzled, helped me to start walking around and never explained what had happened but did encourage me to think of having another child as soon as possible. I suspected that the two groups didn't get along.

After I had been weaned from intravenous feedings and had enough strength to get out of bed with some help and walk to the bathroom, I was able to get a look at myself in the mirror. The face was a frightening sight, thin and pale and the body hardly able to shuffle one step after the other. The eyes had the look of utter weakness and weariness, which evidently matched the voice that could hardly be heard answering questions. Dr. Blumen had commented on this fact in saying, "That's not the voice you came in with, is it?" I knew what a wounded animal feels like when it retreats from harm.

Soon enough the moment arrived for a discharge from the hospital, even though it was the longest three weeks of my life. I was still a bit dazed, perhaps because I had been on morphine until the last moment. My husband arrived dependably by car and drove me to my parents' house. Gradually hints here and there showed what a difficult three weeks it had been for him.

The most emotional moment after leaving the hospital was at seeing my little daughter again to appreciate her more than ever. After I recovered from my outburst of crying, I saw that she didn't quite recognize me, but seeing that I was sad she brought her little doll over to me and put it in my lap. One doesn't or shouldn't forget these little moments of redemption, which if added up over the years, make reason for a holiday.

I was to stay with my parents for six weeks while recovering strength enough to take care of my child and my apartment. My husband visited every day. My mother didn't seem to fathom how serious my condition had been until I asked her to help me take a bath after the bandages had been removed, and to her shock and dismay, she saw the purple scars in all their fury.

Forgive me, but I say these things not out of any personal hatred or desire for revenge, for I understood her hard-hearted behavior. I only wish she had had the opportunity for some psychiatric help to ease the burden of the hurt she carried to give her some satisfaction and tranquility in her life and render our lives with her easier and more satisfying. I hope the descriptions I give will contribute a little bit to the understanding of these problems for those who have it and for those who must react to it, even for those who must treat it on a daily basis.

My daughter and I became reacquainted during this most delicate and trying time. She had been calling my mother Mama, thinking my mother was her mother and had been enjoying herself with her grandparents, they spoiling her because she was their first grandchild. An adorable and talkative little girl, she wasn't like her mother, who was never talkative and often moody and quiet. She soon began to call me Mama, and she made us all laugh with her attempts at talking and asking who was who. She continued in this way growing up and thus lightened my burden of life by being a good companion. Her problems became mine, so that it was easier to put mine aside or make them secondary.

Then suddenly in our own apartment, day followed inexorable day as I did my work slowly and took a long rest every afternoon for about a year. There were stabbing pains especially in the chest area and would be for quite a while. But I was thinking more along the positive line of what to do with this new life I was given. I didn't envision a change, which would show me a new way to be, to serve, to write and even to speak. Settling into a new life with a child, though I was still not sociable, I rather enjoyed it with a thorough sense of duty and obligation and a growing love for my family and my performance as a wife and mother.

Did the gossip on the part of a few of my relatives, giving the impression that I was against the physicians and the hospital though I had never said anything, influence later suspicions about me? Were there other branches on the grapevine that with all this watering grew extraordinarily fast, leaving everyone ready to pick at the ripe grapes?

No one had really asked me what I thought about the surgery, and as usual I was silent. Only much later when I began to talk about the situation or write about the previous suspicions directed at me did the elements of truth began to make the rounds and do their cleanup routine. For I found that in order to conquer gossip and misconception gone out of control, one has to find the original misconceptions out of the past and destroy them so that the rest will fall of their own weight.

"You didn't talk about the operation much."

"I had so much to think about. There were so many tangled emotions from the past and the present."

"How much did the operation bother you?"

"Of course it did — pain, the shock, the unconsciousness, the extreme shortness of breath they gave the oxygen for."

"How about the care you received? Was it good?"

"It was excellent. I can't say enough good things about the doctors who revived me and the nurses who were so kind and compassionate and were always there when I needed them or were just always there. I only wish they had told me more about what was going on. Now I wonder what they may have told me when I was unconscious for those four days because actually I think I was in and out of consciousness. I just remember one moment when I said something like 'I did it,' and there was laughter."

"Did you see anyone then?"

"No, it looked completely dark, but it was masculine laughter. Perhaps they had asked me something, and I replied inappropriately."

"Why don't you just forget it?"

"Things like that can't be forgotten because of the physical and mental scars they leave, which eventually represent compassion, attention and miracle more than that operation. It changed me. It changed my life by giving me hope for something better than the painful emotions that I had been living with and eventually helped me to transcend that."

"And you found that by writing poetry or prose you can express the tangled emotions or untangle them?"

"Yes, and I'm so glad I found the way. What I thought was slight brain damage may have been psychological damage that I'd been carrying with me for years without the 'cure'."

"Did you ever ask anyone?"

"No, because I don't think they have a definite answer, and only I can see into the workings of my brain over a period of years. There was only some little trouble with concentration in reading books."

As I found out only years later, Dr. Lawrence Geoghegan had also been present and had assisted Dr. Kasparian with the surgery. Later, putting what little information I could gather together, I knew that the doctor with the flashlight was looking for signs of brain damage, and I began examining my own behavior and my writing to see if there was anything erratic. There appeared only inexperience and the need for intellectual maturity, and later when I was writing poetry there was an echo in the writing as if I were trying to write two things at once but was unaware of the background meaning. But that had been there before.

Dr. Kasparian continued with follow-up care with three visits in his office, mostly for removing bandages and talking to me. The assassination of President John F. Kennedy occurred ironically on November 22, which was the day of my first appointment. The shooting occurred at about noon while I was sitting in the living room watching television. I was appropriately shocked and sad, though I was still emotionally rather numb and speechless. I had a horrific cough with much mucous in my upper chest and throat, causing pain in my incisions for six weeks until the cough subsided. Of course, the event of the day was mentioned in the doctor's office as would be expected. Giving me little information, he told me of the heroics he had performed without details but never mentioned Dr. Harken's work, which had been crucial. And it never left my mind that he had ignored my complaints of occasional momentary bad chest pain before the operation.

Since I had been with my parents during that time, I don't remember that they showed much shock reaction to the assassination. Perhaps their daily problems were enough for them. Perhaps they had seen so much of that sort of thing, they had only a flat reaction. But that day is forever engraved upon my mind because it became in that way connected to my own suffering.

I tried not to torture myself with questions of responsibility and of damages, but because of difficult recovery, pain and shortness of breath and the guesswork I was surrounded by, it was impossible to stop thinking about the surgery and its implications, and I noticed that some people I came into contact with didn't seem to believe in the complete success of this surgery. Another had looked at me disdainfully and said, "We don't like Jews," a remark that pointed to definite political implications and preferences because the surgeons who saved me were Jews. It was the Armenian way not to accept changes or to be optimistic, my father usually the exception though sometimes he listened to others he thought knew better.

I concentrated more on the positive aspects of the experience because I knew concentration on negative thoughts would destroy my new positive mood. It was also impossible to miss the element of luck in all this. Since I was a thinking person, how could I not think about this or read about it? How can a thirsty person not drink? I'm glad that years later I finally asked for the report after my daughter advised me that I had the right to see it. Thus it became clear who did the actual saving and who else was present at the surgery from Dr. Kasparian's own report.

The bills finally found me, for though Blue-Cross Blue-Shield had paid most of the cost for the surgeries, they didn't pay for blood transfusions or for the surgeons. The initial cost at discharge from the hospital had been $1500. Dr. Kasparian's bill was in the amount of $300. Dr. Harken was initially paid $50, which included his assistants. Then after he sent me a bill every month for another $50, Blue-Cross Blue-Shield eventually paid him another $50. This was another indication of where the care I was getting from Dr. Blumen had been directed from, though no reason for the bill was stated. Now it seems to me that in the four days I had been unconscious that name had been said many times, and it must have been taken for granted that I knew who, other than Dr. Kasparian, had been directing the traffic.

A letter arrived from Blue-Cross Blue-Shield stating that the balance had been paid and that Dr. Harken and his assistants were willing to help me if I needed any. I felt I needed more information. I have that tendency to think too much, but this matter was worth much thought, especially because the old suspicions still seemed to be around. Where did they originate?

My father paid the cost of the blood transfusions, for Hagop and I had no savings left after that trip to Beirut and back. Our jobs were not high-paying, and I had left work more than a year before. My father paid for the furniture also, always generous with money.

I reveal all of these details not to horrify, not to scare, not to indict surgery itself that was more primitive in those days than it is now, and above all not to ask for pity for myself or for anyone else. Understanding and compassion are enough. Such an experience has psychological reverberations throughout one's life, like the ripples in the river when a stone has been thrown into it, except with a bit more permanence. A remark here and there reinforced my emotions in this regard.

But soon I was too busy taking care of a child and an apartment and working in an office to think much about this matter. After this surgery of October 29, 1963, I began working at newspaper in about June, part-time arrangements having been made for me. It may have been taking more responsibility physically and mentally than I had the strength for, but I was willing to try.

I needed to be involved in some work or activity outside of the house, even though house, husband and child were a great comfort to me. The interest in the job and the meeting with people and the occasional praise and perhaps even the criticism began to give me a stronger sense of self and of control of situations with people, though self-confidence was weaker than it should have been.

A Journalist in the 60s

Nubar Aghishian from Beirut, then the assistant editor of the *Baikar* daily as well as business manager while also studying for a Ph.D. in physics, asked me to edit the *The Armenian Mirror-Spectator* in 1964. Since my husband had years of experience working for newspapers and was working foreman of the printing plant, he trained me for the technical parts of the job such as placement of articles on a dummy of what the pages will look like. Copy editing was easy enough, and writing was my forte.

The first woman in that capacity at the newspaper, I was paid $40 a week for part-time hours. I found I had some groundbreaking to do and realized that all editors have friends and detractors. Some people were mystified by my usual reticence and pegged me as egocentric in the sense of thinking myself better than others and not wanting to talk to them. That wasn't an accurate assessment of the reality of the situation, since fear and insecurity had always been my primary motivations.

Antranig Antreassian was executive secretary of the ADL, had been editor of the *Baikar* and was also a prolific Armenian writer who produced many books, which he had to publish himself either at his own expense or sometimes with the help of some Armenian organizations. He was very popular, friendly and a lively speaker whose charisma convinced many people to contribute money for the new building on Mt. Auburn Street in Watertown to house the newspapers that had originally been located on Shawmut Avenue in Boston. The new building was designed by his contemporary, the architect Zaven Baikar of Worcester.

Katherine Tatian was the secretary of the *Baikar* and also a friend. Rose Mamishian, Nancy Bazarian and Arpi Maksoudian were successive secretaries for the *Mirror-Spectator*. Others I knew from the ADL Zovickian Chapter of which I was a member were brothers Ned and George Haroutunian, Don and Margaret Boghosian, Harry Najarian, Katherine's husband Stephen and her sister Rose Yakoobian. Days that cannot be forgotten.

Editor of the *Baikar* Dr. Nubar Berberian, an expert in international law, was also friendly to me, to Hagop and to my father, who later did much volunteer work there. Editors of the English-language newspaper slightly before that time were Bob Vahan and Varoujan Samuelian, both popular in the community. Varoujan, or Juicy as they called him after his column in the *MS* entitled "Juicy Tidbits," was editor for a few nonconsecutive years and was the first editor I had previously met at that newspaper. He had welcomed some of my early poems and articles, which were actually the first pieces I had published anywhere. Bob Vahan was the editor just before I went to work for the newspaper, leading to some unjustified controversy that I had through influence had him discharged so I could take the job.

I edited a great deal of Armenian news from America and abroad, work that broadened my knowledge of Armenians, their woes, their prides and ever-proliferating organizations. I wrote editorials during those two years, some of them on political subjects my only knowledge of which was the reading at hand or reference to my husband's great knowledge of Armenian politics.

But my faith in what I had learned about writing, philosophy and psychology quickened my pen to write on a variety of subjects. I wrote about the value of bilingualism and the importance of preserving languages in America. Many of the editorials were about the Armenian Cause, meaning the Armenian claims upon the Turkish government for its historic crime of Genocide, this because the newspaper was sponsored by the American branch of the worldwide Armenian political party, the Armenian Democratic Liberal Party, which we in America then referred to as an organization.

Traditionally, the Armenian Church leaders led the people of the Armenian communities in Turkey, where they had been dominated for hundreds of years. Thus many hundreds of years without government leaders eroded initiative and left church people and lay people afraid of consequences of displeasing Turks.

This situation of politics and the church was complicated by the fact that there were two conflicting Armenian political parties operating throughout the world. These were the ADL or the Ramgavars with their newspapers *Baikar* and *The Armenian Mirror-Spectator* and the Armenian Revolutionary Federation or the

Dashnags with their newspapers *Hairenik* and *Armenian Weekly*. These newspapers were in our area, and the organizations in question had other publications in various parts of the world. Their ideology was somewhat different, the first tolerating the Communist domination of Armenia in Soviet times for the safety of the people, and the other strictly opposed to this domination and propagandizing for freedom of the Armenian people. For Armenia had always been surrounded by enemy countries, especially Turkey, and Russia was often a safeguard. There was also the smaller Hunchagian Party and a Progressive Party.

Also in this regard the Armenian Church was and still is split along these party lines, the ADL submitting to the Catholicosate of All Armenians in Etchmiadzin, Armenia, and the ARF submitting to the Catholicosate of the Great House of Cilicia in Antelias, Lebanon. The jurisdiction of the former is the entire diaspora, and the jurisdiction of the latter is Lebanon, Syria and Cyprus with other Armenian communities recently added. Each Catholicosate has its historic origins, and since Armenians are traditionalists by nature, these distinctions have continued since 1441.

Tensions diffuse with time and distance to explosive political events, especially when other Armenian problems concerning Armenian immigration and Armenian independence have come to the fore. Few young Armenians these days know much about Armenian politics rooted in the past, so that the subject has become a valid academic study.

Not wanting to get into the controversy, I relented and for a brief period wrote about it in the newspaper. I found the material interesting, and the democratic values of the organization matched mine. Thus, I am still identified with the Ramgavars by my past work, my basic ideals as generalities and by family associations though my life is not geared along any political lines.

There were other editorials about the general social injustices, some about holidays, one about America paying a high price for leadership in technology, some on Armenian schools, some on the meaning of unity between two Armenian political factions, one against the involvement in the Vietnam conflict, one about the meaning of the phrase "old country," another about teens and so forth.

I wrote some editorials on the Armenian identity as well as a general subjects. Following is an excerpt from the October 17, 1964 issue called "Revival of the Armenian Identity":

> The Armenian character is fast reviving now in the new political entity that is Armenia. Its traits that were dormant for centuries are blossoming into cultural and educational activity that astounds many experts with the rate of its progress. Armenians have their identity now, and the world is recognizing it. Many works of Armenian literature are being translated into various languages. The fame of Armenian musicians and artists is spreading in the international sphere.
>
> Armenian voices are also heard from many of the countries including America as some have attained fame in the countries of adoption by bringing what is distinctly Armenian into their work and being referred to as Armenians. For example, Arshile Gorky is recognized as one of the original and most important of American artists, for he brought his Armenian identity into his work.
>
> A new era has begun for Armenia; perhaps we should say an older era has returned in a modern guise. And the politics of the situation has become secondary to its culture.

Another editorial from the same month is entitled "Music in Armenian Culture."

> A basic part of Armenian culture that has been inseparable from Armenian life is Armenian music, which is at this point more complex and varied than ever before. History led to the music that accompanied the exiles with the beautiful *sharagans* sung on Sundays in Armenian Churches . . . and the music of Gomidas Vartabed and a number of other classical composers is on the same plane.
>
> Second, we have all grown up with the familiar village songs that have been recorded in song and adapted by the young Armenian-American generation. They are danceable and singable and have vibrations comparable to American popular music.
>
> But the real folk music is of a different sort. It consists of songs sung lyrically or dramatically and with deep and poetic meaning in their words. Most Armenians have heard the perennial favorites "Groong" and "Vart." The Armenian-

American communities have recently had opportunities to become acquainted with the old and the new songs of a classical folk nature through the concerts given by the National Foundation for Armenian Culture.

Hampartzoum Berberian, the conductor, has himself composed many songs and classical pieces. There are other composers of modern Armenian music in the Dispersion and in Armenia, foremost among them of international fame are Aram Khachaturian from Armenia and Alan Hovhaness from America. There is also an abundance of talented performers, those of top rank including Amara, Chookasian, Doloukhanova, Lisitsian, and others. There are also a number of thriving folk song and dance groups inside and outside of Armenia.

At this newspaper that served the Armenian communities in America and was managed largely by members of the older immigrant generation, I was an inexperienced editor practicing freedom of the press but not realizing how seriously some people would take the ideas expressed there, especially if they were different from those of the leaders of organizations. No one spoke specifically about the editorials, but eventually there was some dissatisfaction even though my projections often turned out to be true in the long run.

I also wrote of my disagreement with the term "white genocide" used by many Armenians to refer to the assimilation of Armenians by intermarriage. This term seemed to me to equate a natural process of a choice with the brutality and bloodshed of a genocide. But time has also solved the controversy, for now intermarriage has become a more accepted way of life and I do not hear the term "white genocide" being used much. There should be a better term for the results of assimilation.

The 50th anniversary of the Armenian Genocide was commemorated in 1965, and up to that point Armenians hadn't expressed themselves publicly or sometimes even privately on the subject because they had been in mourning. But there had been so many unspoken personal agonies of people who had been through this worst of experiences that the anniversary released a flood of articles on the subject to be published in the newspaper. It was the beginning of a movement for recognition of historical facts and for commemoration rather than mourning. Yet I didn't know all the facts, for in a job like this the editors often learn what they don't know from experience and from the articles they receive.

After running article after article on the subject of the Armenian Genocide, I also wrote a number of editorials about it. On April 24, the day of commemoration, I put out a special issue on the subject and sent it to members of Congress, President Johnson and Vice President Hubert

Leon Surmelian

Humphrey. Until that time most Armenians had avoided talking about the subject that was too painful, but some writers had written about it in Armenian and in English.

That issue also contained the article called "Mourning Is Not Enough" by Leon Surmelian, who had authored the best-selling novel *I Ask You Ladies and Gentlemen* and was then professor of English at California State College in Los Angeles. It was a detailed historical and political article, making the point that though the Armenian Church officials and the leadership of the Armenian General Benevolent Union forbade any public demonstrations for the 50th anniversary of the Armenian Genocide, there should be a World Congress of Armenians to lead the Armenian people on their quest for recognition of this terrible tragedy. He added that he was ready for action.

Another important article in that issue was entitled "His Excellency S. Kyprianou Refers to Armenians in UN Debate," in which the Cypriot Foreign Minister mentioned the Armenian Genocide after the Turkish representative had accused the Greeks of genocide. There was an excerpt from the writings of Ambassador Henry Morgenthau, who had witnessed the Armenian sufferings and had tried to defend them from the Turkish onslaught. There was also an excerpt from the book *Bloody Desert* by Hagop Kouyoumjian relating his personal experiences of the deportation and torture in the desert of Der Zor.

The following is the editorial called "Out of Smoldering Ashes" I wrote to commemorate that anniversary, and it was subsequently published in the *Congressional Record*:

April 24, 1915, is the day on which hundreds of Armenian leaders in Istanbul were taken into government custody and killed. But marches in the interior provinces that soon engulfed all villages, towns, and cities, had already begun, and although there was Armenian defense in many areas, 1 1/2 million Armenians succumbed to slaughter after tortures and atrocities. The massacres continued after 1918, when the mask of World War I was gone in Transcaucasia under the leadership of Kemal.

The Turkish government had its way in the complete domination and usurpation of the western part of the Armenian historical land and part of Eastern Armenia. Other Christian nations and people who had shown some sympathy to Armenians previously did not intercede on behalf of Armenians, though they acknowledged with gratitude the help of many Armenian soldiers who fought for the Allies. There were notable exceptions, men who tried to stop the massacres and to aid the Armenian cause, men such as Dr. Lepsius, Lord Bryce, Gladstone, Morgenthau, Nansen, Woodrow Wilson and others.

The Armenians in Armenia and those in the dispersion have not forgotten their friends; nor have they forgotten their Turkish enemies; nor shall they ever forget their mentors. On this, the 50th Anniversary of the Great Crime, they remembered that lives, homeland and $35 billion in savings and property were lost to the grace of the Turkish Government and mob. They remember that the world has not yet recognized the need for restitution, and that Turkey itself will never even admit its crime and its present distortions of history. These Armenians feel that the cause of justice is never outdated.

And they realize that out of the smoldering ashes and the ruins of death and decay, a small Armenia was born and has made tremendous progress in contributions to the universal cause of education, scientific advancement, arts, and the renaissance of its own cultural heritage . . .

This editorial and some others like it were strong when strong was needed and echoed traditional Armenian emotionalism. The self-expression gave me great satisfaction and encouraged some others to write on the subject. I held the innocent belief that justice will triumph in the end, perhaps from the influence of Superman programs on radio I listened to as a child, translating them to Superwoman in accordance with my ideas of equality.

I received many letters of appreciation for this special issue, postage of which was paid for by donations from subscribers. One of these was from Leon Surmelian, replying to my request for an article from him. A portion of the letter follows:

> Good to hear from you, and my thanks and congratulations to you for editing the *Mirror-Spectator*. For one evidently so young, that is an achievement. I only hope you don't get discouraged. Do it for yourself and God . . . I have read and enjoyed your pieces in *MS*. Forgive me, but I am a little touched by the fact that a girl is the editor now. If I can be of any service to you, in an emergency or otherwise, let me know.

The following two letters from the White House pleased me greatly. They are addressed to Mrs. Sarkissian, for I was using my married name, though now I always use Helene Pilibosian as a pen name.

> The President asked me to thank you for the recent issue of *The Armenian Mirror-Spectator* that you sent him. He appreciates your thoughtful interest in seeing that this publication reached him.
> With the President's warm good wishes,
> Sincerely yours,
> Juanita D. Roberts
> Personal Secretary to the President

and from the Vice President:

> Thank you very much for sending me a copy of the special issue of *The Armenian Mirror-Spectator* dedicated to those Armenians killed in 1915. I look forward to reading it. Best wishes.
> Sincerely,
> Hubert H. Humphrey

There were other letters of appreciation I didn't keep from Congressmen, including one from Gerald Ford, who later became president. Needless to say, I regretted throwing some of these away.

Attention to the subject turned out to be foresight, for after that more political involvement for Armenians and organizations such as the Armenian Assembly and the Armenian National Committee began. It was the first processing of my ideas that I had gained by years of hard study and formed the basis of some of my later work in writing and publishing books, many of which were on the Armenian subject in various forms.

Thus the idea stage foretold my future as life led me along its unknown paths. Disagreements were like the gremlins of indigestion and went away when the suggestion was taken to a positive conclusion. I took the American in my Armenian-American identity quite seriously and sometimes stressed what was going on in purely American terms, feeling that even Armenians who live here should be aware of them and consider consequences.

I also did reporting of events such as lectures, plays, concerts and conventions. It was fairly easy and formulaic to write about these, making sure to give credit to all the people who worked for them. My father, my husband and I became like the Three Musketeers going to the conventions of the eastern American area of the Armenian Democratic Liberal Organization, which as a worldwide organization helped the Armenian community with its social and political adjustments.

The ADL is a political organization whose roots can be found in an organization formed in historic Armenia to help the Armenians resist the oppression of the Turks. In America its political character was enhanced much later after the newer immigrants from Lebanon, Syria and Egypt had come in. At the point where it became more political, beginning to use the word Party instead of Organization and using the Armenian language completely in meetings instead of the English we had been used to, I felt I could no longer be involved with the organization but only with the newspaper in a limited capacity.

I had joined the organization when I became editor of the newspaper because at that time it was a requirement that the editor be a member and also because my husband was a member.

My father also was a member, and both of them at various times had served on the District Committee, the highest body of the Eastern U.S. and Canada of the ADL. I did some research into the history of its founding in historic Armenia as a political party and wrote some articles about it in subsequent years.

Following is the Preamble of the by-laws adopted at the organization's 39th Convention held in the Asbury Park, New Jersey, in September of 1959:

> The philosophy of the Armenian Democratic Liberal Organization is based on the traditional democratic principles on which the United States of America was founded, and its members owe allegiance only to the United States Government.
>
> Under the guidance of these principles, the Armenian Democratic Liberal Organization endeavors to serve the welfare of the Armenian people. It is dedicated to the development and preservation of their cultural, charitable and religious institutions and to the strengthening of the vital heritage from which they spring. Although it aspires to the eventual restoration of their historical homeland, its immediate objective is to promote a healthy and varied community life in the free society in which we live.
>
> Its attitude of friendship to the people of Armenia is non-political and derives from a natural attachment to its national, cultural, religious and historical values.

However, during the Cold War difficulties Armenians who had any connections with the satellite republic of Armenia in the Soviet Union were suspect. Armenians generally were afraid to declare that they had any connection with certain organizations that helped the people of Armenia. It was just a matter of who had the courage to be outspoken about valuing a homeland, though it was under a dictatorial regime that was America's enemy. But in the meantime I did my job and I enjoyed the writing in the context with other Armenian-Americans. This organization helped the Armenian people but not the communist system they were forced to live under, leaving no real reason for guilt.

The newspaper became more political in its reporting and interest and thus changed character in the 1970s. The problems it had to deal with had changed according to the needs of the new immigration.

During those years I met quite a few people, whose names I can't completely enumerate or at this point remember. I will mention only a few of the literati, because that is my main interest. Diana Der Hovanessian, noted poet, translator and head of the New England Poetry Club, became an acquaintance early on as did Harold Bond, another noted poet. Michael (Depoian) Casey had just won the Yale Series for Younger Poets award for *Obscenities*, and I met him at a reading.

I briefly met Jack Antreassian, a writer and the first editor of *Ararat* quarterly, the literary magazine published by the Armenian General Benevolent Union, a worldwide cultural and philanthropic organization. He published many of my poems in the magazine, and later the second editor of the magazine, Leo Hamalian, also published many of my poems. I met a few other writers such as Leon Surmelian and Avedis Derounian (John Roy Carlson) through correspondence, in addition to some well-known writers in the Armenian language. I also met Professor Parounag Tovmassian, head of the ADL who lived in Beirut but later emigrated to and lived in Watertown.

I also met contributors such as Carl Zeytoonian and Marilyn Wolohojian and wrote to others including the popular Armine Dikijian and Bedros Norehad of the Diocesan headquarters in New York City. P. K. Tomajan contributed his wonderful epigrams. My cousin Mary Aprahamian and others from New Britain, Connecticut, wrote a column. Notably, contributing news or articles to that newspaper was volunteer work.

In 1966 I left the editorship for an extended trip to Beirut with my family for personal reasons. While there, I was taken to the office at the newspaper and introduced to Kersam Aharonian, editor of *Zartonk* daily, the ADL newspaper there. He was reputed to be a very strong personality.

It was the end of the whirlwind time that taught me a great deal I would never forget and influenced the future course of my writing. Inspiration for writing and publishing books not forthcoming just then, it was a waiting period to live my personal life.

Why Details Are Necessary

In order to visualize what a genocide is like, notably the Armenian Genocide and denial thereof by responsible or irresponsible parties, verbal images as pictures that will describe the situation can help. It is said to be impossible to convey the particulars of the tortures and murders that took place to exterminate the Armenians in 1915 on the pretext that they were traitors to the Turkish state.

A few typical excerpts from what has been written by people who went through this deportation as children and were haunted by those memories for the rest of their lives will suffice. Following is an excerpt from the book *Bloody Desert* by Hagop Kouyoumjian, who lived in Philadelphia until his death in 1961. It was translated from the Armenian by Hagop Sarkissian for the 50th anniversary special issue of *The Armenian Mirror-Spectator*:

> Many starved people fainted and were a hindrance to the soldiers walking in the tent city. One day they gathered such persons and, though they were not dead, threw them into a ditch especially dug for the purpose.
>
> Sometimes when passing by that ditch, I stopped and looked at live bodies of adults and children piled upon each other. I watched them bring new half-dead bodies and throw them upon the bodies still living and breathing. Shaken by the blows of the thrown bodies, some opened their eyes and tried to free bare arms or feet from beneath a fallen body, but they did not have the strength . . . When the ditch was filled, the soldiers covered it with the soil and opened a new ditch for victims fallen every day. But those who died were the lucky ones . . .
>
> The tired and exhausted caravan was ready to sleep when screams and cries were heard. The Turks had come out to hunt in the light of the moon with their beastly passions and were searching for the freshness of a body, no matter how young it was. They plunged their claws into tender brides and young girls. The rest was blood and death.

The victims cried and resisted; some clung to their parents, but the iron fists separated mother and daughter. Many were dragged away by the hair. And the hellish feast started.

The soldiers dismounted and one of them grabbed the beard of a clergyman and drew him away. The second soldier helped to throw him on the ground with his rifle butt and sat on him. At the same time he drew a dagger and holding the beard, cut one side of the face and threw it in the air. The other soldier, following the example of his friend, did the same to the other side of the face. Surprisingly, the clergyman did not utter a word as a sign of pain; only the word "God" could be heard through his teeth.

"Now call your God as much as you want," said one of the soldiers with a diabolical laugh. The other soldier fired his gun. The skull of the clergyman turned to pieces of bone and scattered through the air like broken glass.

The soldiers gave permission to the crowd following us to start the massacre. Thousands of them fell upon us. Some used their swords and, holding the hair of their victims, cut their heads off and threw them away. Others used iron-headed sticks to crush the skulls and smashed bones. Some came with axes and hit all around them, cutting an arm here, a leg there. An ingenious one placed children in a row and passed his spear through their bellies. Some saved their guns and ended the lives of their victims by stabbing and kicking them. Others tied a woman's hands and feet and cut her to pieces. Other beasts slept with dead women and satisfied their souls. If there were no more of living, many killed the dead once more, and again and again tortured them, seeking some life in them. Those who were not satisfied with death, drank the blood of the wounded.

By a miracle I was buried beneath a pile of bodies and thus saved from the massacre.

The following excerpt is from the book *They Called Me Mustafa: Memoir of an Immigrant* by Khachadoor Pilibosian, my father's story and translations of some of his writings, which I co-authored and edited. A brief excerpt of his experiences during the deportation and his subsequent slavery to Kurds who had kidnapped him give an indication of his sufferings:

Some of these Turks forced themselves into Armenian homes to capture any male over 15 years old. These acts lasted until late at night. Then the Turks arrested these males and imprisoned them in the Armenian Church. They also went to the homes and arrested the males they found there, though they were not too many because a large number of them had already been called to serve in the Turkish Army. Those who resisted were taken to the church after being severely beaten.

The husbands of my two aunts and two young sons of one of them were in the church. That night I took bread and cheese to them. The stern-faced guard scolded me saying, "Those inside do not need bread." I returned home crying. (H.P. — The church was burned with the prisoners inside.)

I can never forget going through a valley with a group one day and seeing hundreds of human bodies scattered all around. They must have been killed no more than a day or two before. Among them were many teenage boys.

The gendarme ordered us to follow him. In a little while we reached a place where dead bodies were scattered, and he handed us the rope and told us to pull the bodies into the river. While doing what we were ordered to do, one of the tortured young boys said softly, "Boys, take it easy. I am not dead yet." It was too dark to notice his wounds or his condition, so we left him alone and pulled some of others away. After pulling about 15 bodies to the river, we were exhausted and could not do any more.

. . . As I approached one of the merchants and ate a couple of brunches of grapes, I felt two heavy arms winding around my body. I was then picked up and carried away from the crowd. My kidnapper started to climb the hills as I screamed, trying everything to get away without success as my kidnapper warned me that he would kill me if I did not behave. I cried loudly and often, thinking that my sisters still were waiting for something to eat and would probably starve to death.

And he lived among the Kurds for four years during which time he was often beaten and almost killed. When he heard that World War I had ended, he took off and walked from those mountains and, with the help of an Armenian spared from the massacres because he had turned a Muslim, took a train to

Aleppo, Syria, where he was accepted in Rev. Aharon Shirajian's orphanage.

Aurora Mardiganian wrote about the deportation and especially about the sufferings of women in her book *The Auction of Souls* after she was safely in America.

Below are brief excerpts from this book:

> I think there were more than 200 women whose minds gave way under this sudden impulse, stirred by the crazed widow of the pastor.
>
> Those who were in charge of us could not understand at first. They thought there was a revolt. They charged among us, swinging their swords and guns right and left, even shooting point blank. Many were killed or wounded hopelessly before they understood. Then the guards were greatly amused, and laughed. "See," they said, "that is what your God is — He is crazy." We could only bow our heads an submit to the taunt. Some of the women recovered their senses and were very sorry. Those who remained crazed the *zaptiehs* turned on to the plains to starve to death. They would not kill an insane person, as it was against their religion.
>
> I tried to conceal myself when the little party of Kurds came near. But I was too late. They took me away, with a dozen of the girls and young wives this band had caught. They carried us on their horses across the valley, over the hills, and into the desert beyond. There they stripped us of what clothes still were on our bodies. With their long sticks they subdued girls who were screaming, or if they resisted, beat them until their flesh was purple with flowing blood . . . When the Kurds were tired of mistreating us they hobbled us, still naked, to their horses. Each girl, with her hands tied behind her back, was tied by the feet to the end of a rope fastened around the horse's neck. Thus they left us — neither we nor the horses could escape.
>
> As the regiment closed in, thousands of the women, with their babies and children in their arms, scrambled up the cliffs on either side of the narrow pass, helped by their men folk, who remained on the road to fight with their hands and sticks against the armed soldiers.
>
> But the *zaptiehs* accompanying the party surrounded the base of the cliffs and kept the women from escaping. Then the Kasab Tabouri (Butcher Battalions) killed men until

there were not enough left to resist them. Scores of men feigned death among the bodies of their friends, and thus escaped with their lives.

Part of the soldiers then scaled the cliffs to where the women were huddled. They took babies from the arms of the mothers and threw them over the cliffs to comrades below, who caught as many as they could on their bayonets. When the babies and little girls were all disposed of this way, the soldiers amused themselves awhile making women jump over — prodding them with bayonets, or beating them with gun barrels until the women, in desperation, jumped to save themselves. As they rolled down the base of the cliff, the soldiers below hit them with stones or held their bayonets so they would roll on them. Many women scrambled to their feet after falling, and these the soldiers forced to climb the cliffs again, only to be pushed back over.

The Kasab Tabouri kept us this sport until it was dark.

The women and girls who were left were to be sold into Turkish harems for the highest prices on condition they would accept Islam. It seemed then that civilization was totally absent, except in the minds of the defenseless Armenians . . . Word from Talaat Pasha: "Anything you do to the Armenians will amuse me."

Four Armenian towns were able to withstand the onslaught of the Turks with ammunition that had been smuggled in to them. These were in Zeitoun, in Deurt Yol, on the mountain of Musa Dagh in Alexandretta, of which Franz Werfel wrote his great novel *The Forty Days of Musa Dagh*, and in the city of Van in the province of Van, of which Dr. Clarence D. Ussher wrote his eyewitness account *An American Physician in Turkey*. The battles in Van were clever and heroic, but the Armenians ultimately lost, though the people who fought them were rescued. An excerpt from Dr. Ussher's book follows:

Dr. Clarence D. Ussher

Why had not the Armenians emigrated in greater numbers to escape this oppression and fear of massacre? The Turkish Government would not permit them to emigrate without first renouncing their citizenship and inheritance rights in Turkey, selling all their possessions and promising not to return. Passports would not be issued to men trying to return. Armenians are passionately attached to their native lands and to their ancient traditions. Property has passed from father to son for generations.

The supply of ammunition was small. Jewelers, tinsmiths, coppersmiths and blacksmiths set to work to increase it, turning out with the primitive tools at their command 2000 cartridges and case bullets a day. An Armenian professor, graduate of an American university, made smokeless powder. Unskilled labor built walls and dug trenches, often under fire. Women made uniforms and other garments for the soldiers and cooked for them. The normal school band marched about the city playing military airs when the fighting was heaviest. Even young boys did their bit, and a big bit it was, too.

These Boy Scouts now became the sanitary police and fire patrol of our little municipality. They kept the various buildings supplied with water for drinking purposes and for use in case of fire, acted as messengers, reported the sick to me, and brought patients on litters to our hospital. They dug Turkish bullets out of the ground by the hundreds and took them to the munitions workers to melt and the recast.

Following is an excerpt from an article I wrote as part of a series entitled "ADL - The Living Ideology" published in *The Armenian Mirror-Spectator* of June 15, 1963. It is only a summary of the vast and complicated story of the Armenians in historic Armenia.

From 1375 to 1920 the Armenian people were subjected to the tyranny of the Turkish Empire. It was not until the latter part of the 19th century when the ideas of freedom infiltrated from Europe, that the Armenians made an organized attempt at liberation. Conditions were unbearable in Turkish Armenia. An Armenian could expect no justice by law, he was treated with utmost contempt and derision by the Turkish people, and if he tried to gain freedom by any revolutionary activity or even possessed a gun, he was instantly and without question killed.

The Armenian Democratic Liberal Party was formed under those conditions with inspiration from the minds of men such as Mgrditch Portukalian, who preached liberation in his newspaper *Armenia*. In Van, Mgrditch Terlemezian-Avedisian led the Armenagan Party, the first branch of the present ADL, in the preparation for democratic ideals and the use of arms to defend those ideals. He led the resistance to the massacre of 1896, but was killed later in an ambush as he and others were leaving the country under a promise of safe conduct.

The Armenian Revolutionary Federation was formed under the same circumstances and for the same purposes but with somewhat different views of actions that were necessary. These groups produced heroes and martyrs and were the beginning of the present Armenian political organizations.

In the present Armenian diaspora, formed mostly after the tragedy of 1915, there are active and thriving communities of Armenians with many outstanding individuals and achievements, proud of national heritage, but not forgetting the painful history that brought them to where they are and tried to dispose of their ancient civilization.

Lebanon Again

We traveled to Beirut via Europe on Icelandic Airlines for a second visit in 1966 on an economy flight which stopped in Iceland before setting down in Luxemburg. Hagop's brother Hovsep picked us up at the airport and proceeded to his house in Germany, where we intended a short stay with him. Our four-year-old daughter Anoush (meaning sweet), had not been feeling well before we left and unfortunately became quite ill on the plane, vomiting a number of times. First Hovsep and then a German doctor diagnosed her as being dehydrated, and her uncle did the intravenous treatment while she was in a bed in their house. She soon recovered with the help of the chicken soup her aunt Mechtild made and with the care she received.

Then the cousins had a good time playing whatever games children that age like. Even though they didn't have a common language, they seemed to understand each other well. After all, they were very close in their years and most likely similar in their dispositions. On the first trip in 1960, we had seen Arpi at three months old, and in 1966 we saw an older Arpi and Alexandra, who was about three years old.

In Beirut, Anoush was friendly with her cousin Hagop, who was close to her in age, and though she doesn't remember, she was baptized in the Armenian Evangelical Church of Ashrafieh by Rev. Vahram Salibian, its minister, along with another cousin Hratch, who was exactly her age. Actually the two children had thought, with a charming and remarkable kind of comprehension, that they were going to church to get married.

Hagop did some work then for a printing establishment, so that I was often home with my daughter and the women. Sometimes we would go walking near the house to get *booza*, the Lebanese ice cream, which we both found quite delicious and an excellent treat in the hot summer weather. Then we might have dropped in to Alice Khanigian's house nearby to talk to someone we were familiar with. My Armenian at that time was in practice

View of Beirut in the 1960s and its fabled Hotel St. Georges
in the foreground

because I was surrounded by people who spoke the language. Anoush also spoke Armenian then, though she lost it when she was in kindergarten in America. She was once terribly embarrassed when she couldn't answer a boy who had spoken to her in English.

We saw condo culture in practice there, for my in-laws lived in an apartment they owned with a working automotive garage below and an apartment above owned by another family. The practice was common in that crowded atmosphere with houses that were made of stone and cement, considered quite durable and with floors and walls that were easy to wash. The women there, particularly the Armenians, were very exacting about cleanliness in the house and also about food, that perhaps being the reason why they cooked such excellent meals.

In the marketplace customers haggled with vendors over the prices of merchandise, a practice I was told was expected and necessary. The seller offered a high price the buyer refused, offering a lower price. After this went on for a few minutes, they agreed on the more moderate price. A huge marketplace occupied a space downtown and sold all kinds of wares as well as meat and vegetables, and the local bazaar nearby consisted of some fresh produce brought in from the mountains or outlying areas.

Traffic lights abounded throughout the city, but drivers didn't seem to pay attention to them and raced around the streets.

Sometimes, but not as often as one would expect, there were small accidents that resulted in what looked like fierce arguments and a great deal of shouting. Emotions soon cooled and the word *maalesh* (that's all right) covered the damage and the blame, and the parties parted in a friendly manner. Once when we were taking a bus to the outskirts of the city, the driver started racing with another bus, making our safety questionable. In those years most people there had no insurance coverage for traffic accidents. But the residents of the city seemed to trust their drivers.

Much of the culture, the customs and the manners of the people appeared to be the opposite of those of Americans. Though my country was idolized by some as a perfect country and one they would like to go to, many others thought of it as a place of evil for reasons of sexual permissiveness and openness about personal issues. Puritanical values still held and were part of Middle Eastern culture, as they still are, and girls were usually chaperoned when with a date.

Visiting each other was the usual social life, since most married women didn't work outside the home and younger women tended to marry young. My in-laws were always sociable, so friends and relatives would often drop in unannounced because they had no phone and expected no announcement. Democratically, they welcomed all types of people from the least educated to the highly educated and treated them all with respect.

Most of the company were Armenians, and they shared the custom with Arabs of serving coffee to every visitor, the host family also drinking coffee at the same time and perhaps a number of times a day. The strong Oriental unfiltered brew, powdered black-roast with some sugar, was poured into demitasse cups. Mary, then 19, taught me how to make this coffee and serve it on a tray, a skill which would later be valuable. She had been making coffee for company for a few years. If the gathering were of women, sometimes one of them would read the dried coffee grounds to tell the fortunes of the others, a game more of amusement than of serious portent.

Hagop and I took a few trips outside of the city to see some of the extraordinary historic sights in Lebanon. One of these trips was with Aram and a neighbor Hagop Hamamjian by automobile to Baalbek, the Phoenician and Roman ruins of temples made of lovely pink stone. Glimpses of this very ancient history were intellectually stirring and emotionally mysterious.

We visited the town of Zahleh in the midst of quiet nature. On the way Hagop and I saw a couple of camels sitting down and tried to take a picture of them. Immediately, a man jumped up as if out of nowhere and chased us with a stick in his hand and a shout that meant we should pay him for the privilege of taking the picture. We didn't pay but ran.

We went to the city of Jbeil, or Byblos in antiquity, 26 miles north of Beirut, where the Crusaders Castle of the 12th and 13th centuries stood. It was made of solid rock with narrow windows for fortification from attack. Nearby

Columns at Baalbek

we went to the Birds' Nest Armenian orphanage, which had been founded by the Danish missionary Maria Jacobsen in 1928. In 1970 the Armenian Catholicosate of Cilicia took over the management of this institution.

We also visited the Armenian Catholicosate in the small village of Antelias, 20 miles north of Beirut. It is the seat of the local head of the Armenian Church and the locale of the Saint Gregory the Illuminator Cathedral, next to which a Memorial Chapel houses bones of the victims of the Armenian Genocide dug from the sands of Der Zor in the Syrian desert. The sight of these tragic bones left me with a sense of tragedy at the unrelenting past they represented.

We took the *tramva*, meaning streetcar, to the American University of Beirut, which had been founded by American missionaries in 1866. The buildings were sedate and dignified and the campus was beautiful. There we walked to the American

Embassy on the Corniche, the broad avenue that stretches for miles along the Mediterranean.

From the sublime of these tours to a less-than-ridiculous illness when with my eyes and ears alert, I found that much can be learned anywhere. I had contracted a severe intestinal infection, resulting in much vomiting and diarrhea with the weakness that follows. My sister-in-law Alice took me to a medical facility called CMC or Christian Medical Center where Dr. Puzant Krikorian gave me some pills to alleviate the condition. However, since they didn't work very well, I consented to try the folk cure concocted by brother-in-law Joseph Ashjian — a teaspoon of dried sumac mixed with water a couple of times a day for a while, the dose to be adjusted according to need. This did work, and I always keep some in the cabinet of my kitchen, having used it on occasion and having recommended it to others.

During this visit, which was for six months and mostly in the long summer, a newspaper editor was murdered, causing much talk. As a political move, it seemed to bode trouble to come. Some months after we had returned we heard the news of the Six Day War between Israel and Arab neighbors Egypt, Jordan, and Syria, leaving eastern Jerusalem, the Gaza Strip, the Sinai Peninsula, the West Bank, and the Golan Heights under Isreali control. The results of the war affected the geopolitics of the area, and the instability of the region became more obvious.

When I became homesick for America, I left with my daughter, stopping in Germany before going home. Hagop stayed on for a few weeks to complete a business transaction for his family. After we had boarded the Lufthansa Airlines plane, Anoush had asked where the ears of the plane were; then she was on dramamine with limited success to try to avoid airsickness. The trip was very comfortable, and the stewardesses were accommodating as we were changed from tourist class to first class for some reason and were given some special desserts and coffee.

Now values in Beirut are more Westernized. There is less visitation because more women are working at jobs, leaving them less time and energy to prepare for company. Even the strictest adherence to the rule that Armenians must marry Armenians has changed and reached another extreme of frequent intermarriage with Arabs, nullifying the rule that Armenians must speak

Armenian or study in Armenian schools. That fact has become a source of worry for Armenian leaders, for assimilation dilutes the essence of Armenianism and produces fewer identifiable Armenians in a country and diaspora that has only about eight million people with an additional three million living in Armenia.

It is estimated that less than one million Armenians, including those who were born in America, live in the United States at this time, though there is no exact figure and no way to arrive at one. Those who immigrated from Middle Eastern countries brought with them a closeness of family ties and a cohesiveness that existed in America some years ago but somehow got lost in the materialistic shuffle. Hagop's relatives exemplify this trait very well as we have occasional large family gatherings with young cousins who know each other well and love to get together and other family members who cooperate without question to make their lives together fulfilling.

Family gathering, 2009, Alice Ashjian's 80th birthday

1960–1975, A Crucial Period

In the decade of the 1960s and onward, I watched the news on television more than I ever had before and certainly with more sadness and conviction because tragedy was in the air as well as on the news. The Vietnam War was raging by 1968, and Lyndon B. Johnson wouldn't seek reelection because of the controversy over the war. Young people were demonstrating in the streets, and some were forcibly arrested. The civil rights movement was in full swing, and Dr. Martin Luther King Jr. was assassinated as its leader on April 4 of that year. Robert Kennedy was fatally shot after giving a victory speech celebrating his winning the California Democratic presidential primary.

American history was literally on the march. We couldn't miss it, for television alerted us all by its very detailed reporting and analysis. It presented very graphic and very dramatic scenes, providing more fodder for the news. It was an exciting time to be alive if one could ignore the untoward events that were being played out every day.

But we concentrated on our daily lives, which were only indirectly affected by the continuing war since we had no one in the armed forces. Yet, I was personally rather depressed by the assassinations, beginning with that of John F. Kennedy in 1963, and by the seemingly endless war with rather graphic photography on the news reports, since I already had that tendency to feel other people's pain deeply.

In this decade of civil rights, President Johnson had created the Kerner Commission to study the widespread riots that were going on throughout the United States. Their conclusions included this quote: "Our nation is moving toward two societies, one black, one white — separate and unequal." This was part of the American Civil Rights Movement of 1954-1968 in which blacks, especially in the South, were marching and campaigning for equality under the law and an end to segregation in schools, buses, restaurants and so forth. Later groups like the Black

Panther Party, the Young Lords, the Weathermen and the Brown Berets became more militant, trying to start a revolution that would result in self-determination for American minorities. The revolution failed due to government intervention.

The Women's Liberation Movement began with statements such as in the Virginia Slims cigarette ad that read as follows: "You've Come a Long Way, Baby." This movement went hand in hand with the civil rights movement as a natural consequence of it. Women had long felt themselves treated as inferiors in the working world and were demanding the equality that was due them. The early movement clearly expressed itself in more militant terms than it does now when women have in large measure attained their goals of being hired for high-level employment, of being respected leaders and being paid on an equal scale.

However, family life was never the same again after women became fully integrated into the working world as opposed to the domestic world they had been living in. Day care centers became necessary, and schools adjusted their hours to accommodate younger children for a longer time and older children in after-school activities because the majority of mothers were working in offices, in factories, in stores in an ever-increasing variety of jobs. Some opted to work from their residences or worked part-time in order to take care of their families. The adjustments for all of society were tremendous in this shakeup of traditional values. By this time we are all used to men helping with children or the housework or taking the baby out for a walk in a carriage, unthinkable before 1970 (with notable exceptions).

This development affected us in that more women became bosses than ever before. Hagop had a woman supervisor named Miriam Palmerola at Harvard University Printing Office, where he was employed after our return from Beirut in 1966. Working at HUPO was certainly a step up for him with better pay and good benefits and after a few years a chance to gradually master the field of cold type or computerized typesetting after the Linotypes were retired from use. She was extremely professional and accomplished in the fields of graphic arts, strict with those who worked with her but also easy to get along with.

When he was hired, the person in charge of the plant was Carl Getz, a gentleman of the old school. I met many of Hagop's coworkers over a period of time. One of them was Charles Fulton, his mother an Armenian from the same area of the old country as my parents. I also met Dick Ford and Charlie Woods, Mary Anne McCarthy, Leo Ferland, supervisor Peter Imrie and many others.

Around 1976, new systems of typography began to be used at Harvard, and Hagop and Dick Ford both agreed to take a pay cut of $50 a week and be trained in the new equipments. First there was the TTS (Teletypesetter) where punched tapes were fed through a phototypesetter called VIP by Mergenthaler. Then came the computerized Penta system. At the same time, the Cathode Ray Tube-based digital typesetters called Compugraphic flooded the industry. Finally, Macintosh and IBM computers put an end to all the above. Hagop trained and retrained on all of them, becoming one of the most valued employees in the plant where he worked for almost 29 years. Jim Gill managed the plant in the last few years before Hagop retired.

Miriam gave me a job when I needed one as a part-time proofreader there, a job I held for about 10 years , and I would go to the plant when called on a casual basis if their proofreader was absent or needed extra help. The perfect arrangement for me for a while, I terminated it after my father died and my mother needed daily help.

The beatniks were around in the late 1960s with their long hair, sloppy clothes and rebellious attitudes and offered outstanding writers such as Jack Kerouac with his novel *On the Road* and Allen Ginsberg with his famous poem *Howl* to defend them.

This long poem set forth the beliefs of the beat group, then called "hippies" with emphasis on a positive approach to taking drugs and having sex to the point of hallucinating. Some Buddhist teachings underlay the anti-materialist and anti-conformist beliefs in the work. However, a brilliant but misguided poetic mind had been at work here, presenting many powerful images and some insights into our society in that very troubled era.

Ginsberg's long poem was directly an expression of rebellion against the conformity of American life, a rebellion gone to an extreme in praise of drugs and hatred for the country without any constructive suggestions for improvement. Ginsberg called it "a lament for the Lamb in America with instances of remarkable lamb-like youths." Containing writing about oppressed people and full of psychedelic experiences including the taking of drugs and psychiatric characters, the work was the shocker of the decade but has maintained its popularity as representative of the Beat Generation. However, in spite of his leading rebellions and demonstrations against the American government, he received the National Book Award for his book *The Fall of America, poems of these states 1965-1971*.

Jack Kerouac was a very popular writer who missed great critical acclaim during his lifetime. Writing about the crowds and the escapades of the Beats and those who were prominent among them, he provided great detail into their lives and mentalities. Thus he has been an influence on subsequent writers and on the school of writing called the New Journalism. He died at a fairly early age of the alcoholism that had been his escape from a difficult reality.

Though I disagreed with the type of life this group led, I sympathized with their problems and suffering as I read the works their writers left. Some elements in my life could have led me in a similar direction but never to that extreme for the discipline I met through the strict code of my parents and relatives as well as my school and my psychiatrist. My future life depended upon internalizing these codes, or reinternalizing after the break, and recovering from imbalance.

The Beatles were a happier sensation of the day with songs that never went away like "Don't Pass Me By" and "Octopus's Garden." One of my favorites is called "Yesterdays," the lyrics of which are as follows:

> Yesterday
> All my troubles seemed so far away
> Now it looks as though they're here to stay
> Oh I believe in yesterday
> Suddenly
> I'm not half the man I used to be
> There's a shadow hanging over me
> Oh yesterday came suddenly
> Why she had to go I don't know
> She wouldn't say
> I said something wrong
> Now I long for yesterday

The Beatles were a pop and rock band from Liverpool, England, and were the most successful and popular band in the history of recorded music. Who can forget the names John Lennon and Paul McCartney and the charm of their songs and lyrics? They enjoyed tremendous success in the United States and in the world and were a great influence on all subsequent bands and songwriters as well as a great inspiration for many millions of people. The music defined the creativity of the Beat movement and had many followers. After their era, hard rock as well as hip hop, rap and other variations entered the scene.

Richard Nixon was elected president in November of 1971, and after more years of war and demonstrations and part of a second term, he resigned as president under pressure in 1974, and the unpopular war came to an end that was considered ignominious by some. But it was 1975 and about time, for the country was in a psychological turmoil as anger and failure turned many people to taking illegal drugs that had been entering the country during the war, a serious problem that has beset the country ever since.

The scandal called Watergate began with the arrest of five men who broke into the Democratic National Committee headquarters at the Watergate hotel complex in Washington D.C. in June of 1972. Investigation by the FBI, the Senate Watergate Committee, and the House Judiciary Committee provided evidence that this burglary was one of the many illegal activities perpetrated by Nixon's followers. There were other crimes connected to the administration such as campaign fraud, political sabotage, illegal wiretapping and a secret fund to pay those who conducted these operations to be silent about them. Facing the Watergate scandal and possible impeachment, Nixon left the presidency to Gerald Ford who had been Vice President. Subsequently as president, Gerald Ford pardoned Richard Nixon.

An anecdotal aside: also in the 1970s I ended up in group therapy at Mass. Mental Health on Fenwood Road in Boston, probably due to anxiety and panic caused by hormonal changes of perimenopause. I mentioned some events out of my past to the psychiatrist in charge, at which he assumed a stunned and almost incriminating look that said I was being delusional or deliberately lying. I said no more about the incident, thinking that it would only cause more disbelief or even trouble. I got the same stunned and silent reaction when I mentioned that I had had a cardiac arrest once during surgery, so I maintained silence. Again, the fear response and lack of self-confidence to explain or insist. What had been expected of me?

There seemed to be conflict everywhere, the usual human condition.

A Larger Family

Having finally conquered my fear of renewed cardiac problems with much reassurance, I became pregnant again. For the hidden fear of dying in sleep had been with me for a long time because of memories of my previous double surgery. The mind also bears scars, thus making memories questionable.

Our son Robert was born and grew into the turmoil of the country in 1970, part of Generation X. He was a husky baby who became noted for his red hair, unusual among modern Armenians but traced back to my grandmother and perhaps other relatives and to ancient Armenians before that. As his sister had, he also spent extra time in Waltham Hospital for jaundice. We never told him that the outside world was in turmoil, and he would learn about it soon enough on his own. We could give him a philosophy to live by only by our own outlook on life. Years later he would read books of philosophy by the score in depth, thus finding the meaning of life and religion in his own way.

The family was now complete with two children, one of each gender, and the dependability of a constant husband who worked very hard for all of us. Our daughter had been an only child for almost eight years before I became pregnant, and even when I returned from the hospital temporarily without the baby, she thought I had been lying to her. However, the situation was soon resolved, and she helped me care for her brother for a long time.

We had bought and moved into a small bungalow on Maplewood Street in Watertown, a very pleasant and peaceful neighborhood away from traffic or businesses and near the Oakley Country Club and close to Belmont. We often took walks in that area and imbibed the pleasant atmosphere on the walk to Cushing Square or to my parents' house, for we were on one side of the country club and they were on the other.

I fell in love with its rather large and recently modernized kitchen. The house needed other renovations, which we made over a period of years just enough for our needs, but in the long run with some upgrades it was an excellent investment. The changes began with the conversion of the sunroom into a bedroom by making walls where there were large windows that let in a tremendous amount of cold air and by installing a radiator. We made it a real room, though small, which served as a bedroom for Bob until his sister married and moved out, a storeroom, then an office with two desks and one computer, the birthplace of Ohan Press.

We installed vinyl siding on the outside of the house for $3000 and added new shingles on the roof, a repaved driveway, a new chain-link fence, outside cement stairs replacing the wooden ones, two new finished rooms in the basement and many more small changes to make the house more livable. We had the ceilings redone for about $1200. We had the bathroom redone for about $3000, and it was the only one we ever had. We had the electrical system updated, fixed the chimneys and changed the furnace. So that with an initial investment of $23,000 plus another nearly $55,000, we now live in a house that is worth nearly $500,000, recession notwithstanding.

Conveniently there was a ready grape vine, which always lost its grapes when they were tiny but had tender leaves for me to use in making *sarma*. A small yard space allowed for a garden on one side with many flowers, which we constantly tended for the sake of the beauty of the area and our own love of flowers. In one corner a patch of spearmint grew to provide the fresh herbs for use in salad or for drying and subsequent use during the rest of the year. My parents also had a grape vine and a patch of spearmint to use as other Armenians and Greeks did.

I had learned the value of dried spearmint from my mother, who used it also to make mint tea, a great medicinal aid for digestive problems. Having used it as tea, I knew the power of it and also the taste of it added to soups and stews as well as hamburgers and *sarma* when it was crumbled into them and cooked. Of course, I also used other herbs, especially parsley and basil for the richness of flavor they gave to many foods.

I loved the process of cooking, following recipes but also making creative changes. This interest led me to many hours of watching all the cooking programs on television, Emeril being the overall favorite for his use of humor as well as his showing the cooking techniques of excellent food. Julia Child was an early favorite, my mother's indispensable guide.

A story about the grape leaves seems amusing in retrospect. When we as an extended family went on vacation in the summer, my mother-in-law, my sister-in-law and I would go around searching public areas for grape vines that had tender and usable leaves. We always found them, picked quite a few leaves and took them home with us. If the grape leaves were more than we could use at one time, we would package them and freeze them for future use. And on one occasion, I saw Emeril making stuffed grape leaves.

Fortunately, my two children got along well and became friends in spite of the eight-and-a-half years age difference. I had seen too much of people in families not getting along to be comfortable with that situation. Then when the two grandchildren came along, they followed the lead and have always been the best of friends with each other and also with their uncle Bob. They all enjoyed playing board games and watching comedies on television together as well as playing basketball games in the back yard with friends or cousins, bicycle rides and games downstairs in the unfinished basement.

My children attended the same schools as I had: the Hosmer School, the East Junior High School and Watertown High until they graduated, the girl to continue at Mass Bay Community College and the boy at Northeastern University. We took the challenges and demands of parenthood very seriously because of our deep love for our children. I thought it was an honor and a privilege to do so.

Thus my small family gave me a foundation for emotional comfort, which was upset only by occasional conflicts connected with work or the lack of it and some conflicts in my original family. These days people are decrying the lack of contact of family members especially at mealtimes to solidify a feeling of oneness. In my family we always had meals together, and to this day we get together often for meals at home or in restaurants for birthdays and other celebrations.

When we gather, we discuss many subjects, though most often computer-related matters in the later years. For my husband

Newlyweds Gregory and Sharon Anoush with his parents Krikor and Julia Hekimian (left) and her parents Helene and Hagop Sarkissian (right)

Hagop and Helene's grandchildren Emily and Joshua Hekimian

was a professional in computerized type-setting, our daughter works with medical records on computer at Beth Israel Hospital-Needham, our son-in-law builds engines (Hekimian Racing Engines) in his own business but does his office work on computer at his home and is also the pastor of Believers' Baptist Church, I do my writing on computer, our son Bob trained in electrical engineering but does

Newlyweds Bob and Audrey (Dow) Sarkissian

technical writing for a scientific company called Atmospheric and Environmental Research in Lexington on computer as well as writes satires to publish on his web site and in books, our daughter-in-law Audrey Dow is a trained engineer with a complete knowledge of computers turned tutor of high-school-age students, our grandson Joshua studied computer programming at Pensacola Christian College in Florida and is working at Draper Labs, and our granddaughter Emily, former pianist for the Heritage Baptist Church and now her father's small church knows computers very well and attends Pensacola Christian College. They all emphasize the relaxation of humor, which I learned slowly to enjoy because my upbringing had been humorless.

We used to go to my parents' house for Sunday dinner, which my mother would cook with the delight she took in being useful. They would expect us with a desperation that made me feel guilty if I and my family didn't go there every Sunday. My husband and my father had long conversations about Armenian political views and about religion, Hagop egging my father on by questioning his views and encouraging him to talk more about them. My father usually had a lighthearted manner and drank whiskey moderately with Hagop's company.

I was able to conquer my fear of driving and get a license to be of further service to my family, and even though my driving was local, I drove my son to school and appointments and also drove to and from my mother's house during the eight years she outlived my father to help her in many ways, especially food shopping and medical appointments. At the end of her life, I drove back and forth to the hospital and to the nursing home to visit her,

Joseph Ashjian

the tension of those last weeks leaving me almost ill. Now that my parents are gone, I don't feel the guilt of abandoning them to their loneliness of facing only each other and their painful past memories.

By contrast, Hagop's mother, two sisters and their families, who also lived in Watertown, were sociable and loved to party. Hagop's older sister Alice, her husband Joseph and their children Sona, Apo and Hagop had immigrated here in 1970 and lived first in Cambridge then in their own home in Watertown. His younger sister Mary with her husband Panos and her mother arrived a year later and also bought a house in town, where they raised three children, Viken, Hratch and Salpi. This large family always had many visitors, and we used to gather for a number of years every summer for a week or two to vacation in New Hampshire or New York or other locations that were easy enough to drive to.

Our first such vacation was in the summer of 1973, a week at Twin Mountain, New Hampshire, staying in some of the two dozen or so cottages there. The children greatly enjoyed the swimming pool, and the parents enjoyed each other's company. We always pooled resources and had grilled *shish kebab* or steak with trimmings, Hagop's mother being the most eager cook. The next year we went to Vermont and stayed at Sleepy Oaks Cottages on Lake Dunmore, swimming in the lake and sightseeing in the Adirondack region of upstate New York near the wonder of Ausable Chasm. The third vacation was at Lake Sebago in Maine, and the fourth was at Chanticleer Lakefront Cottages on the shore of Lake Winnipesaukee in Gilford, New Hampshire, with the addition of Hovsep and his family from Germany and Hagop's aunt Araxi from Australia.

I often envision the scenery at the Flume, that natural granite gorge at Franconia Notch State Park populated by so many plants and many stairs that present a challenge going down then up again. It extends 800 feet at the base of Mt. Liberty, and its walls rise 90 feet for an irresistible attraction. Then I see the utter peace of the Kancamagus Highway with its small river flowing over so many rocks near the white birches that drop yellow leaves upon the area in the autumn. We stopped there a number of times, as well as at the site of the Old Man of the Mountain, which collapsed in 2003.

The next vacation was to Niagara Falls, another wonder of nature and water, and Toronto. We saw the American Falls and the Canadian "Horseshoe Falls," the "fossil water" left from the Ice Age flowing mightily over the rocks of the Great Lakes Basin from the Niagara River. And we found Toronto to be a very big city with some of Hagop's relatives in it.

By this time the older children had started jobs and didn't come with us. The next was at Falmouth, Massachusetts and on to Sargent's Lakeshore Cottages in Georges Mill, New Hampshire. Hagop greatly enjoyed making all the capable arrangements for these vacations. We stayed in cottages, motels and condos in all the New England states and in New York and later traveled to Kansas, California, Nevada and surrounding territories and also Florida, which all became grist for my poetry mill. We met Hagop's cousins, Zaven Hatutian and his family in Kansas and Jasmine (Hasmig) Hazeldine and her husband Michael in Florida, and my cousin Roxie Bold and her husband and mother in California.

After vacations in Pennsylvania, Cape Cod, Lake George, New York, the final joint vacation was at the Green Harbor Motel in Gilford, New Hampshire. The children all much grown then, the joint vacations ended, and we began taking vacations with either Bob and Audrey, or with Anoush and her husband Gregg and the grandchildren. During that time we visited California, the Grand Canyon and environs, Florida and Kansas City. Since then we have concentrated on the New England area.

But my favorite of all for its nature and inspiration was the Grand Canyon in Arizona. Belonging to the National Park Service, it consists of rocks of the Colorado Plateau a mile deep and 10 miles across with spires, buttes and amazing artistic coloration. The rushing Colorado River below it has carved this canyon through millennia, and nearby hotels and motels are ready to accommodate the many millions of visitors who come to see this miracle of nature. I still love to see films of this place on television, giving me a chance to stare at this beauty as if to fully absorb the atmosphere of its peace and meditate.

An additional favorite near the Grand Canyon and other amazing canyons is Bryce Canyon National Park. It consists of a series of amphitheaters in Utah where erosion has carved limestone into orange-red formations called hoodoos. One would think that a very original sculptor had been at work there. I have seen it twice and a number of times on television, but the sight of it never ceases to thrill me. We were accompanied by Hovsep and Mechtild or Bob on these trips out West.

Hagop and I can never forget the many trips we took to Tanglewood in the Berkshires of Massachusetts to hear orchestral concerts by the Boston Symphony. We attended many choral concerts by the Berkshire Choral Festival in the nearby town of Sheffield held on the beautiful grounds of the Berkshire School at the base of Mt. Everett. These events presented the height of musical thrill and performance, and visits to the Clark Museum in Williamstown and the Normal Rockwell Museum in Great Barrington fulfilled our artistic expectations.

So these American vacations left me with as much revelation as my trips abroad had and truly deepened my insight into the geography of the country and also of the variations in human nature in different states.

Variations Among Armenians

Having observed Armenian communities in America and in Beirut and also Armenian immigrants from Iran and Armenia, I've found that many cultural differences exist among differing groups, some people being more accepting of them than others. Some of the older immigrants don't accept the values of America, so unlike the customs that they have been used to, but others have learned to live with them. Their children going to American schools are quite well adjusted and also show respect to their parents by speaking Armenian to them and to their relatives and by participating in Armenian events because the mood of the country has changed from the days of emphasis on speaking English only.

My greatest dedication had been to family and less to learning the Armenian language, though some Armenians from abroad subscribed to the thinking that one couldn't be an Armenian who didn't speak Armenian to other Armenians. However, I understand spoken Armenian rather well, and I do have great respect for the Armenian language and for the Armenian Church, evidence of which can be found in some of my books. I also read and write about Armenians, am very much aware of my heritage, associate with many of them and often cook Armenian food.

Since this new group of Armenians has more education and more wealth than the first influx of Armenian immigrants in 1915-1930 and have been accustomed to private Armenian-language schools in their countries of origin, they have established Armenian day schools in many Armenian centers. Their children sometimes attend any of the Armenian schools that have been established in the communities of Montreal, Detroit, New Jersey, and a number of schools in California for the largest Armenian population of any of our states.

In my town, some Armenians sent their children to the Armenian General Benevolent Union School, which had six grades plus a pre-school but closed after some active years. Now the parents send their children to St. Stephen's Day School, connected with St. Stephen's Armenian Apostolic Church. The Armenian Sisters' Academy in Lexington also accommodates these students.

The first such school in America was established as the Armenian Sisters' Academy in Philadelphia, Pennsylvania, later moved to Radnor. Their teaching is rigorous and includes many Armenian subjects along with language and the usual English curriculum. Its kindergarten and pre-school use the Montessori method of teaching, which emphasizes self-directed teaching with the teacher as a guide.

Some of the Armenian day schools in California, Southfield, Michigan, and Montreal have classes through the last grade of high school and others have classes through the fifth grade, after which the students usually transfer to the public schools. These schools bent on using the language of the immigrant parents are seen as a safeguard against the threat of assimilation.

This quote is attributed to Heraclitus of ancient Greece: "The only permanence is change." Some change worked for the better; some change didn't. The changes of the children growing up and finding their direction in life were certainly better in that they relieved us of many worries inherent in bringing up children in this modern era.

Changes in the country such as the youth acting with unusual disrespect for authority were not better and led to some of the social rebellions that followed and shaped a new mood for America. Some of the changes worked also for the better, depending upon the perspective of the individual who was entrusted with the powerful tool of judgment. However, the judgments of one generation are usually different from the judgments of another.

My mentality was more like the Armenians than what we thought of as the Americans, though the differences were often surmountable. I didn't have a mainstream mentality and didn't know what the American or even Armenian mainstream was all about.

Also in my youth I had an inferiority complex about being an Armenian, that is, the child of immigrants whose language and ways were ethnic. It was a common complex among the American-born generation of earlier years, not helped by the fact that the Americans in business and institutions such as school frowned upon the speaking of foreign language and thought that students whose parents spoke a foreign language had more problems in school than others, a fact many of the newer Armenians didn't accept. But through the years I gradually found my way out of that complex, for the more Americans accepted Armenians as a valuable ethnic group, the more I felt proud to be an Armenian.

Artistic Gatherings

In the early 1970s, a few gatherings assured me I was still a respected writer of the Armenian community in America and my name had also reached literary people in Armenia. At a small gathering of writers I attended with my father at the Watertown apartment of Edmond Azadian, the writer and editor from Egypt who was executive secretary of the ADL, I saw Diana Der Hovanessian, the Armenian-American poet, and met Kevork Emin, a very popular poet from Armenia. Emin didn't know much English, and I lacked fluency in Armenian, so I listened to his pleasant, understanding and rather humorous remarks. He was working under the Soviet system, which supported poets and artists and published their books while also favoring some over others and so didn't speak about other problems that existed in Armenia.

During those few years when my father was doing much volunteer work for the *Baikar* newspaper as well as writing for it in Armenian, he also hosted a number of dinners for Armenian visitors from Armenia and countries in the Middle East. The few of them who stayed for a day or two at his house included the brilliant and humble Alexander Saroukhan, who was well known and much celebrated cartoonist and caricaturist from Egypt. He was about my father's age and fatherly in his manner.

Mother had to work hard to keep up her perfectionist cooking for all of these people. One of these gatherings was for Lucineh Zakarian, a famous soprano from Armenia and her company who had arrived here to give concerts. She was surrounded by her retinue and some friends.

In the 1970s, we all enthusiastically attended a performance of the Armenian Jazz Ensemble at St. James Armenian Church. This marvelous group, including singers Raisa Mkrtchian and Roupen Matevossian, had been invited from Armenia to give a few performances around the country. The concert was in the large cultural hall of the church in order to accommodate the very

From left, Diana Der Hovanessian, Helene, Khachadoor and Kevork Emin

large crowd in this central location of the Armenian community here. We were all very much inspired by the sounds of Armenian jazz with its own particular nuances of Armenian sound in music, itself an extension of our own personalities.

Also in those years, an organ concert of the compositions of Alan Hovhaness took place in the sanctuary of the St. James Armenian Church. The organist was the famed Berj Zamkochian of the Boston Symphony Orchestra. The concert was impressive and emphasized the early connection Hovhaness had with the church as its organist.

The composer Hampartzoum Berberian had his own choral group, in which Hagop sang for a short while. Then we went to a performance of his work *Requiem Aeternam* by the Masterworks Chorale of Boston conducted by Allen Lannom at Cary Hall in Lexington. An impressive piece, the chorus had learned it very well and performed it in the original Armenian. Perhaps this performance whetted our appetite for more of this type of music, for in later years we attended many concerts with a preference for choral music. Two of our favorites were the *German Requiem* by Brahms and the *Requiem* by Mozart.

Eventually, the interest in music led to my attending many classical music concerts with my husband at Symphony Hall in Boston, Jordan Hall in the New England Conservatory and in many other concert halls. After his retirement, we made many trips to follow the concerts we thought we would like — a wonderful experience encompassing many of the works of Bach, of Beethoven, of Handel, of Purcell, of Brahms and many other choral or orchestral pieces from the great legacies.

By that time I had also learned to like and really appreciate the songs of Frank Sinatra, as well as his acting in the many movies he made, probably because my husband always liked the popular American music as well as classical music. We influenced each other. I loved Sinatra's rendition of the songs "Strangers in the Night" and "My Way" and was inspired by those songs and others as well as by his winning an Academy Award and many Grammy awards.

Dramas were also performed in Armenian by various cultural groups that were either local or from other Armenian communities. Our brother-in-law Joe, a fine actor, directed and acted in a number of dramas. Hagop also acted in at least one drama as did our daughter Anoush.

Dance programs by various dance groups became very popular at this time, and there were a number of Armenian folk dance groups that traveled for performances in Armenian communities. Subsequently, our nephew Apo Ashjian and others formed the Sayat Nova Dance Company of Boston, which he directed and danced in with his brother Hagop, his wife Arlet and other relatives and friends. Their sister Sona did the administrative work. Armenian literary programs, evening dances, and conventions of many organizations all made for a lively social scene.

In addition, there were the many continuing programs going on in Cambridge and Boston as part of the American cultural scene, though the majority of Armenians usually preferred the Armenian scene with the college crowd attending programs in their own schools as well and forming Armenian clubs. Some of the schools in this area contributing to this continuing activity were Harvard University, Boston University, Northeastern University, Wentworth, Bentley, Babson, UMass, community colleges, and many more.

The parties we attended were serious, conversational and sometimes humorous. Most of our parties were family gatherings, usually with members of Hagop's large family. They kept adding new members all the time, since there were so many children who married and had their own children. We were invited to many showers and weddings and baptisms with subsequent feasting on Armenian delicacies. My family was not so celebratory, though there were weddings of relatives to attend.

In those years there was much cultural activity in the Armenian community of the greater Boston area, including dances, dinners and programs with an occasional poetry reading in English or Armenian. A number of organizations flourished that are now centered in the New York-New Jersey area, in the Detroit area, in California and a few other areas. The churches were and still are very active with their many programs as is the National Association for Armenian Studies and Research.

But generation succeeded generation, each with its own preferences. Armenian organizations proliferated into groups for dentists, doctors, businesspeople, artists, etc. The Armenian Library and Museum of America now houses works of art in its busy gallery as well as books and Museum artifacts. Art exhibits that had flourished in the 60s and 70s continued in the many art galleries in and around all the major American cities that house Armenians. So many fine Armenian artists exhibit their paintings that it is difficult to compile a list of favorites.

Since serious and dedicated Armenian art began with manuscripts illuminations of the Middle Ages, there have been many outstanding artists in a number of countries. Ivan Aivazovsky (Hovhannes Aivazian) of Russia was famed for his seascapes. Martiros Saryan and Minas Avetisyan were famed colorists in Armenia. Hovsep Pushman was famed in America for portrait type paintings, which are still being sold. Arshile Gorky was an original and great abstract-expressionist whose reputation benefitted both Armenians and Americans.

In addition to these most-known Armenian artists, the mood and production of art continues in all Armenian centers with many exhibitions being announced at galleries. In this time period, I wrote about a couple of shows of my ex-brother-in-law Martin Barooshian's work, which was influenced by the abstract-expressionist movement. Some of his paintings had graced the walls of my parents' living room, the most impressive an abstract rendition of an Armenian archbishop. He also taught art history in a New York City high school and continues painting at present.

I also wrote about the paintings of Nora Azadian, Edmond's wife, who had immigrated from Egypt a few years before. A few years later she went with her husband to Detroit when he was appointed secretary of the Alex Manoogian Cultural Fund established by the great industrialist and philanthropist.

Also on the American national scene, the Armenian Assembly and Armenian National Committee arose then to do work for political influence with the United States Government. This type of activity thrives in the present political climate.

However, there has been marked decrease in Armenian artistic programs in and around Watertown and Boston since those active years.

Hampartzoum Berberian (left) and Lucineh Zakarian
at the home of Khachadoor Pilibosian circa 1975.
Martin Barooshian painted the abstraction
that hangs on the wall.

Editing Again

After another term for Varoujan, Barbara Merguerian became the editor of *The Armenian Mirror-Spectator*; Ara Kalaydjian and Alin Grigorian followed. I then returned as part-time co-editor of the newspaper with Barbara as editor in 1975.

My son was five, and I wanted to work around his hours at school because my parents were getting too old to do constant babysitting. The change in people meant a different atmosphere, and the committee in charge of the newspaper was comprised mostly of the new Armenians, who were usually well-educated and had the slant on life they had brought with them from their various cultures learned from living in Middle Eastern countries and Armenia.

In the years between 1975 and 1980 I wrote quite a few articles, such as the piece on the life of Lord Byron's study of the Armenian language when he was at the Mekhitarist Monastery in Venice, the piece on the history of Watertown, the article on the Armenian collection at the Watertown Public Library and others. Many books were being published by Armenian-Americans and sent to the newspaper for mention or review. I reviewed many of these, finding my true calling in this sort of writing where I could evaluate the style or subject matter of the books according to what I had absorbed in my studies of literature. I made a mental collection of compliments I received for the reviews and also a collection of grateful letters from the authors of the books.

I particularly liked writing articles such as the one entitled "A Few Armenian Proverbs and What They May Mean" in the November 27, 1976 issue:

> It took thousands of years of Armenian history, or hundreds
> if you prefer, to facilitate the folk wisdom of generation after
> generation living in a stable and slowly-changing environ-

ment. Part of this wisdom has been handed down in the form of proverbs, some hundreds of which can be considered purely Armenian without the imprint of other peoples, except in the influence of cultural or business contacts upon the mentality of the Armenian . . .

These proverbs peppered city life as well as village life, though some may apply more than others. They are exceedingly apt, and some apply to modern situations. They can stand trial with any of the best proverbs of the world . . .

These are particularly traceable to the general area of the state of Kharpert:

If you do not have honey, you do not have honeyed speech.
One who sells honey licks his fingers.

Some of these proverbs are similar to other Near Eastern proverbs, like the similarities in the beat of folk music. They pulsate with similar circumstances and the rhythms of life there quite peacefully and simply compared to modern technological society. But they do reflect more awareness of the lessons of the past, of the realities (often harsh) of the present. These next few proverbs reflect misfortune in a philosophical light:

The blind man does not care how expensive the candle is.
The defeated drunk gets drunk twice.
If I am boss and you are boss, then who will grind coffee?
The poor man's boss ate a snake; they said he was hungry.

I only neglected to mention who the translators were because I usually didn't know, though no one complained. If there were any errors in what I wrote, it was because sometimes mistakes happen in that kind of speed work where a deadline looms every week.

I wrote quite a few feature articles, one on the federal grants given to a bilingual program for the Watertown public schools, for which I interviewed Stella Malkasian Boy, director of foreign languages, ESL, and bilingual education. She had been my high school French teacher, so that writing this article meant something special to me. I also wrote many reviews of the literary quarterly *Ararat*. The reviews were quite long and, I think, quite positive.

Then I had the chance to write about the federal grants for Watertown Library materials in Armenian, another point of interest to me because I had worked in the library system when I was in high school. The article was accompanied by three delightful drawings, one from a children's story by Vaghtank Ananian, an illustration from a story by Hovhannes Toumanian and a third satirical illustration for a novel by Yeghishe Charentz. I enjoyed writing these feature articles more than I had enjoyed writing editorials, which were after all a burden of thinking with which people could agree or disagree.

Book reviewing at the newspaper provided me with some enchantments. This was an exposure to books I probably wouldn't have read otherwise and certainly wouldn't have reviewed unless I had been required to. It was part of my education on what Armenians are all about, as if my being one were not enough. Yet it had not been enough.

I also wrote an occasional editorial, and the one quoted below is entitled "Books, Books, Books" written in July of 1979 with the prophecy at the end. By this time it should have been obvious to anyone who was reading my writings that I had a great love for books and felt that without them my life would certainly have been quite empty and meaningless.

> Books in all categories by or about Armenians are a boon to Armenian studies and also a growing and thriving enterprise. For much data in these publications, which are seldom a profitable venture and usually a costly one, are a basis for the study of Armenians and their character . . . Translations are included. There are also many books in Armenian being published in the diaspora, some of which appeal to the readership in Armenia as well as to Armenians in dispersion.
>
> And we often get news from Armenia about the many books being published there by academicians, by poets, by novelists. They also are of value to Armenian studies here, as they provide research data for which there is less availability and also provide the thoughts of Armenians with profiles of their lives past and present.
>
> We consider ourselves fortunate to be immersed in this veritable sea of knowledge at the time when the multicultural approach is popular in the US. It was not always so, as many of us remember. And this change in attitude, this

desire on the part of Americans that began at the time of the presidency of John F. Kennedy to learn of the various heritages that built this country, is a catalyst for this new movement of Armenians in Armenian-American to write and publish as much as they can on Armenian subject matter.

The books, though not quantity sellers, have been welcomed in many public and university libraries as well as private libraries of those who appreciate them. The trend will continue; there is no doubt of that.

Perhaps sometimes I was writing too philosophically, more than would pique the curiosity or comprehension of the average newspaper reader. The material was interesting and varied, too varied for some and too intellectual for others. But you can never please everyone. If I had it to do over again knowing what I know, I would try to be easier to understand and not quite so bold. Even though other newspaper editors have been? I knew it was the style of editors, certainly the Armenian editors, to "hit the subject on the head" by being strong and forceful in expressions and beliefs. Otherwise how could one convince or influence readers?

Perhaps I ignored some of the up-to-date news that should have been reported, but even that is a matter of interpretation of the circumstances. My agreement with my bosses was that I would work part time, no more than 15 hours a week because I didn't have the stamina to do more and I had a child to take care of. The work I did was fast, furious and unhesitating with never a break for chatting or for lunch. The payment was commensurate with the hours, in other words less than half of what a full-time editor would be paid. For these reasons I couldn't pursue the news more actively.

I also honed my writing abilities by writing editorials, articles on intriguing subjects, news reports and book reviews and also sharpened the knife of my metaphors with some poems so that they could cut cleanly and mysteriously into consciousness without leaving blood. This intensive writing schedule, especially in the later years of 1975 to 1980, left me with a great need to write daily.

In 1975 the Civil War in Lebanon had begun. There were a few interpretations of how and why it began, but basically the Palestinian group in Lebanon and their Muslim allies were fighting the Lebanese Christians for control of the country. Each group had its own small army, including the Armenians who stayed neutral during this war, a neutrality that saved them from hostilities and also from fighting each other for political reasons. In 1982, Israel, which had been from a distance allied with the Christian group, invaded southern Lebanon to fight the Palestinians there. Wearily after 17 years of fighting, the Taif Accord mediated by Saudi Arabia was signed by all the discordant parties agreeing to peace.

The war was big news at the newspaper because of the large Armenian community in Beirut to constantly contact and worry about. Many prominent Armenians and business people had left Lebanon for various countries around the world. Many sad stories of what people had lost before leaving the country were told so that one could fathom a great need for social services and a new understanding that Armenian-Americans were not used to.

My two sisters-in-law with their husbands and their mother were safely in America, but my brother-in-law Aram, a high school principal, and his family including his wife Asdghig and four sons, Hratch, Hovig, Ari and Azad, were still there for some years until 1989 when they arrived in America. I learned all that the Armenians of Beirut were going through from my own family and their worry about their son and brother. The other brother Hovsep in Germany also worried about those in Lebanon during the war.

I left the newspaper in 1981, to concentrate on writing poetry in order to find a niche in the poetry world. Having found the discipline of writing every day and having the need to write, I could make this switch with a great deal of practice and concentration. Of my impressions of working in journalism, the following quotation from the book *Double Vision* by Ben Bagdikian, a leading journalist who became dean of the graduate school of journalism at the University of California at Berkeley, will serve very well:

> With all its roller coaster alternations of frustration and satisfaction, of the joy of working in the newsroom full of good ideas and enterprise, and grief when it falls into dull bureaucracy, for all the eternal politics and conflicting ambitions within newsrooms, of breathless excitement followed by

grinding tedium, of endemic under-payment because they know you like the work so much — it is still full of opportunity, excitement, individualism, and accomplishment.

I met many more Armenians from abroad in those years. One of these was Dr. Haroutiun Arzoumanian of Montreal, one of the foremost leaders of the organization and also of the Tekeyan Cultural Association, a cultural offshoot of the ADL. He had immigrated to Canada from Egypt. Hagop Vartivarian, a writer and businessman, was from Beirut. Bedros Piandarian, business manager for a while, was also from Egypt. Assadour Devletian, another writer and teacher, was from Cyprus. Kevork Marashlian, who still serves as secretary of the Tekeyan Cultural Association, was from Argentina. Thus I became acquainted with many aspects of the diasporan Armenian mentality.

"From the standpoint of the present moment, were you glad or sorry that you were associated with this organization and its newspaper?"

"All in all, I am glad for the association and the opportunity to learn so much about my people, for learning about my people is a way of learning about myself."

"And learning about your husband's and father's social and political beliefs."

"Yes, indeed, to meet the people they knew. It made me feel as if I were running along the same track as they were, a sort of cooperation and coordination of feeling, of a close friendship that meant a great deal to me."

"I imagine you also enjoyed giving readers information and ideas that they could use."

"Of course, a thousand times of course."

"In spite of many difficulties and some curses?"

"Of course again."

"After you left the job, would you have served again for a few more years?"

"After I left the first time, yes. After I left the second time in 1981, no, though I did appreciate the opportunity to hone my writing skills."

Returning to Poetry

Coincident with editing at the newspaper, I had been publishing a few of my poems in *Ararat* quarterly, which had an important place in the intellectual life of Armenian-Americans as one of very few English-language literary magazines in existence. Publication was sparse and sporadic, but nevertheless lent a spark to my life. From the newspaper and from this magazine I learned to focus on Armenian subject matter and explore its possibilities in poetry.

Then I vowed to branch out and publish more poems in American journals, and I began to publish books of my poems. Publication would still be sporadic with the consolation that I was competing with thousands of poets from all categories of life, many of them very well trained. I withdrew from community life for a number of years and wrote copiously.

"You were publishing poems occasionally in *Ararat*. What did that mean to you?"

"It meant a great deal. It meant that maybe I could call myself a poet after all, after I had been denying myself that name because I had a personal complex and felt my work wasn't good enough to compete."

"You have written a great deal about Armenian subject matter. Did your poems in the magazine follow the same line?"

"Not at first. General subject matter was okay until Leo Hamalian became editor and requested Armenian-oriented material."

"Were you willing to go along with that?"

"Yes."

"How often did they publish your poems?"

"About once in four of five issues or sometimes less often."

"How many poems each time?"

"Usually one. But at first it had sometimes been two or three."

"How did you feel about that?"

"I felt that I wasn't their favorite poet. And in the reviewing my books, I had the impression they didn't think the matter through. In other words, they didn't take me seriously."

"Then you redoubled your efforts to get poems published in literary journals."

"Right."

"Did that work?"

"Yes, to my great delight. I eventually got used to all the rejection slips poets always get, and even got used to the idea that I was competing with thousands of other poets. For as the years went on, there were more and more poetry workshops in colleges and universities and elsewhere that produced many poets, making the system slow and difficult in some ways. For though writing modern poetry presented great difficulties, it had become a popular thing for writers to do."

Keeping concentration on only poetry with its exacting use of language and metaphor was difficult because I came up against many mental blocks. I kept writing diligently in order to overcome some of the communication problems I had and to be able to please the editors of literary magazines. I'm not sorry for this, for it lent my mentality a warm glow, kept me company, put me in touch with some fine literary people and gained me some publication credits.

Then two incidents occurred which influenced the subject matter of my poetry and also shook me and all Armenians to our roots. The first was the Armenian earthquake of 1988 in which at least 25,000 Armenians in Armenia were killed and very many were seriously injured. The city of Spitak was virtually destroyed, and immediate appeals were made to Armenians in America and other countries to help people who were homeless and destitute. People and Armenian organizations responded immediately and very generously, adding to my sense of pride in Armenian-Americans.

Then in September of 1991, the Soviet Union, of which Armenia had been a part as a satellite republic completely dependent upon the Union, fell apart more for financial reasons than political. The Iron Curtain that had scared so many people suddenly dissipated. Armenia became free, a turn of fate that had not been expected, leaving it with a trend toward democracy and capitalism without preparation. Complicated problems existed, and again the Armenian-Americans rallied and poured money and services in accordance with those needs into the small country.

Pride and also some relief replaced old attitudes of shame and fear. With new political circumstances, Armenia was independent and had a president and parliament at last, even with the inherent instabilities. We were all relieved that a major factor that had been dividing the Armenian community, the communism of Armenia as part of the Soviet Union, was gone and that the two political sides of the Armenian community could feel freer to associate and cooperate.

The division between the Armenian Democratic Liberal Party or Ramgavars and the Armenian Revolutionary Federation or Dashnags, changed with the political situation. It lost its old dimension and loosened some of the disagreements that had existed in the communities. Still there were some disunity along those party lines such as the division in the Armenian Church and the continued existence of two Catholicoses, one in Armenia and one in Lebanon, but the new alignment promoted a general feeling of more cooperation and friendliness.

I had worked with this subject matter somewhat from the ADL perspective. So with this new development, I was encouraged to write about Armenia and Armenians in any country in the world from my own point of view. In other words, Armenia was now an independent country, and I was now an independent free lance writer.

I had found the subject of Armenian history interesting, and writing about it had been a learning experience affecting my poetry in that I found myself writing a poem about the new Armenian freedom. The poem was part of a number of poems which were declared a finalist group in the important poetry competition of the literary journal *NEW LETTERS*. An excerpt from one of the poems called "I Chose the Poetic" follows:

> The old rules had crumbled
> on thin and outdated paper.
> Statues of ideologues were crushed
> and mixed with soil of United Nations,
> the homeland knot a newer fruit.
> Armenians here, Armenians there,

> spread thinly like jam
> on the bread of many lands.
> The new democracy was taking root
> like a wild daisy in a field
> recalling the heaven dimension
> to be popular as a jazz tune.
> My fingers were newspaper gray
> with hesitant views and news
> of skeptical brooms made public
> being seized after a Stalin purge,
> a Khrushev reform with thump of shoe,
> the cleansing of toil and inheritance,
> Gorbachev's new wording
> melting the iron with new demands.

Later I wrote another poem called "Earthquake Monument" in response to the earthquake of 1988. In part it reads as follows:

> They ask me to be involved.
>   I send 50 blankets,
>   100 bars of unscented soap
>   and 1000 pencils for schoolchildren.
>   I can't send my shock.
> They ask me to shed tears.
>   My river overflows.
>   My dry eyes sigh.
>   My morning juice sours.
>   I see double sometimes.
> They ask me to spread the word.
>   I type too fast.
>   My images are pasted on the past.
>   My daily trek is vexed.
>   Memory still consults my mind.

Both these poems are included in my book *History's Twists: The Armenians* published by Ohan Press in 2008.

I thought writing these poems about Armenian happenings that also reflected the Armenian character was enough to satisfy my craving for expressing my Armenianism and would also please those who had been following my articles in the newspaper. For I isolated myself from the community I had been serving in order to work a great deal on what I felt was bringing my thinking self to a gradual fruition. But I was willing to do the work and take my chances on getting the recognition I thought I would be entitled to if I could produce good work.

In the meantime some of them made me feel a bit guilty for abandoning the community.

"Are you writing for yourself?"

"My work is meant for anyone to read. Publishing poems is not immediate with its appearance like articles in the newspaper."

"You really should write for the *Mirror-Spectator*."

"But I'm not employed there anymore."

"Why should that stop you?"

"I really love what I'm doing now in poetry and feel I owe it all my concentration."

"That's too bad. We liked your articles."

"I'm going to publish a book of poems about Armenians."

"I don't read poetry."

Thus I realized that my words were not reaching and couldn't reach most of the people who had read my previous work. It was obvious that expressing oneself in poetry was nice but not a service to the community.

"Am I a traitor then?"

"Why?"

"A number of people have wanted me to write articles for the newspaper, probably reports on this happening or that or expressions of opinion."

"Why do you feel bad about that? You can do what you want."

"But I'm still a writer and often writing about Armenians. The poem I wrote about the earthquake of 1988 had a great deal of concern and sympathy in it."

"Some of the Armenians liked it, didn't they?"

"Fortunately, yes. It was published on *Literary Groong* online by Grish Davtian and on the *Armenian Poetry Project* blogspot by Lola Koundakjian."

"That should make you feel better."

"It certainly does. It seems the Armenians who like my poems most don't usually speak up on the subject."

"Reticence can be a virtue."

One has to keep abreast of new developments even in poetry, and much of my work is narrative in this sense of the new narrative that will not displace the postmodern work of today but may exist beside it. With so much experience in journalism and its political and social subject matter, my work in poetry would inevitably be influenced by it to be a sort of journalistic poetry. I liked individuality in the writing of poetry and varied approaches to it, making the subject a variegated study in books available to readers of poetry.

Some people thought I had inherited my father's talent and improved upon it with study, though I was never sure about the heredity part of this. Certainly I was influenced by his habit of writing and reading, but this seemed rather minor compared to the influence from school and all the study of literature. I hoped he would be happy with what he saw of my work, even though he didn't understand the poetry because his English wasn't up to it. He never said much about it.

Then I gained great comfort from the anthology *Forgotten Bread: First Generation Armenian American Writers* edited by David Kherdian and published by Heyday Books. I had gotten to know David, a poet and also writer of prose books and his wife Nonny Hogrogian, a famous illustrator of children's books. Sixteen of the poems from my first two books were included with an excellent and positive evaluation by Alan Semerdjian, a young poet and musician. The other 16 authors had all been through more or less the same types of ethnic experiences of immigrating to or growing up in America as I had, and all were introduced by a young Armenian-American writer.

The writers included were all bilingual or bicultural, and I was in the company of people such as William Saroyan and Leon Surmelian as well as David, Marjorie Housepian, Diana Der Hovanessian, Harold Bond, Michael J. Arlen, Peter Najarian, Peter Sourian, Gary Braver and others. Some of them had written best-selling novels. For us, the bicultural subject provided a superb challenge, for it gave us a chance to plumb its insights and describe its meanings. Though I had met David before only briefly in person, I corresponded with him when he was an editor at *Ararat* and expressed interest in publishing my poem "The Anti-Rebel" that had won a first prize from the Armenian Allied Arts Association. That poem was also included in the anthology.

I didn't join many organizations, for I often felt out of place with groups of people. But I kept my membership in the National Association for Armenian Studies and Research, a group of Armenian-Americans under the leadership of Manoog Young who dedicated themselves to establishing chairs of Armenian studies at various universities, beginning with Harvard, including UCLA and ending with Boston University. They have a Book Clearinghouse, a bookstore that helps distribute my books, at least to Armenians and perhaps some libraries. After many years of service, Young retired and ceded the post of director to Nancy Kolligian.

Finally writing about my topsy-turvy life added a deeper dimension to my mind and emotions. The methods of journalism and newspapers in their daily and weekly pressures gave me a more disciplined approach to writing, though I felt liberated to be free of deadlines.

"Did you enjoy writing this memoir?"

"I absolutely loved the experience of writing of prose again, and the freedom to write about anything I wanted to in my own life without being structured by limitations."

"More than writing poetry?"

"Probably yes, because of less reworking. I was writing and rewriting poems an average of about 10 times for each poem before I could please myself and the editors of magazines. However, prose rewriting, rearranging, editing and proofreading also needed a number of times to insert facts and take out endless repetitions."

The Mystical Experience

My cardiac arrest and recovery became an obsession that wasn't evident to anyone around me. For I saw the scars every day; they were many and large and couldn't be hidden. I didn't feel any particular anger but only some guilt and thought I must communicate an indefinite something to Dr. Harken. How and why had I always felt that he would understand what no one else had? Why did I always feel an odd sense of worship when I tuned in to any of his television appearances at which he spoke with such great dignity and wisdom? I was unconsciously back in the operating room, and he was speaking to me or to the others there, back in the hospital and breathing in the atmosphere of compassion as if it had the pleasant scent and sensation of oxygen. But I didn't remember.

One day years later in 1984 when I became annoyed at something, I took a long walk to Mt. Auburn Cemetery in Cambridge, a beautiful park-like place. I often carried the memory of that surgery with me in the back of my mind in order to try to fully realize the fact that I had the gift of life and to appreciate it in a positive way, so that while I was walking along those lovely paths I was suddenly overcome by a strong emotion. I had entered the cemetery unhappily and uncaring about the world, but then I began to recognize a lighter emotion as though dark clouds had been lifted.

As I walked up the hill looking around me feeling lifted emotions, I wasn't quite able to define, I heard a masculine voice calling my name and realized that it was only an echo in my consciousness, not an auditory hallucination but imagination. Then I walked back renewed in a mood that seemed to be permanent.

After that I was more likely to smile at my family and be cheerful and loving. I soon noticed that I was returning more often to the typewriter (before I started using the computer) and either typing poems after writing them out first by hand. The inspiration went back to that incident of heightened emotion that

I call a mystical experience. It could be interpreted as a religious experience, an epiphany, if that mindset were present.

I knew there would be misunderstanding if I explained this to anyone. So I kept the experience to myself and used the newly engendered positive emotions as inspiration to write more and more poems. At first they were not hugely successful, for I had some problems with lack of clarity, writing too many ideas at one time so that the results seemed confused or jumbled with many repetitions. I could also trace an echo in the background of my writing that seemed to be a spilling out of the contents of my unconscious, as if a chink of it were open when it should be closed. But I had quite a few poems published in American literary journals, which was very encouraging especially as some of them were either prizewinners or finalists in literary competitions.

"You seem to be thinking of the psychology of surgery."

"It must be a new discipline."

"Yes."

"I didn't know what to think about the experience at the time, only when I did some reading into the work of C. G. Jung and found his ideas about creativity very positive and liberating. Much later I read *Skin Deep*, a novel by Gary Braver, which described the psychology that went along with plastic surgery. That was enlightening."

"Especially after what you have been through."

"Yes indeed."

"The experience is certainly giving you confidence."

"It's a wonderful thing to have. At least I have intellectual self-confidence, though my social self-confidence is still lagging."

"Has being married helped you with social self-confidence?"

"It certainly has because the social life is there, and I don't have to search for it. But our social life centers mostly around family, his and mine."

"Has your work experience as an editor helped you socially?"

"More intellectually than socially, though I've met many people I like as acquaintances."

"What held you back from being more friendly?"

"My usual introverted self."

"As I can see it, the ice is beginning to melt a little."

"It is."

Realizing that I worked better by intuition than by instruction, I returned to my own analysis of how my mind was working or not working well. We all know the unconscious mind consists of senseless and confused impressions that don't make any sense as in dreams. This background echo in reading my work that lasted for years seemed like the voice of someone talking at the same time and was rather like some nonsense syllables. Sometimes my readers showed unexpected anger at me because they thought these were innuendos that indicated spying or sending messages to people, even with personal connotations. For me it was a totally involuntary wording, and I had trouble perceiving the meanings of what I had written. After years of trying and of effort, I succeeded in changing the pattern of the almost-hidden hostile words and expressions that some people may have taken as angry expressions meant for them and of other echoes of words that indicated a more personal approach than necessary.

Then as I was reading the *Boston Globe* literary section, I came across an article written by poet and publisher Peter Davison, who was then poetry editor of *The Atlantic*. In the article he mentioned that he had been an assistant to Professor Howard Mumford Jones, one of my favorite professors from my student days, in his American literature course at Harvard. The time frame would have been approximately the same, but the assistant in the course I took was someone else whose attention and presence with some literary advice I had then valued and missed later.

The fact of Peter Davison being a similar presence, though not in my life, intrigued me and renewed all the excitement and emotion I had when I was taking the course. This led me to write some poems as a fictionalized and generalized version of my times as a student at the Harvard Extension School with unusual aplomb and fired ambition. As I finished the manuscript, it was announced that he had passed away. I might have wished to contact him about the manuscript for comment if nothing else, but as usual I was too late.

I had written to Mr. Jones at a time when I was at a low point in morale regarding the writing of prose or poetry because I thought I had done something terribly wrong in that regard. He answered me immediately on his old typewriter in his wonderful style that always carried such a pithy message, and I realized that he had had faith in my work all along as he reassured me that I had done nothing wrong but had only been misunderstood. This was a year before his death at the age of 88, and I have never regretted writing that letter and would have liked to show it to Peter Davison. Instead, I posted it on my web site for a while. It reads as follows:

December 15, 1979

Dear Helene Pilibosian:

If my note was stern, I am sorry, and I am not conscious that you have wrought any wrong that needs to be righted. As to what you say regarding the literary establishment, I think we people who teach what is quaintly called literature probably mislead most of our hearers because we perpetually overlook the sad fact that the book's a book although there's nothing in't (I think this is Byron, but I'm not sure). By this I mean that we perpetually perform as though there were no economic activities in the literary world, no rushes of fashion for this or against that, no discharging of editors when magazine circulations go down or book companies fail to show a profit. Peter Davison, who runs the Atlantic Monthly Press, tells me he has recently written a letter to the editor of the *London Times* literary supplement sternly asking him why he doesn't review more books of poetry. The latest issue reviews eight poets, whether as a result of the letter or no I can't say, but the difficulty with poetry is, I suppose, that the poets have invented a secret language of their own satisfactory in their circles and unintelligible to the great, good, stupid public. Ah, well! I'm glad my letter of praise got to the linotypers at Harvard University Press.

After his passing, I reread some of the work he had left and realized that it was a great legacy that would probably lose some of the appreciation it had enjoyed as fashions of literature change along with new personalities. But the wisdom of his words and the knowledge of literature and modes of analysis are still in the older books that probably form a basis for the new ones whose authors had learned from them.

My Unusual Personality Type

It took me a while to be able to perceive the poems I wrote with the clarity of meaning a literary reader would. Often I misjudged my own work, throwing away the better poem and sending out the worse poem to magazines or conversely destroying the good version and having it accepted by a magazine it had been sent to, dismayed that I didn't keep a copy. But over time I kept writing and rewriting, stubbornly sending my poems out to magazines for consideration undeterred by criticism and indifference with always the occasional acceptance in one of the many literary magazines. That fed me hope. Others would read and react to what was mysterious, thus giving the necessary feedback that helped clarify my own writing to me.

I am grateful to the editors of the magazines for being so patient with my endeavors, often taking the time to comment that they liked one poem or another but space constraints or different preferences kept them from accepting these for publication. I suppose they identified with the process of creativity as a search for self and with the struggle for achievement and publication.

Thinking more about the emotional experience at the cemetery, I wanted to analyze it while still keeping it to myself. For how in the world does one explain a mystical experience to others? Reading about the 16 different types of personalities, I learned that only one or two of those types are capable of having mystical experiences.

The 16 types are the 16 personality type patterns that are often referred to by a 4-letter code developed by Isabel Myers based on her understanding of the personality typology of Carl Jung.

From the articles I inferred I was an INFJ, a complicated person with a great deal of empathy and intuition. These comprise one percent of the population, are good students and creative but prefer to exert influence behind the scenes rather than be overt leaders. Private people with complex personalities, they find conflict disagreeable, have vivid imaginations and lend themselves to composing complex works of art. They are poetic and can be mystical, often selecting liberal arts as a college major, and may be attracted to writing as a profession, notably using metaphor in communications. Noted for enthusiasm, concentration and originality, they can understand human systems but are crushed by too much criticism and can become physically ill in hostile working conditions. They want harmony in their family lives, and as parents they are extremely devoted.

"What are you reading there with such intense concentration?"

"I'm reading about different kinds of personalities and trying to figure out which one is mine. I'm sure I didn't invent it."

"What is the article called?"

"'The 16 Personality Types.' The name of the book is *Please Understand Me: Character and Temperament Types*, written by David Keirsey and Marilyn Bates."

"Did you find your personality in it?"

"I certainly did. The description is unmistakable and very accurate, to the letter, you might say."

"I don't believe it."

"You can read it for yourself."

"It certainly sounds like you. Where did you get this?"

"Bob gave it to me after his boss gave it to him at one of his co-op jobs, the one where he was working for a mechanical engineer. Imagine, he didn't even care for the work, though he did like the boss, and he gleaned such wonderful and revealing information not only for himself but also for me."

"And you had this on file?"

"I have this one section on file, but unfortunately I threw away the rest of the article because I simply don't have space for all the articles I want to keep. I'm quite taken by this subject. But I can't quite figure out whether they mean personality when they write about character and temperament or whether they mean that the personality arises from character and temperament."

"Maybe you'd better read the book."

I read the book and was illuminated by its perceptions. The personality types set forth in this book are the results of the research of C. G. Jung, the Swiss psychologist whose works have recently become important in the fields of psychology and psychiatry. The authors present an interpretation of his works and of others with the addition of an analysis of the four temperaments, originally discovered and listed by the ancient Greek Hippocrates.

The four temperaments set forth in modern terms are first, The Dionysian Temperament. These people devoted to action in their lives without much regard for duty. People of The Epimethean Temperament live to be useful to their social environment. People of the Promethean Temperament try to control and predict realities, like the scientists they often are. Persons of the Apollonian Temperament live by intuition and feeling and are often dedicated to a search for self. These are the writers, except for the scientific writers. Such inborn traits influence the types of personality, singly or in combination.

Mutual understanding between or among people working together or married or in the relationship of parent and child could benefit from this information to better understand each other and be more tolerant of each other. For, as emphasized, the person of one personality type tends to erroneously think others should be of the same type and have the same preferences. The authors mention that the material is being used in some business courses to help employers and employees better understand the people they work with.

The differences between introvert and extrovert, again descriptions of types set forth by Jung, are also explained in detail and with great perception. My life would have been easier if those around me had understood that I belong to the 25 percent of the population who are introverted, that is, those who are more likely to think than speak or to avoid people and crowds and public speaking and to the one percent of my particular personality type. The world has traditionally been geared to the other 75 percent of the population who are extroverted, that is, those who have no trouble speaking to people, are more aggressive and like crowds and public speaking. It would have been better to have been understood rather than ridiculed or thought of as stupid or abnormal. Hence, the name of the book *Please Understand Me*.

I and a few other introverted people I know grew up with the phrase "Why are you so quiet?" or "Did someone cut out your tongue?" The second phrase usually emanated from an Armenian of the older generation, for the tongues of Armenians were in some areas of historic Armenia cut out by the Turks, who in a their national fanaticism resented the speaking of Armenian. Be that as it may, these phrases were humiliating to the introverts and caused them to develop inferiority complexes and to further withdraw into their protective shells. On the other hand, the people who made these statements thought they were being helpful and encouraging. But their comments sounded like saying, "You can't talk and socialize as well as I do, so there is something wrong with you."

I have simplified the complex but understandable subject matter of the book enough to convey the essential meaning and purpose. In reading the book I was able to see not only myself but the personalities of many acquaintances as if they had been sketched upon a screen.

"What about conditions like mental illness or autism? Do they deal with that subject matter?"

"No. Whatever they write about is within the range of normal personality differences."

"Do they write much about shyness?"

"They hardly use the word shy. I know that many Armenians in my experience have thought that shyness is an abnormality in itself and might treat the child in question as an abnormal child. Perhaps this is a more general attitude."

"But it might be wise to have the extremely shy child checked out by a psychologist."

"I agree with that, so that early problems could be treated and not develop into large problems. I can imagine the early days when lack of comprehension resulted in humiliations and even punishment."

"You care much about children and how they are treated."

"Indeed I do. They are important for the future if they are brought up with kindness and understanding."

The Pills

What could have led to the mystical experience involved a hysterectomy to cure severe physical problems, taking the beta-blocker propranolol or Inderal daily for high blood pressure and feeling very happy about these circumstances because I had had trouble for a few years with a slight but constant shortness of breath. The beta-blocker immediately relieved the problem which nothing else had seemed to help and put me more at ease with myself and everyone else. Suddenly I was able to speak without effort, and I craved the use of a microphone so I could practice public speaking. I was thrilled with this new luck and skill.

The pills were originally given to me by a cardiologist named Burton Rabinowitz, for I had asked the gynecologist Anthony DiSciullo at Mount Auburn Hospital to have a specialist present at the hysterectomy just in case something went wrong. Not that anyone expected anything to go wrong, but I was always nervous about going into surgery, especially since I had previously been seeing a gynecologist who said surgery for me would be certain death. Not in a particularly good mood because of difficulties, I'm afraid I wasn't very nice to the cardiologist, though I was grateful to the gynecologist for releasing me from suffering.

I didn't expect Dr. Rabinowitz to be part of my later life, but during this surgery I was taking these pills as he directed and felt quite at ease. My breathing was fine, but then I dropped the pills he had wanted me to continue taking. I went to another general practitioner, for Dr. Rabinowitz was a specialist only. Then after a couple of years my blood pressure was consistently a bit high, so I asked for those pills. My wish was granted, and almost immediately my breathing problem was better, leaving me very grateful because I had seen a few doctors for that problem to no avail.

My stage fright also was better after taking the medicine, and I did a few public readings with moderate success. Though not as successful as many other poets at doing this, I felt a great sense of accomplishment at having conquered not only depression, which is the mafia of the mind and also chews away at the emotions, but also my fear of public speaking. However, I still get jitters when I have a reading, though even practiced public speakers have them.

A few years later, I was to have a small operation to take out the benign tumor in my salivary duct. Just before that I had written a note to Dr. Harken with a hint as to what my communication problem was about, assuming that he remembered me and my case. The note stated that the brain damage had been caused by the previous shock treatments and that I had been to two psychiatrists and still couldn't talk. It certainly didn't explain much, but I felt much better after I had sent the letter that was never answered. It had been a worry for me that I had some brain damage because my mind didn't always do what I wanted it to, especially in the matter of communications. However, the report of the surgery of 1963 stated that the minor brain damage had been reversed, so that I was curious.

Then just as I was waiting to go into the current surgery, a man who looked something like Dr. Harken and must have been a volunteer at the hospital walked over to me, stopped, and said, "Everything's going to be all right, Little Lady," in a very kind and caring voice. I smiled with appreciation then wondered if I were dreaming or hallucinating in thinking that this could be a message from Dr. Harken, who had affectionately called me "Little Sister" during an office visit after an assistant had examined me. Even if it were only a spontaneous comment from this unknown man, I never forgot it and repeated it to myself when things appeared dismal. The operation was brief and very successful.

Gradually over the years I was to realize what an astounding innovator Dr. Harken was. His career began in World War II where he had great success operating on the hearts of wounded soldiers. He was a valued professor at Harvard Medical School and chief of thoracic surgery at Peter Bent Brigham Hospital in Boston and at Mount Auburn Hospital in Cambridge. He developed an implanted device to assist the heart's pumping and also the first internal pacemaker. He was cofounder of Action on

Smoking and Health and wrote many books and articles in his field. And the list goes on.

Some facts about my resuscitation were set forth in the report of the surgery and the follow-up care, part of which Dr. Kasparian wrote. I read the report a number of times in order to fully digest its meaning. Like, what happened and why. My subsequent efforts to uncover the truth may have put the doctors up against a mystery when trying to figure out what's wrong, when I was only following my curious bent.

It was ironic that Dr. Kasparian had come from the same area in historic Armenia as my parents had and through similar circumstances. My mother had been in the same orphanage in Euphrates College as he had and at the same time. If he had encouraged almost everyone in the hospital to come and see me as a "miracle," I am grateful to him. But perhaps it was someone else.

Ten years before that incident when I was a student and being treated for despair, I took a part-time job in Dr. Harken's office, personally hired by him for the routine job of typing letters and reports. I had been there a couple of months when a doctor who shared the office returned from a vacation. The other girl in the office had warned me that this man was hard to get along with, which I soon found out when he whose name I can't remember shouted at me for no apparent reason telling me to get out of there. It was a bad turn for my condition of despair, fear and paranoia. I left the office and never returned, feeling that perhaps Dr. Harken shared his sentiments.

Consequently the emergency surgery was the greatest coincidence anyone could ever imagine. The anxiety of whether he had turned against me was gone, and I came to the conclusion that perhaps he had not known anything about what had happened in that office. The other doctor in question may not have liked me for any reason or may not have liked Dr. Harken. Since at that time we had been going through the McCarthy hearings in Congress to find and discredit any suspected communists, many of whom were innocent, there was also suspicion against Armenians because Armenia was part of the Soviet Union. Or was it simply a manifestation of negative feelings toward the female gender? Or a bad reputation following me around? Or all of these? But I will never know.

Leaving the employment suddenly without warning was wrong, but I thought I had to. No one knew about this because I was always a very secretive person and hadn't told anyone.

In my book called *At Quarter Past Reality*, I included a long poem entitled "Matters of Survival" I had written about that trip to the cemetery containing a flashback about the surgery and whatever I knew about it in very abbreviated poetry form. I should have foreseen that no one would really be able to follow what I meant.

I had unexpected reactions from accusations of self-pity to attempting to destroy the hospital's reputation to egocentrism for daring to write about a brilliant surgeon and his work on me, this from indirect hints. While others tried to avoid mentioning the poem or the book itself, some people liked it and were impressed with the care the hospital provided.

Following are a couple of clips from that poem:

> Operating room lights,
> anesthetic scents like flowers,
> voices talking through dark . . .
> Emergency, 1963.
> The code . . . the code . . . the code . . .
> They tried twice; nothing.
> Cut . . .
> He happened to be in the next room.
> Only he could have resuscitated . . .
> Recognitions later,
> another father of my life.
>
> Elixir of truth, a tablespoonful.
> Cardiac arrest remains my description.
> The scars wear clothing.
> Jot down appropriate lines.
> Pain turns inside out, blossoming into verbs,
> red, yellow, orange meanings.
> Gone, it becomes the invisible Muse,
> dancing into some forever-thought
> here where there is no argument.

Though that part of the poem could be considered post-modern styling, I learned my lesson about indirection in poetry and made much more effort to read my writing as someone else would and write poems from the point of view of the reader to make them more significant and appealing. Other poems in this book are easier to follow; this poem got away, perhaps for too much inspiration and enthusiasm on my part. It can be very frustrating not to be able to get an important idea through to the people it is intended for. Conversely, it is emotionally very rewarding to get the idea through after much effort and some failure.

Feeling strongly that here was someone who would take my side against false accusations, I had written three poems previously about the surgery and its aftereffects, hadn't tried to publish them but with my characteristic shyness had mailed them to Dr. Harken, imagining that he read them and knew what I meant. Imagination is very helpful sometimes, or it can get one into trouble. At least the poem did attract some attention to my work, which made me work harder to produce a number of other manuscripts of poetry and finally this manuscript of prose.

At about that time I also wrote a letter to Dr. Harken because I had felt that I had to tell him about my past problems and my suspicion that they had something to do with the cardiac arrest he had saved me from. In that letter I related consulting a couple of psychiatrists but still not being able to talk, meaning that I couldn't express myself very well and that the brain damage was from the shock treatments of some years before. It had taken me some years to get my thoughts and memories organized and think the problem through at least in order to get the understanding I needed from the doctors who were treating me. I had the mystical experience in the cemetery where I felt my mood lifting and my emotions freed from the negativism of so many years very shortly after writing that letter.

Three years before that, my hysterectomy had also relieved me of some physical and emotional suffering. So why the sudden change of emotion and outlook I felt should have happened long before? I didn't question it but rather used it for the energy and inspiration it lent to my life and to my writing. Though I never received a direct answer to that letter, I felt that it had found its logical place.

So if one is inclined not to get discouraged with the bad hand life deals out, much can be done with the writing of poetry, the writing of prose and also with one's personal life. If the sense of personal accomplishment is there, all those rejection slips don't seem to matter so much and are just an expected part of the activity of being a writer.

The life of a poet, especially a modern poet, can be quite difficult with her alienation from the public. People usually don't show an interest even in getting to know the form and its particular uses. Poets are usually content with the audience of other poets and some people who feel challenged to read worthy modern poetry.

Subsequently, prose loosened my thoughts to recite all the facts I wanted to and more in order to reach those who had not understood and to convince them of a certain way of sympathetic thinking. Yes, the beauty of metaphorical language was missing, but instead there was the ability to dramatize fully and to quote endlessly with the inclusion of letters and parts of my previous writings to clarify certain points. I relived those moments more vividly than I ever had before as my entire life marched along in front of me day by day and year by year with tears at reliving certain dramatic moments. Best of all I found that the problem I had had with lack of self-confidence was gone, since I found some encouragement and started believing in my abilities. So much for self-hypnosis.

Thus prose helped poetry, and poetry helped prose, each developing skill in itself and in the other. Also truth was on the witness stand in its own defense. Evidently, people wouldn't perceive the truth from the poems because they were so indirect, truth presented as an analogy to something else without definite statement of fact.

Trying for accomplishment in the field of poetry, was I really trying to hide my story or withdrawing from a great deal of attention to it out of fear of not being accepted? The old taboo against mental illness really had been paralyzing until I convinced myself that it no longer existed among intelligent people and that we were all better educated than we had been. For in this very complicated modern world we live in, whose life has not been touched by episodes of these illnesses among family or friends?

Mother's Cancer

My husband retired from working at Harvard in 1995, after which he was able to help me take care of my mother and her house. I treasured my degree from the University and also his years there as an employee at its printing plant and always read *Harvard Magazine* and the *Gazette* to see what's going on there in news and research.

"Mother Harvard is taking care of us."

"Now don't you think you were lucky to work there?"

"Now that I'm not under stress."

"Always remember the Printing Office or HUPO as you called it. With thanks for the benefits."

"They gave me plenty of chances to work overtime."

"It sure helped a lot."

Then to get further treatments for a blood pressure problem, I returned to the doctor who had originally given me the propranolol, finding him welcoming and helpful after I had put him in the background of my mind for a number of years. This was after an unusual reminder. I had taken my mother to see Dr. Guy Rochman, a plastic surgeon whose office was next to that of Dr. Burton Rabinowitz in the same office suite. Upon entering the waiting room, I felt a strange and pleasant nostalgic twinge as if I had been there before. And indeed I had, for there was Dr. Rabinowitz.

My mother had a small cancer, a basal cell carcinoma, on her nose that had to be removed because it was growing, even though at the age of 92 she had many conditions including a weak heart prone to heart failure. She was also quite blind and deaf and had a severely impaired memory. But this small cancer was considered easily curable with a small surgery. Three years earlier, she had had an episode of heart failure after which her doctor predicted that she would pass away within a year. The small operation was quite successful, but she died three months later, not because of the operation but because she was already failing badly. The decision for surgery was made because we were caught between a rock and a hard place, as the saying goes.

The loss of my mother and the memory of the loss of my father as well as the joint ownership of the house with my sister, whose solutions didn't agree with mine, caused me anxiety and exhaustion. It took a few months to sell the house at my insistence, for it was a burden on my nerves. Taking care of my mother in old age and illness for eight years had weighed upon my emotions, especially when with her loss of memory she hadn't recognized me when I was caring for her and asked my husband to call the police and "get this woman out of the house." But forgiveness was my usual way.

I had felt a terrible sense of guilt when my father had offered the downstairs apartment in their house to me and my family. I had refused, knowing that it would start my emotional problems all over again in the same house with the same people, especially my mother (my sister was in New York), as when my problems had begun. Comprehension of my problem seemed to elude him.

However, my husband and I miss my parents and feel that they are near us in spirit. I dreamed about them for a while and knew the sometimes hesitant and difficult love, satisfied that I had taken care of them in their last years and had made sure they reached the hospital for the help they needed. Losing parents thus to old age became only a natural progression.

Seeing Dr. Rabinowitz

I was happy to be able to talk to Dr. Rabinowitz about some of my problems but had to wait a few months to change my health plan from one that didn't allow me to choose him as my physician. With a specialty in cardiology, he also took general patients and showed an unusual interest in attitudes and emotional problems. He has been one who will defend his patients when there is need for defense in keeping with the dedication and compassion of most of the doctors at that hospital.

Finally at the appointment, I asked him if he would tell me why I had my previous cardiac arrest, this after I had given him a copy of the report of my surgery because I sensed it would be in line with his work. He never accepted everything that had been said in judgment in a bland manner. By that time most of the doctors who had been involved in the surgery were either deceased or retired.

"He has helped me a lot."

"Then continue with him."

"He talks to me."

"He talks to all his patients. He's just friendly and concerned."

"Does he talk to you too?"

"Of course. Sometimes he gets a bit frazzled."

"What do you mean by frazzled?"

"Just that he may get a bit nervous from the pressures of the work."

"That's acceptable."

So the elation returned like a river of dammed emotions released, and I wrote poetry with great enthusiasm, overcoming mental blocks by stubbornly writing and rewriting, an extremely good exercise for my brain. With all that effort and with the emotional implications of the medical help given to me, I was able to conquer even the memories of sadness and hopelessness. The block of mental ice melted, and the river of creation flowed freely.

I shared some of the work with others, including Dr. Rabinowitz, to affirm the mystical experience. I discovered more and more positive meanings that made excellent imagery. The metaphors flowed, though sometimes in reverse, but when they were adjusted they fired new shades of emotion.

As Albert Einstein stated, "Imagination is more important than knowledge.

Burton D. Rabinowitz, M.D.

Knowledge is limited. Imagination encircles the world."

Or as Joseph Joubert stated, "Imagination is the eye of the soul."

Or Henry Miller, "Imagination is the voice of daring. If there is anything Godlike about God it is that. He dared to imagine everything."

Though I can't swim in water, I can swim in this sea of quotes.

My emotions developed so and grew when I was conscious of them and not afraid to plumb into the depths of the unconscious to find and uproot the problems there. That's how I came out of my shell, and my personality seemed to be more outgoing than it had been. However, I still often avoided much sociability for devotion to my thoughts and to my work.

I explained this unusual experience to Dr. Rabinowitz with only a mention because there was never time to delve into the subject. For a while he seemed to be confused about my behavior and my dependence upon metaphor, because the subject of mentality of poets is so unusual and the experience of my kind of personality quite rare. I wanted to find a way to tell him that he had saved my life, my soul and my work, because one depends upon the other.

Though he is kind, understanding, very highly trained and rather brilliant, this matter is out of his field. We seemed to invent a new treatment for my condition to help me clear my communication effectively. Or did I just see the situation one way while he saw it another?

Though his office is in the same hospital where I had the emergency surgery, I have not usually avoided the hospital and have had constructive discussions with some of the personnel as well as much care for a number of conditions I or some of my family have had. Some of my older relatives have died in the hospital after good and adequate care, but that has left me only with a feeling of gratitude that they had the care they needed and that the emergency system was working well.

The doctor appreciated the background information I provided about my former stressful circumstances. This problem could be seen by my slow responses to the conversations around me or my inability to respond at all, not being able to think of an appropriate and quick answer. If I lacked clarity of expression in the writing of poetry, I did better with prose as a less emotional approach. Thus it looked as if there were more of a problem with right-brain or intuitive thought, the basis for poetry.

I wrote many details of my life as if I were writing it for his perusal. Perhaps I was unrealistic, as I have often been, but it did work out for me in the matter of cleaning up the problems of expressing myself completely and effectively and also in the matter of getting his complete sympathy. I hadn't previously been treated for communication difficulty, for it hadn't been recognized by other doctors. Is it possible that such a problem wouldn't be investigated in the books?

I wished that my psychiatrists had had as much curiosity to ask endless questions and demand answers with as much caring and dedication to my ultimate comfort and happiness. I wished they had had the imagination to see beyond the surface behavior as Dr. Rabinowitz did, or when he didn't, to agonize over the problem to find the right answer.

The subjects we talked about included my writing of poetry and the presentation to him of one of my published books and then another. Since he had once been a rabbinical student, he had some literary background and could understand my motivations, which had needed a jolt with encouragement. He provided this by telling me he had read my poems and liked them and by often talking about poetry or calling me a poet with never a negative word. He was quite strict about matters of discipline, however, and his reprimands helped me also.

In the process of untying my literary knots, I began to wonder more and ask some questions, especially of my husband because we had never talked about the subject much. So I found out after 45 years that I had been unconscious with perhaps brief moments of awareness for four days instead of the two I had previously thought. I had never thought to inquire about it after my definite assumption, nor had anyone thought to straighten out my thinking on the subject.

The report of the surgery stated that I had awakened after 36 hours, while actually I had been in the recovery room for four days after which was taken into a private room. I only remember awakening in that private room, for I was usually heavily anesthetized, thinking it had been 48 hours since I was taken to the operating room. The report also stated that Dr. Harken and his crew had watched me carefully while I was in recovery. Then my logical deduction was that I had heard the doctors talking about possible reasons for the cardiac arrest other than the prime culprit of the anesthetic. Perhaps they spoke to me in my unremembered moments of clarity, not realizing later that I might recall it.

Thus, an unconscious memory was nagging me while trying to express itself in conscious terms. I had known instinctively that this was at least partly a psychological cardiac arrest and later read that such things could happen. I wanted to confess this to Dr. Rabinowitz, and the only way I could was to write out the significance of the entire story.

The doctor encouraged my writing with a few words when I had nothing to prove that I could do the work and do it well as Dr. Harken requested when he had said, "it has to be good." After that I had seen one of his assistants for my problem of shortness of breath, but neither of us seemed to want to pursue the matter of writing the story. Later I completely recovered from my discouragement and was on my way toward concluding the project that I had earlier conceived but never followed through.

My health did well considering my age. I felt that the doctor gave me the right medicines and treated me in a professional manner. My husband, also his patient, felt the same way. The doctor was also treating a number of other Armenians, including acquaintances and some relatives. He was an example of a newer generation of leaders and doctors building on the successes and failures of their predecessors.

Then having developed painful osteoarthritis in my spine, for which I depended upon acetaminophen and cortisone injections, I received an additional medicine that worked on nerve pain called gabapentin, the generic of Neurontin. It helped relieve the pain without discomforts and also boosted my moods when I felt discouraged or slightly depressed. I could then indeed feel a triumph over some troubles and could also speak to a group with more confidence.

I have no more unconscious memories that nag me and have reached the point of tranquility in my life. But it was internal nagging that led me into creativity, so I am not complaining. Even my unrealistic expectations seemed to propel me into positive emotional territory as opposed to my previous negative mood. In order for creativity to burst forth free, there must be some dichotomy of thought and feeling, some tension or anger from the past that can be resolved by the catharsis of writing about related subject matter or actually hitting the subject over the head as tactfully as possible.

I worked at being more tactful, because sometimes I wasn't. It took some years of studying other people's poetry and comparing it mine to adjust it to achieve poetic maturity. I believe I have gone through all the stages of the evolution of the human psyche in my search for full consciousness of mind and its expressions in writing.

"Did your mind ever seem blocked and not able to think of what to write next?"

"Many times. Sometimes I would totally give up trying or just wait until I felt more like writing, never knowing what I was going to end up with. And through the years I gave up writing poetry completely a few times but always came back to it. About this need to write poetry, which could be called a compulsion, it's like climbing the emotion instead of the mountain because it's there. Similarly, you become an artist because you see colors and shapes and can visualize effective scenes. Creativity is part of us."

"I'm glad you did return to poetry."

Ohan Press

A humanities education gave me the background to work at poetry and publishing. A great deal of writing as part of my employment as an editor gave me the practice I needed and added strong motivation to continue. It was as local as I was, though as it became more ambitious and more political, I became more ambitious and poetic, having published quite a few poems in literary magazines.

I had started Ohan Press in 1983 to publish my first book of poems, *Carvings from an Heirloom: Oral History Poems*. It was like a jump into the ocean after a small press that had almost promised publication refused it for either personal or political reasons. Not a refusal, it was only a statement that they would publish it if I paid the cost. I thought if that were the case, I might as well publish it myself, though I was disappointed in not having a publisher.

The book has sold over 500 copies with at least 200 given *gratis*, its subject being scenes and customs out of the old-country village my parents had come from. I had interviewed my parents a few years before and collected ethnographical material, which I had intended to use for prose. Since that didn't work out then, I wrote some of the information into poems. Perhaps people related to the subject matter, which contained some information about natural medical practices that were used in remote villages at the beginning of the 20th century and are still used in certain rural areas of the world. Or perhaps they reacted to the low price of $5 a book. Perhaps they were curious about the Armenian customs described, and some may have liked the red color of the cover. Whatever the reason, the number of books sold was more than expected for a first book from a tiny micropress run by someone with no experience in marketing or publishing books.

I used some symbols and many images of a rather primitive type of living as compared with our complicated social structure.

Perhaps I shocked some people in presenting basic scenes of village life rather than glorifying my heritage. But I had been taught to present reality as it is or was. The writer Leon Surmelian had written the advice, "If you will write about Armenians, you should not live among them." I saw proof of his statement among some people, even those who followed trends in literature, as they tried to nullify the value of the work.

I found out later that there was a religious ban on writing about the natural medicines and cures used by self-trained doctors of villages isolated from more advanced medicine, which in modern times hadn't been strictly enforced but did leave an attitude and an impression that had become firmly ingrained in some people's minds.

The poems in the volume were about the poor and unsophisticated villagers. I found this oral history to be fascinating, especially since some of my relatives had a part in it. My purpose was not to recommend these practices but only to write about some colorful people and what is considered primitive and unusual practice in medicine. Some readers must have thought I advocated those old attitudes or that I would influence others to advocate them. Or perhaps those who judged were simply disdainful of my style, which was so different from those of more sophisticated poets. It is so difficult to guess at motivations that are never explained.

Many readers accepted the subject with interest in the oral history aspect of it, especially now that there is a need in America to find and prove as many natural medicines as possible. And some have been proven, like glucosamine for joint pain of arthritis or sumac for diarrhea. Probably more non-Armenians bought the book than Armenians.

Then I was asked by a relative why I was writing about my mother when others disliked her basic pessimism, her temper and her awkwardness. It would have been useless to argue with the relative because of her lack of knowledge in those matters, but I felt that writing about difficult personalities was a great challenge to any writer and that writing about problems one had with them was a way of solving emotional conflicts — in other words, a catharsis. In writing about family and problems with them, I could manipulate situations to come to a resolution that was actually

from my own mind, imposing conclusions to neutralize the conflict and accept it in a mature fashion.

"Why do people question the choices writers make in choosing characters for their books?"

"They don't know the rules, which include the presentation
of difficulties for analysis of personality and conclusions that come
about because of them."

"Even if they do, they question the choice, the wisdom of
the choice or the meanings we have arrived at."

"You just have to keep explaining forever."

Of course, many did accept what I wrote in that book and
knew the reasons why.

"How do you feel now?"

"At last I feel that all of the work I did hasn't been wasted,
and I do feel appreciated."

"Will you continue to work as much, even though you may
have some doubts?"

"I will."

Most likely, I should have made clearer that I was writing in
the various voices and through the personality of those who actually lived in the village at that time and practiced these customs.
To the trained literary mind, this should have been adequately
clear. But then, I was often hazy in my intentions.

I had written these poems in a simple and rather direct style,
later lost when I was working in pursuit of style in the modern
idiom. The later poems sometimes turned out to be dense in
expression as complicated poems not to be easily read. A great
deal of work helped to simplify what I had written in a way that
had charm and depth. The process took years, but I did finally
produce a few manuscripts.

The book gleaned a couple of good book reviews, one by
Harold Bond and another by Professor James Etmekjian. Both
were positive and the second emphasized the subject matter,
which the professor had enjoyed because it reminded him of his
childhood in that general area. The Tekeyan Cultural Association
in Watertown gave a reception for the book, at which Professor
Etmekjian delivered the review in a speech. I was gratified for
having published that book, though I realized that there were
going to be some negative comments as well as friendly ones. But

Prof. James Etmekjian reviewing Helene's first book of poems
Dr. Nubar Berberian at left, Helene, Khachadoor and Yeghsa at right

like a person who had just come from a desert with a terrible thirst, I would gladly then accept any comments as long as I felt I had a book under my feet to steady my step.

Family comments were not to be taken too seriously. My mother had no grasp of the process of creativity or its value, and told me after all had been done, "No one knows these stories but us," implying with Old World pessimism "Who would be interested?" My father, seeing that it got some attention, had a more positive attitude towards my writing, though his reading English was inadequate for understanding it.

Publishing and distributing the book provided a source of joy and a feeling of accomplishment, my sales being made either through the Internet or as the result of flyers I sent out to libraries. Amazon.com proved its dependability then and through the years.

One of the poems in the book is called "With the Bait of Bread" and was republished a number of times, notably in the anthologies *Anthology of Magazine Verse* and *Yearbook of American Poetry 1981* and *Forgotten Bread: First Generation Armenian American Writers*, the latter named after an image in my poem.

These small successes gave me a great deal of gratification and encouragement. Most recently, my poetry in an early anthology edited by Lorne Shirinian of Canada and this book have been cited in the new *Greenwood Encyclopedia of Multiethnic American Literature* in the section of Armenian-Americans searching for identity. Many other Armenian-American writers have also been cited with their work in the generous section about Armenians in this five-volume set. My years of work hadn't been wasted.

"How did you get there?"

"I ate humble pie."

"What did it taste like?"

"Sometimes like blueberry pie or sometimes like apple pie, sometimes like salt water or sometimes like mud."

"How far did you travel?"

"Far down the Amazon River of mind. Also around America, Europe, and the Middle East."

"Did you feel deprived?"

"Sometimes in spirit. Otherwise I always had someone to support me financially and always had good food and decent housing. I had more luck in my later years."

My computer has certainly been very helpful in my endeavors, and I wouldn't have been able to do as much work as I have without its large and retentive memory as well as its searching and its cut-and-paste ability. Hagop taught me the use of the computer with his expertise in that field and came to my aid when anything went wrong with my use of it. We have worked together on producing books by word processing, editing, proofreading and all other skills that go into book production. So I continued with another book of poems, gathering many previously published work and new work into another slim volume.

Winning a first place award from *Writer's Digest*, a popular magazine for writers that is not too well respected in the Northeast because it is rather down-to-earth and commercial, the second book called *At Quarter Past Reality: New and Selected Poems* had more limited sales, either because the subject matter was partly about family including children, which was out of fashion, or because with a more elaborate style it was more difficult. There are so many factors in distributing books, and what appeals to one will not appeal to another, the writer left to try to comprehend reasons. Many will misinterpret poetry and others will judge unfairly. It's a built-in part of the endeavor.

I received a long review in the now defunct literary magazine *Raft* from Prof. Leonard Trawick, who was then at Cleveland State University. The review was critical in that it decried over-use of the confessional form and pointed out some minor flaws in the book, including the risk of sentiment in writing poems about children. He liked and quoted from a narrative poem about my impressions of the picture of a grandmother I never saw and also a short lyric poem about a green dress.

However, with its negativism reversed, the review graphi-cally outlined the paths I could travel in the future as far as subject matter and style were concerned. I was disappointed that he totally dismissed my long poem about my surgery, and I attribute that to his missing the point. The absolute need for more clarity asserted itself. I changed my approach to style and turned the negative to its logical positive with some good results.

Being so close to the subject of surgery and knowing it so well, I had meant only gratitude and idolatry. Somehow I did get the significance through to some people.

"They tell me to persist and not get discouraged."

"Who tells you this?"

"Articles for writers such as in *Poets and Writers* magazine, which I subscribe to and read faithfully."

"Then why are you discouraged?"

"Well, sales of the book often stop and don't start up again with the flyers I send or with announcements on my web site or at bookstores like amazon.com. The usual bookstores don't take self-published books of poetry at all because they don't sell. A few specialized bookstores will take them on consignment with doubts."

"Why are you working so hard at writing poetry when you know poetry in general doesn't sell in large numbers?"

"I'm working on another manuscript that I can publish. It should be better than the ones before so that maybe it will sell more."

I was by that time glad to be a poet and publisher, even on such a small scale, and completion compounded. More attention, more incentive to keep trying. Indeed, I was writing and rewriting as if my life depended on the quality of the poems and trying to win more contests. A few times I achieved the rank of finalist or honorable mention and won a few minor first prizes. Then with anger at myself, I worked even more diligently, even though I had no career to go to, no teaching or magazine editing. The emotional counterpart was my main interest, the finding of personal identity as well as communication on a deeper level than usual and on subjects not in ordinary conversation. In other words, enrichment of life experience.

John F. Kennedy had some ideas on the subject:

> When power leads man toward arrogance, poetry reminds him of his limitations. When power narrows the areas of man's concern, poetry reminds him of the richness and diversity of his existence. When power corrupts, poetry cleanses, for art establishes the basic human truths which must serve as the touchstone of our judgment.

And so did Sigmund Freud, whose rare humility I enjoyed:

> Everywhere I go I find that a poet has been there before me.

I was pleased with some of the results of my writing, though I was shy about reading to groups, feeling isolated and never attending poetry slams or frequenting poetry clubs. These seemed to be for younger people, for they were the majority in such places. I attended a poetry workshop with poet Gail Mazur when she was teaching at Harvard, which helped me to feel a little more connected and gave me a little more clarity and conscientiousness in the writing of poems.

But it was the original explication of the forms and terms of modern poetry by Professor Paul Engle that gave backbone to my interest in writing it in the modern idiom and finally following through. Years later, all the lessons returned with a new dedication and with a rereading of the book that was used in that course. By that time much had changed in the world, in the poetry world and in my mentality. It took all that for me to gather myself together to be a poet.

Adding More Titles

We kept the micropress going since we liked the work we were doing and believed in its power. It was named after my father-in-law — Ohan is an Armenian form of John — who was a writer for the Armenian press, as my father was. We learned as much as we needed to know, and we continued.

My husband, being a retired professional in the field of typography and book design, designed the books I published, adding some books he translated from the Armenian. Our son designed the web site at http://home.comcast.net/~hsarkiss, and we have had some small successes with a couple of prose books. One is *They Called Me Mustafa: Memoir of an Immigrant*, my father's story beginning in 1915 as a child survivor through the later years of employment at the Star Market and proprietorship of Huron Spa in Cambridge, Massachusetts.

The many stories my father told about his work at the Star Market and the people he met there made fascinating anecdotes and turned out to be a valuable copy for the book I partially wrote, edited and published about him through his mentality and from interviews plus a short written piece he had left. He had struggled to handwrite the story of his 1915 experiences and survival in English — he wrote it more easily in Armenian — for me to read and perhaps edit and publish.

After my father's death my husband was given all of his writings and papers in Armenian to sort through and choose what was most important to keep or to give away. Among the papers he found the story of my father's experiences during the Genocide written in laborious English, as if meant for his children and grandchildren to read. The story impressed me, for it was written simply and dramatically in such a way as to draw the reader into the action with its extremely vivid depiction of the deportation of Armenians from the town he was living in. I fell into the old country and its story while I was writing about it.

I had just learned to use the computer and began typing the manuscript into a file and simply couldn't stop typing, editing in the process to keep basic story he left more or less as it was and adding to it. Since I was in the period of grief, the work seemed to absorb those feelings as a sponge absorbs water. I continued the story with my own memories and what I could decipher from notes he had left on paper, adding all the information from a taped interview by Ruth Thomasian of Project Save. Her work is with vintage Armenian photographs and the information that goes with them. More facts bubbled to the surface of my memory about his store on Huron Avenue and his retirement years as well as information about Watertown.

This made a small book of 96 pages, which my husband and I published under the imprint Ohan Press in 1992. Seeing that the book was doing fairly well selling to people and to libraries, my husband translated and added some of my father's writings from Armenian into English, and we published the second edition of the book in 1998. It was soon republished by Alexander Street Press, a small scholarly publisher of electronic databases available to the academic market by subscription, in its *North American Immigrant Letters, Diaries, and Oral Histories*. The book was to be accompanied by an unpublished letter my father had written to the *Wall Street Journal* protesting America's defense of Turkey in the matter of Armenian rights. However, only the first section of the book was used without the letter. The database, intended mainly for large academic libraries and researchers, began in the summer of 2003 and continues.

Then we published our second prose book, *From Kessab to Watertown: A Modern Saga*, my husband's translation into English of the memoir his father had written in Armenian. It contains an autobiography of the teacher and writer from Kessab, noted during his life through his writings in the Armenian press in Beirut, Lebanon, and in America, with additional accounts by the educator Kevork A. Sarafian, and the lawyer Dickran Boyajian. It also contains facts about the Armenian Genocide (1909 and 1915) in Kessab (an Armenian village in Syria), Adana (a former Armenian city in Cilicia), and elsewhere in Cilicia; descriptions of Kessab, Mt. Cassius, the city and the state of Alexandretta (an area alternately belonging to Syria and Turkey); facts about the Armenian Legionnaires in Cilicia and the Kessabtzi volunteers; facts about the Vartanian School of Aintab, St. Paul's College in Darson (Tarsus), School of Religion in Athens, and Near East School of Theology in Beirut. It concludes with a short narrative by Vahan Mamalian, M.D., Hagop's mother's cousin. With 236 pages of narrative with pictures, maps, family trees, Index and Bibliography, it sold quickly. Unfortunately, we had only 200 books to sell and didn't print more for financial reasons. The book was still in demand for its information as well as the charm of the story of a young man in search of higher education when it seemed impractical.

So dramatic prose won for popularity. The subject matter of the published books has been partly Armenian life and history in its many aspects, remembrances of life in historic Armenia and experiences in Beirut, Lebanon, in the middle of the 20th century. My husband added two more books in Armenian, comprising the works of his father and of my father that had been published in the Armenian press and another translation from English into Armenian that had been left by his father.

The name of last small volume in the Armenian language is *Character, or The Guide to Life* by Henry Varnum, translated from English with additional material by Hovhannes H. Sarkissian in 1938 and published in 2003. The print version not meant for sale, the book of aphorisms on 100 subjects is presented on the Ohan Press web site in PDF format. The web site is bilingual and parts of the other Armenian books are posted as well as descriptions and reviews of all the books.

Then Hagop added another large volume he wrote in English, including all his highly detailed memories in Beirut and in America, letters, his diary, and many photographs. He called it *The Sarkissian and Pilibosian Families: A Guide for the Curious*. It is mostly about himself in relation to his and my families and relatives, but it also has sections of work at newspapers in Beirut with historical background and computerized typesetting at the Harvard University Printing Office. The project took him five years to complete, and it was printed in a very limited edition to be distributed to family members, some of whom were very happy to read it.

My work has been in English. I completed three published books of poetry and three poetry manuscripts of varied subject matter including Armenian-American experiences, art works, places here and abroad, fantasy and characters in narrative poems, all the while trying to be more accessible in style and subject than I had been. One of those manuscripts is now published as *History's Twists: The Armenians*, poems on highlights of Armenian history and art, including a number of narrative poems featuring the fictional friend Nazeli of Armenia with descriptions of some history concerning the defunct Soviet Union, of which Armenia had been a part. Concern with the past kingdoms and

Cover of *History's Twists: The Armenians*

oppressions and their subsequent effect upon the present day Armenians in Armenia and in diaspora form part of the subject matter along with poems on Armenian-American life and Armenian artists. Now this memoir.

Year after year the list of my published poems grew slowly. At first I hardly dared call myself a poet, but I gained confidence with the years, with more publications, with the fight for the truth and with the valuable moral support of a few dependable people who believed in me. I could hardly understand how the peace and truth of poetry could also meet hostility and total misreading. Matters of style, perhaps. Matters of choosing unpopular subjects. Matters of trying to enlighten. Matters of lack of training for readers of poetry.

My readings of books of modern poetry have been extensive and inspiring, leading me to try to emulate the best of the work of poets such as Pablo Neruda, T. S. Eliot, Marianne Moore,

Donald Hall, Mary Oliver, supplemented by anthologies and works of many other poets whose names are not that familiar. I felt a deep need to read modern poetry of all kinds, to immerse myself in it.

"Why did you get up at five o'clock this morning?"

"Because I had a poem working in my head since four o'clock."

"Couldn't you just go back to sleep?"

"Then I would lose what I was thinking about."

"You wouldn't be able to remember it?"

"The train of thought would leave me completely. It has been suggested that poets keep pen and paper near the bed to scribble down such thoughts, but I have found that impractical because at night I'm just too sleepy."

"So your mornings all begin early."

"I guess I just think too much."

My readings in prose were less, or I should say less in the later years, either for lack of interest or lack of identification. Or perhaps it was lack of concentration, though as a young girl I had read many novels such as *Cry, The Beloved Country* by Alan Paton and *The Man in the Iron Mask* by Alexander Dumas. But we change, and now my readings in prose are more likely to be short stories or articles pertaining to my particular interests, though lately I have read a few novels and a few books of nonfiction whose subjects have caught my fancy.

Progress in perfecting poetry was slow, as it tends to be in that area of writing. Patience and love were with me, for without that latter quality, there is no magic for sifting metaphors out of a jumble of thoughts and impressions and getting them on paper. And by love I don't necessarily mean the act of sex but love of family, love of children and grandchildren, compassion given or taken, gratitude, idolatry, worship of intellectual capacity, etc., all of which I have practiced.

My expectations for myself and for the three additional unpublished manuscripts of poetry I have produced are now more realistic as through my web site and personal connections I try to win new friends for the art of poetry. I love to write it as much as I love to write about it, for I find that writing prose about poetry is as satisfying as writing the poetry.

Matters of Styling

With my editorial experience, I had gained an international mix of Armenian subject matter in the English language. Luckily, the Baikar establishment gave me a job when I needed it and have always provided a ready outlet in the newspaper for my articles on Armenian subjects and publicity for my books.

Through Ohan Press I managed to turn out some books that were of general interest as well as of Armenian interest, and I was determined to carry them as far as I could with a great deal of work. I knew my methods of writing were different from most of the poets I knew or had heard about, and I knew that I should have to explain them at some point.

The difference can be summed up in a few sentences. My poetic guidelines would require me to get in touch with my inner self and delve into some of the workings of the unconscious mind as much as I could perceive them. They would also encourage me to be individual and at the same time identify with the people I admire or have admired the most for intelligence and personality and try to incorporate some of their traits into my personality.

I followed this formula. My conscious mind in writing depended upon the cooperation of my unconscious mind, just as actions of the present depend upon the teaching of past experiences. Those who have encouraged and showed compassion left a residue of positive emotions that helped my conscious mind to make optimistic decisions and to do better work. Those who tried to discourage or made disparaging remarks over time left a residue of the anger and negativism that worked against positive decisions and good work. It sounds simple, but it isn't easy to balance emotion and intellect when circumstances are tricky.

I adapted to the extreme difficulty of finding a publisher for any book, especially for poetry that is not mainstream. My work is not mainstream, being different in subject and style, though I have found an individual style I like and others seem to like. Now the difference is beginning to look like a plus in spite of former difficulties, for I have published and distributed my own books as much as possible with my limitations in aggressiveness and public speaking, and differences in style seem more acceptable now.

I concentrated on optimism and constantly tried to do better than expressing the pessimistic tone. For by consciously identifying my problem phrases and words and turning them more positive, I created better concentration and results and achieved a more mature approach to style and subject matter.

The mystical experience propelled me to go forward with my work and with reaching out for the compassion and depths of friendship. It was the emotional release I had sometimes read about, the greater self that grows out of the limited lesser self. This takes a great deal of thought and effort, which most likely only an introvert would undertake.

That done, the matter of writing poetry became easier than pushing the proverbial boulder uphill with forced writing. Obviously, my intuition serves me better than conscious efforts in this undertaking. A preconscious state, a term Freud used for the shady area between the unconscious mind and the conscious mind, often seems to write the poem for me. For example, sometimes but not often I will feel a poem in my mind that seems to be totally written before I get it on paper, leaving me with the impression that I'm only the scribe. I take that to be the preconscious upheaval of a poem in the inspired mood. As most good poets do, I usually have to go over most of the poems many times in an effort to perfect them, if there is any such thing as perfection in poetry.

I did much reading in poetry and in psychology, especially of the work of Carl Gustave Jung, who had been working with Sigmund Freud and adjusted those early theories to achieve a more positive outlook and provided some theories of his own. He had some strong ideas about creativity as a positive and even spiritual activity in life. The following quote is an example of his theory from *On the Relation of Analytical Psychology to Poetry*:

> (The creative artist) is wholly at one with the creative process, no matter whether he has deliberately made himself its spearhead, as it were, or whether it has made him its instrument so completely that he has lost all consciousness of this fact. In either case, the artist is so identified with his

> work that his intentions and his faculties are indistinguish-
> able from the act of creation itself . . . sensing that his work
> is greater than himself, and wields a power which is not his
> and which he cannot command.

A work begun will in time be finished because what has been started tends to go toward completion.

Freud is credited with discovering the subconscious mind, though he actually uncovered it because it was always there. His theories on art and behavior tended to be sexually oriented, and he gave symbols of poetry and art some generic sexual interpretations. Jung gave these symbols more personal and individual meaning, each work of art thus being created by a different individual with a different set of circumstances and preferences having its own meanings. Creative people have seen more sense in this broader representation.

In addition, Jung classified human behavior in terms of introvert, meaning the inward personality, and extrovert, meaning the outgoing type of personality. The former talks little but thinks a lot; the latter talks a great deal to everyone but has less time or inclination to meditate or look inward. This is not to imply that all poets or artists are or must be introverts. There is and must be a great deal of variation in human behavior in order to fulfill the needs of multiplicity of work and social dealings. Mutual understanding can thus be difficult sometimes, and international understanding is always demanding in many ways.

Jung also contributed a different concept of the unconscious mind than the subconscious of Freud, which was a collection of repressed desires. In Jungian theory, the unconscious is a vital world in itself and part of the life of an individual as much as the conscious world and even more complex. The language of the unconscious is symbolic, as we can see in dreams. These theories are explained and analyzed in the book *Man and His Symbols*, edited and partly written by Jung in a captivating study.

The entire subject of the psychology of art or the philosophy of art is very complicated with many proponents of varying interpretations. The two subjects overlap at certain points. The philosophy of poetry seems constantly to waver between two extremes, poetry for the people or poetry for art's sake. In the days when poetry was more popular than it is now, narrative poems like those of Walt Whitman dominated the scene, being poetry for the people with great value as art also.

In writing my own poems I am in this constant conflict. Shall I keep the poems and language simple enough so that they will be read and understood by more people, including my own family, or shall I follow newer styles like the postmodern or experimental and be understood by very few people, hoping that the poems will be accepted in magazines? I find that unless I make a conscious effort to be understood, I will go off on a tangent and either write about something that is unfairly difficult without explanation or pack too much meaning into the sentences. The conflict has kept me occupied enough to persist in studying my own style in relation to the style of other poets.

I unearthed too many unnecessary questions in my poems, though I like the effect of questions in poems, and criticized my own constant sound of immaturity. I was embarrassed to sound like a high school student writing for an assignment, and this resulted in discouragement, anger and frustration, especially when I read some high school poems that were quite a bit more mature and stylized. This matter of jumbled thoughts and lack of discipline is evident in the following poem, an older version of another:

DRESS TEST

Are you dressed for the lecture?
Are you dressed for the tresses
that comb your mentality
to an e e cummings
or a finagled Vachel Lindsay
(ready for "The Congo"
and its bongos that sing)?
Are you ready for the glitch
on the authority
of the skyscraper
that shadows the street
with that iambic beat?
Your preference may rest
in the tilt of it,
like an electronic whiz
with the power of speech

in its offices and TVs,
it may reach
for the pessimistic stance
that doesn't believe in it
or for the optimism
that takes it to brimming.
The lecture is dressed
in purple, then in brown
with shimmers of change
to dazzle or frazzle.
Are you ready to meet it?

I knew I could do better, rewriting poems many times after I had sent them out to magazines for consideration and possible publication, receiving rejection slips for them and continuing to hope for acceptances. I received my share.

My Writing Guidelines

I finally accepted myself as an individual creative person entitled to have subject matter that is different from that of the others. In admitting that I haven't been able to do as much for poetry as many have, I realize how much poetry has done for me in my lifetime. It began as therapy when therapy was needed, then fizzled out for a while, then returned with full inspiration. I minimized my endless repetitions and some dark brooding thoughts that had found their way into my sentences and called out my full capability of emotions from some unconscious area of my mind.

This art form has often given me fortitude, has never betrayed me even when it has been misread and has led me to be part of an endeavor that is greater than my life and also important to the world. Every time I see one of my poems published, it reaffirms my belief that I am included in this international creative field. Concentration, clarity and discipline have turned my life around and gained me some praise as well as access to friends who share this interest. After I learned not to take rejections seriously, it gave me much joy in self-expression and in my own improvement. Finally, it has provided me another subject on which to write prose.

Now I keep these viewpoints in mind and called them my guidelines:

* Concentrate deeply like deep breathing.
* Find appropriate images and discard the less appropriate.
* Be careful of line endings and review them constantly to catch any strays.
* Don't get too complicated.
* Pretend you are someone else reading this.
* Remember, no end rhymes. Internal or irregular rhymes are okay.
* No autobiographical or family poems unless fictionalized.

- Minimize sentiment and emotion with indirect references using nouns rather than adjectives.
- Avoid using the first person singular, or use the impersonal I.
- Read constantly the kind of poetry you wish to be influenced by, in this case either modernist or postmodern. Be influenced but don't imitate.
- Reread and rewrite often while trying to attain the next level of perception.
- Keep working on clarity.
- Keep subjects global or social rather than personal.
- Accept only fair criticism based on understanding, but don't be too sensitive.

Maturity set in, and so did the need for change from so much poetic thinking, which can be exhausting. Writing prose about the high and low points of my life, I broke out of some constraints such as doubt that I would be able to reach publication in the best poetry journals. I had previous skill, comprehension and experience but needed to know that I had communicated with others after years of being asked, "What does it mean?"

"Why do you write poetry? There are so many easier things to do."

"You could write poem a day. How nice to do so much."

"It wasn't easy and it took a long time. I felt as if I were in a dark tunnel trying to reach the light at the end."

"Most people don't care, so they don't make the effort to read poetry. Why should they when most of prose is easier?"

"They don't recognize emotion translating itself into readable words."

"These days people don't often have much time to or don't want to make the effort to read."

"It's a kind of neglect that robs one of many wonderful experiences."

In free lance writing, it wasn't worth worrying too much what kind of magazine is going to want to market it, because worry tends to paralyze thoughts. But I knew the market quite well by then, and I thought I could navigate even its difficult streams. Like enjoying the sun and flowers that beautify our days.

Like sailing on the warm ocean and enjoying the sight of the waves and the various shores. Like enjoying a visit to one country and then to another. Like enjoying being at home and then enjoying a vacation.

My guidelines for writing memoir prose are similar to those for poetry, because after all writing is writing with some variations. The differences are in the fine print, in the formatting, in the style, in the metaphors, plot for prose, characterization, conversation and a true story line.

- Write about your life only after you have digested it and can write about it calmly and with reason.
- Get your will and ambition to cooperate and stay committed to the task.
- Have your audience in mind.
- Try to be chronological and as you write about yourself with the facts, anecdotes and conversation.
- Draw characters for fiction or memoir and describe or fictionalize actual experiences.
- Research as necessary to illustrate or prove any point you wish to make.
- Explain each point more than adequately to make sure it can be understood by all potential readers.
- Take information from reliable sources and add quotes, acknowledging the sources.
- Set up chapter headings as an outline and follow them.
- Write what you remember quickly at first, then go back and add other data.
- Try to avoid repetition of parts of the story or of words and delete repetitions after finishing.
- Sound upbeat and optimistic, even when the subject is sad.
- When presenting people's actions or attitudes, be careful to be fair and not to offend. Meet arrogance with friendliness and anger with a smile.
- Don't write out of anger but only with an improved disposition.
- Reread often to edit, proofread or to cut and paste parts of the story to other chapters that are a better fit. Then edit and proofread again for other mistakes.

- Spell check often.
- Reread and edit again at the computer and on a printed version.
- Compete with yourself in trying to make it better and compete with others in the marketplace, remembering that there are many thousands of writers out there.
- Have others read parts of the manuscript, and get their opinions. If they respond positively, then continue.
- Research the market that publishes essays and memoirs.
- Send some to publishers of magazines.

Then I wish myself good luck in interesting a publisher or an agent in the manuscripts to be submitted, keeping self-publishing in mind if necessary.

My Journalistic Score

I was privileged to experience first-hand the workings of a newspaper from the editing phase to the proofreading, the correcting, the making of pages and the actual in-house printing. The smudge of fresh newsprint. The aroma of the chemicals used on the printing presses. An individualistic aura. In the earlier years the fascinating process of the Linotype held my attention with its particular clicks and slugs locked into place, whereas in later years computerized typesetting produced another quieter atmosphere.

I haunted the public library for facts out of encyclopedias when I was researching articles to write for the newspaper, the time-frame before the era of the Internet when information of all kinds is available for a few clicks of the mouse. My early editorials tended toward philosophical meanings of events. Some quotes I exhume from my youth bring back an atmosphere forgotten, a friend, a voice, a course. For example, "People worship miracle, mystery and authority," from *The Brothers Karamazov* by Fyodor Dostoyevsky. I pondered the quote for years that only experience could explain.

Under those circumstances poetry was the eraser, prose the clerk, newspaper the wrapper, and readers the trappers of the spark. For poetry did erase the power of the word and its immediate impact on the readers with its aesthetic indirection. Prose was indeed the clerk who would deliver the messages and write the letters that helped get things done, shoveling meanings into their proper places. Then the newspaper wrapped the work into a finished product that could be delivered to residences. The people who read the articles and book reviews with all the attendant pictures tracked the spark of thought into their own minds and were influenced by it.

Newspapers, editors and reporters perform an important function in educating the public to what is going on in their particular corner of the world as well as revelations from distant places. Analysis of the news is just as important. In addition to news from Armenian communities in America, there was always news of Armenian communities abroad, particularly in Armenia. I absorbed all this with its familiar ring and felt the heavy influence of it.

Why else would I want to quote T. S. Eliot's profound words, "This is the way the world ends,/ this is the way the world ends,/ this is the way the world ends,/ not with a bang but a whimper" from "The Hollow Men?" Why else indeed when so much of the social and political events an editor writes about are controversial with often a pessimistic turn or tone of voice? Too much negativism. Too much sameness.

An apt quote from Cyril Connolly (1903-1974) in the book *Enemies of Promise* of 1938 states:

> Literature is the art of writing something that will be read twice; journalism what will be read once.

Imagination doesn't belong in journalism, except to imagine a better ending or a better world where people are more likely to cooperate. Newspapers are organized and predictable in arriving either every day or once a week on Sunday, the writing to meet deadlines speedy in trying to keep up with all the information given. Editorials may be controversial for presenting a single opinion, but the daily realities we must face need sensible opinions. Now I seldom read editorials, though I can't dodge editorializing on television news programs. However, some people live by the opinions expressed and are tremendously influenced by them.

My Sunday paper is my morning relaxation with a cup of coffee. Advertising in the coupon books intrigues me as the mainstay of any newspaper and a help for my shopping. A few coupons I clip from these books pay for the price of the paper. The magazine sections with short comments and the longer articles about lifestyle issues or physical ailments or about some prominent people hold my attention. Satisfied that I have learned something or have been entertained, I continue to peruse other sections of the newspaper. The want ads, the rentals and the houses for sale do not apply to my situation, so I put those sections aside for anyone else who might want them.

The book section magnetizes me with its reviews of some of the latest books written, the variety of the opinions being expressed about them and the style in which they are expressed, for I too have written many book reviews. The subject matter of the books also interests me, adding more dimension and scope to my total picture of what to write about or think about. Whenever there is an article about a book of poetry or about a poet, I peruse it with enthusiasm to add to my knowledge of the subject, which is adequate but not vast. The methods of analysis interest me as I try to imbibe the turns of mind they explore with their comments. An excellent way to use time.

I like the variety of the Sunday paper, including pages on sports, on automobiles, on properties, on metropolitan news and issues, on developments in the financial world, advice columns and so forth, though I don't read all of these. I read little news of national or international politics, not liking to go into details unless an event of great consequence has happened or may happen.

In addition to this large Sunday paper, I also sometimes buy the local paper for necessary local information. My Armenian-American newspaper arrives by mail once a week to keep me apprised of all of that is going on in the Armenian diaspora and Armenia as the homeland, a different set of concepts than many others around me follow and a different set of facts and politics. This may or may not involve chauvinism; I've never had much of that mentality in my particular dealings or writings.

The Internet news that I read every morning is a good supplement with items more of positive interest and outlook than in the usual news pages of the newspaper or on the television news. The latter often overemphasizes the shocking, the tragic and the criminal to the detriment of happier subjects and usually repeats each item many times with interviews in order to fill the hours of time they broadcast.

I am often shocked by the stories of crimes that have been committed on that day or the day before, and I read about them because I feel I should know what is happening in the world. But who can ignore the news? There are too many dangers to be made aware of and also advances and progress, especially in the fields of medicine and science. And if my Sunday paper doesn't arrive by eight o'clock in the morning, I start pacing the hallways.

Therefore my score on the writing of journalism is limited to the total of the seven and a half years I worked at *The Armenian Mirror-Spectator* plus some volunteer publicity work I did for the same newspaper. But my score on the reading of journalism totals many more years.

I still like the friendly feeling of picking up the newspaper from the front porch every Sunday morning and bringing it into the house as if it were a guest, even though projections are that newspapers will have a more online presence in the future. I like foraging for the coupon books and perusing them to clip coupons for use. I like having my ethnic newspaper mailed to me. The physicality of these acts has a particular personality that I favor.

Sentiment vs. the Postmodern

Probably the first poet known to have written about children was the ancient Greek poet Sappho, who was born on the island of Lesbos in Greece in 630 B.C. She was born into an aristocratic family, and when they were exiled from Lesbos went to the Roman island of Syracuse. She was considered bisexual on the basis of her writings, which were mainly lyric love poems that concerned the goddess Aphrodite, women, weddings or herself. Unfortunately much of her work has been lost except for fragments. She did however have a daughter about to whom she wrote the following poem:

> Sleep, darling
>
> I have a small daughter called Cleis,
> who is like a golden flower.
> I wouldn't take all Croesus' kingdom
> with love thrown in, for her.
>
> Don't ask me what to wear.
> I have no embroidered headband
> from Sardis to give you, Cleis, such as I wore
> and my mother always said
> that in her day a purple ribbon
> looped in the hair was thought
> to be high style indeed.
> But we were dark:
> a girl whose hair is yellower
> than torchlight should wear no
> headdress but fresh flowers.
>   —Translated by Mary Barnard

A charming poem that only a mother could have written, it is sentimental yet not overly so. It traces the maternal instinct back to ancient times, and it has survived many centuries to mirror some of our emotions back to us. Sappho wrote on these subjects that many poets avoided. They wrote more about heroes and gods and warfare, the stuff that concerned them. Sappho, the first woman poet on record, introduced the more feminine subject matter with such a powerful meaning that it has reverberated throughout these years in many books that have been written about her with quotes taken from the poetic fragments that have been found.

She inspired the coining of the word lesbian, though it is not definitely known whether she had sexual affairs with women or whether the affection she described in her poems was more concerned with Platonic love. It is theorized that at that time the customs of her society allowed for bisexual behaviors without chastising them. Yet most important, she started the tradition of the lyric poem and poems that were concerned with the lives of women and children.

Many centuries went by without any particular concern about children in poetic terms. Yet upon reaching the 19th century, there were many poems written about children, and they were often quite sentimental. For example, the poem "The Children's Hour" by Henry Wadsworth Longfellow, one of the most famous of 19th-century poems, ends thus:

> I have you fast in my fortress,
> And will not let you depart,
> But put you down into the dungeon
> In the round-tower of my heart.
> And there I will keep you forever,
> Yes, forever and a day,
> Till the walls shall crumble to ruin,
> And moulder in dust away!

In its time and later this poem was a glorious achievement for the young, and it is still a popular piece to read to them.

However the current literary taste in modern poetry does not allow much writing about children because it shows too much sentiment for the modern style. This newer style exists on a tight emotional budget, which decries excess emotion and replaces it with "objective correlative." The term simply means replacing the adjectives and verbs describing emotions with nouns and metaphors that will induce a sensation of a similar emotion. This tends to draw the reader's mind into the poem as an active participant rather than the more passive reader.

Sentimentality means a cloying sentiment overdone and not controlled enough for the needs of modern poetry. Sentiment, however, is not such a strong dose of the emotion as to turn the reader away as from a chemical that is too strong but only like a bit of its perfume. Yet even that seems to be too much of modern poetry for some purists. The early modern poetry shows more emotion than does the later.

The narrative poems of the 20th century great poets show emotional involvement with the action. One of our perennial favorites is the poem by T. S. Eliot called *Old Possum's Book of Practical Cats*, which resulted in the wonderful musical *Cats*. Perhaps this poem was meant to be read primarily by children, for it is not as difficult as most of Eliot's poetry and is an imaginative piece suitable for children. Yet children's literature is often adored by adults also.

Among the modern poets who have written about children successfully are Anne Sexton and Sylvia Plath with each writing a few poems that mentioned their children in the typical indirect or oblique manner. Their poetry showed their anger, especially towards their parents, who had abused them either physically or psychologically. As such, Sylvia Plath's "Daddy" poem is well-known for its indictment of her father as the Nazi type and was promoted by the women's liberation movement. They also wrote a few highly stylized poems about their children. They were part of the confessional school of poets, those who wrote about their mental illness. Both of them committed suicide.

The famous poet Rilke wrote about children as did the more recent Sharon Olds, Richard Wilbur, Judith Pordon, Sarojini Naidu and others. They contained a modest amount of sentiment but are not sentimental. Where do we draw the line? Should the mention of children be ousted from poetry altogether?

Poems about children don't have to be sentimental. The emotion can approach the reader through the words indirectly, leaving a picture of the mother with child as a painting would do so that the reader can make an interpretation and take as much emotion as necessary from the viewing. I wrote a number of poems about children in two books I published, and some of them gained good comments. The following is an excerpt from my poem "Blue Mother," which may illustrate this point:

> the blue mother
> thumbs through a book
> and through her children's looks,
> settles in a study chair
> after the sand and mud
> have returned to their places,
> and clicks on the light
> she ladles there
> after the tousled ones
> have drawn a picture
> of sleep.

Why is the mother blue? It attracts the reader's attention, and perhaps the reason she is blue is only because I love to work in color. Everything in poetry doesn't have to have a logical explanation, for it is the logic in illogic that we are after, the construction in deconstruction, the meaning out of the meaningless.

Poetry illustrates illogic in action as children do, and children are more lovable for the fact of being bumbling in a brilliant way. Children in poetry can be a charm, even in the modern form because they are a treasure and inherently understand the nature of poetry. Who else but a five-year-old child could look up at the sky and say in an incriminating manner, "God, why don't you come down and talk to me?"

Of course, poems for children become another category in which there are many books written in this time and others. There are books for small children and others for teens and also poetry written by teens for teens, which can be quite popular. These days poetry is branching in many directions.

Lack of sentiment in poetry when carried to its extreme becomes postmodern, a style that is based on destruction of meaning. Actually when reading through these poems, they seem to have an undercurrent of meaning that sometimes comes through in a sporadic way. They seem disjointed but also have some brilliant lines and insights. This movement began as an experiment in form and has had an ongoing influence on the general poetry style.

Practitioners of this sort of poetry include Lyn Hejinian, Kenneth Koch and Mary Jo Bang whose book *The Eye Like a Strange Balloon* includes the following representative lines:

> Some vigorous enactment.
> Is it three o'clock or twelve fifteen?
> Either is only an estimate.
> Myth equals fate
> plus embellishment.

Some prominent literary journals employ this style exclusively, and others use some of this style along with the more usual styles of poetry. It has been an interesting foray into using words or phrases in a very different way to achieve effect. The movement came about when the confessional style became stale, and the rebellion was in order. No one can predict where it will go.

There are many styles of poetry coexisting at the present time, and the following list includes most of them: alliterative verse, concrete poetry, erasure poetry, found poetry, free verse, imagism, modernist poetry, objectivist, postmodern, symbolist, minimalist, surrealist, cowboy, beat poetry, lyric poetry, language poetry, and narrative poetry. They are for the most part what their title indicates, and readings into each form are readily available. For the only way to appreciate these forms is to be enlightened about them and exposed to poems in each genre.

The question now is of all these forms with their oblique approach to subjects, which is the most desirable and which the least. The answer can only be following one's own preferences and the dictates of one's mind in approaching what is offered by book publishers and literary magazines. I say the best approach is variety.

Basically the motivations of writers and ways of working are quite similar sometimes though different in the particulars of life. The resulting work differs with the structure of the geography of each mind with its variations in storms of emotion. They can be storms either of despair or of anger at one's self or at circumstances or of an overwhelming love for all persons in the emotions that link us together.

I hope this is part of the progress of civilization, which I certainly want to be part of. The mistakes I have made seem to impel me to be angry at myself and to "break my brain" rewriting to make any particular work better. Many times this anger has been as effective as that cup of coffee or that fantasy of a kiss.

But whatever the impetus, it should be one that leads to an increased enjoyment of the experience of writing and the experience of life.

A Toast to Poetry

Since some of the best quotations I have encountered are from the works of poets and poetry has always nourished me by helping me to keep my soul in shape, I hereby pay tribute to poets with thoughts and selected quotes. I emphasize selected, for that is the meat without its fat, the lean comparable to the gist and the enjoyment of the toast. Like a bit of champagne, not overdone in order to keep possession of one's wits, these pithy words encourage uplift.

Poems stir the intellect also, the modern poems with indirection and its significance, the older poems with the largesse of direct emotion. The twentieth century has required more of comprehension and concentration to grasp the meanings of metaphors and indirect allusions that are the only way modern poets can write to fulfill the needs of literary magazines. For old styles of rhyme with a set meter with more direct statements have had their day and have peaked and petered out after saturation. Just as modern art has gone into abstraction and surrealism, so modern poetry has gone into similar ways of expression to further challenge the mind.

Modern poets and artists have taken us toward and into the future, still a haze that we drive into with our more urbane cars and our more complex poems, hoping that we can meet the technological feats like exploration of the moon and of Mars halfway. We have already met the computer, and the marriage is a success. Though many people seemed puzzled by these works, they are a necessary part of expressing the mentalities of the 20th and 21st centuries.

The effort of creating poems satisfies, and publishing them in any of the myriad little magazines that exist now for that purpose is a kind of closure. Truly the proliferation of literary magazines is not nearly enough to adequately accommodate all the practicing poets. Then at the point of publication of a book, it seems like the birth of a person who goes on to try to win friends, becoming an entity all its own and somehow hopefully growing on people.

This meeting of minds holds a mystical kind of sympathy through these miles of magazines and books. For some the check may be the high point, certainly an encouragement, though money isn't an essential part of the process. Indeed, there isn't much money to be had except through the best of prizes, teaching and readings. Poets and writers endure the frustration of the thousands of rejection slips along the way and are divided from non-poets by an invisible wall of magnitudes of possible misunderstanding. They gain power and meaning in the heights of emotion and thought they are able to stimulate. The process rather than the poem carries us along as inspiration feeds on inspiration, though fame often eludes.

Philip James Bailey in *Festus, Proem* wrote at about the turn of the century, "Poets are all who love, who feel great truths, and tell them; and the truth of truths is love." He means the emotional love that stirs us to the depths and heights of thinking and expression. Some of us are poets without realizing it, sometimes sputtering an image without rhyme or meter that is raw material, the uttered message without a form. Poets are simply those who work at this, usually for a lifetime, stylizing these moments of inspiration.

I know poets well by their books. The pie of what has been written about them cuts into wrong, right or cynical. Sir James Matthew Barrie, for example, stated: "Poets are people who despise money except what you need for today." The statement is like a potato, for what it means depends on how you fry it or bake it or even mash it. To me it means that poets, if they are poets with no other occupation, work in their field with great devotion and sacrifice. But poets are so dedicated to their art that they gladly accept the limitations that poetry puts upon them, sometimes feeling like martyrs to a cause. Those who are very successful become professors or teachers in the many poetry workshops or win big prizes.

Risking an alphabetical trek through a maze, I found that Roy Campbell offered in *Poets of Africa* a less cynical statement:

> Far in the desert we have been
> Where Nature, still to poets kind,
> Admits no vegetable green
> To soften the determined mind.

He equates the harshness of the desert landscape with the determination of the poet. The vegetable green would soften that harshness, thus diminish determination. Perhaps the harshness of the poetic life leads poets to be more determined. Nature's kindness to poets in providing so much of their subject matter is a compliment, which does not have to be an unqualified rave. Poets are also, metaphorically, very kind to nature.

Is poetry a need or an art for the poet? Or the need for art, or the art of need? It is easy to ask unanswerable questions. Yet philosophers and other writers have usually been sympathetic to the poet's basic drive. Thomas Carlyle, the philosopher, stated in *Burns*, "A poet without love were a physical and metaphysical impossibility." Writer Elizabeth Rundle Charles sympathized thus: "To know how to say what other people only think is what makes poets and sages," in *Chronicles of the Schönberg-Cotta Family*. It would be difficult to add mathematics to these ideas, for the poetic mind usually works in an antithetical way to complete logic, poetry being subjective and depending upon emotional states.

A poet without love? Though most poets seem rather content, there are many who write out of alienation, despair or poverty, seeking the answer or triumph over pain. Some ultimately find the way. Writing out of emotional anguish can produce good work, though somehow it shows through but can be very convincing, as in the anguished Edgar Allan Poe's "The Raven."

> Take thy beak from out my heart, and take thy form from
>   off my door!
> Quoth the Raven, "Nevermore."
> And my soul from out that shadow that lies floating on the
>   floor
> Shall be lifted — Nevermore.

Yet many poems that are written after a transition to a state of happiness where the poet writes about difficulties from a distance in time, place and mood, can be very convincing for seeing tragedy or difficulty from two perspectives at once. They find the depth of double thoughts needed to complete the expression. Fortunately, between suffering and ecstasy lies a great deal of subject matter for poets.

Prose gives a marvelous and dependable contrast to poetry. It is the practical counterpart, the realistic everyday allusion to life around us, all subjects, the bedtime story,

Edgar Allan Poe

the daytime story set out for anyone who can read or cares to, the technical fact, the historic fact, all fact without its special feelings, the how to, the cookbook, the how to get well, the warning, articles and chapters of magazines and books. It explains without condensation or fancy.

But metaphor and simile, hyperbole and alliteration add something special, magical, a moon of dreams over a world of seeming, a third eye perceiving what many do not. How can you not be fascinated at what shines like magnetic silver? It is possible to have both worlds by alternating writing prose and poetry. The saying, "Where there's a will, there's a way" applies here, though it may be a difficult one as in any field of endeavor.

Poets weigh each word on its own and against all the others in the poem. It is critical that this be "right," and the beginning or even advanced poet words and rewords the poem many times to develop it with a sense of what works. Even after much reading and writing and some training, it is necessary to have either an editor's comments or a coach in a workshop situation to focus the mental lens more sharply. After all this work, poets perhaps should be called word experts.

Prose writers of nonfiction do not have to weigh each word against all others for that delicate balance. They must be wordy to water down any possibility of indirection or allusion and weigh pages and chapters instead, repeating the idea in different words as needed in order to develop it. Fiction is a different matter. It hangs in the balance between poetry and descriptive prose within lines of characterization and plot.

Writers or critics have said much about poets throughout history. Thus it appears that the subject has its own particular kind of importance or relevance to our lives. Some of these allusions have been humorous, such as this quote from *A Fable for Critics* by James Russell Lowell:

> There comes Poet, with his raven, like Barnaby Rudge,
> Three fifths of him genius and two fifths sheer fudge.

The poem is the ripe fruit; we do not need to eat the seeds. The planting is done by life, and the tree is nourished by workshops, study, or reading. The publishers do the harvesting, and we eat the fruits. The afterglow is me, is you, is a sip of champagne or grape juice, if you like. In her lovely and genteel way, Edna St. Vincent Millay wrote in *The Poet and His Book* the following:

> Stranger, pause and look;
> From the dust of ages
> Lift this little book,
> Turn the tattered pages.
> Read me, do not let me die!
> Search the fading letters, finding
> Steadfast in the broken binding
> All that once was I!

Poets can also be humorous about themselves or the world around them. So Alexander Pope, poet and satirist who is noted for such statements as "To err is human, to forgive divine," wrote pointedly rather than tragically in *Epilogue to the Satires* the following:

> We poets are (upon a poet's word)
> Of all mankind the creatures most absurd;
> The season when to come, and when to go,
> To sing or cease to sing, we never know.

Some comments on poets are not so favorable. However, that has not deterred any poet from writing poetry. One such comment is this: "Who writes poetry imbibes honey from the poisoned lips of life" from the preface to *Man Possessed* by William

Rose Benét. Another is from *Dying Young* by A. E. Housman, himself a poet:

> Why if 'tis dancing you would be,
> There's brisker pipes than poetry.

The controversy bites like a lobster's claw unsheathed to be taken as is before or after meals as part of the prescription of life or as the delicacy of the lobster meat itself. For those who love it and whose lives have been shaped by it, poetry is not medicine but a kind of glory for which there is no substitute.

Walt Whitman

Percy Bysshe Shelley, the nineteenth century poet, made a few more delightful comments on poets. He wrote in *An Exhortation*, "Poets' food is love and fame" and in *A Defence of Poetry*," Poets are the unacknowledged legislators of the world." From one of the best-known American poets, Walt Whitman, "The United States themselves are essentially the greatest poem" in Preface to *Leaves of Grass*.

This toast to poetry wouldn't be complete without a few quotes from the modern poets. They tend to wake the imagination from its slumber and reinforce the point that modern poetry shapes passion into words in such an indirect way that they express a tender irony. From W. H. Auden as quoted in *The New York Times*: "A poet is, before anything else, a person who is passionately in love with language." From John Ciardi in *Saturday Review*: "Poetry lies its way to the truth." From Paul Engle in *A Woman Unashamed and Other Poems*: "Verse is not written, it is bled;/ Out of the poet's abstract head." And from the popular Robert Frost as quoted by Edward Connery Lathem, editor of *Interviews with Robert Frost*: "A poet never takes notes. You never take notes in a love affair."

As the older personal confessional style gives way to the broader concerns of interpersonal moments in the world around us, we find subjects renewed or revived with a variety meant to enhance interest and intellect. Add a bit of rhyme and meter or free verse and some surrealism for new poetic growth that blooms, leaving analysis to the prose of critics and humorists.

Comments from the poets themselves as aestheticians are often as flavorful as their poems. From Robert Graves as quoted in *Monitor*: "There's no money in poetry, but then there's no poetry in money either." From Marianne Moore as quoted in *Ladies Home Journal*: "In a poem the excitement has to maintain itself." From the patriotic Carl Sandburg, planning for his 79th birthday: "I'll die propped up in bed trying to do a poem about America." From Edith Sitwell: "I am an unpopular electric eel in a pool of catfish."

Some novelists and nonfiction writers have expressed feelings that also apply to poets. From Katherine Anne Porter on completing *Ship of Fools*: "I finished the thing; but I think I sprained my soul." From John Steinbeck in a diary, quoted in *The New York Times*: "In utter loneliness a writer tries to explain the inexplicable." From Barbara Tuchman in *Author's League Bulletin*: "Books are humanity in print." From the poet William Carlos Williams in *Newsweek*: "I think all writing is a disease. You can't stop it." Poet Joseph Brodsky added (as quoted in *The New York Times*): "Bad literature is a form of treason.

I reluctantly state that I have no favorite poem. Among the published modern poems I have read, there are some I have not liked in the sense that I didn't respond to the style or subject. Certainly the editors did, or it wouldn't have been published. But choosing carefully among what is considered the best, I favor the entire field of poetry and have by this time read thousands of modern poems I love. They stir me by their sounds, their imagery, their vital thought or emotion that I identity with, their subtlety of approach, their intensity. They sometimes stir thought and emotion so much it becomes necessary for me to drop the book to go to the computer and write or revise some poem I have written, ashamed that I have not done better. I suppose that one who is addicted to golfing can feel the same sort of excitement at competing with other golfers or competing with a personal previous level of skill at the game.

When I first studied modern poetry years ago, the influence of imagism as in the poems of Amy Lowell and Ezra Pound was fading and the poems of T. S. Eliot were being studied. A new social interest was beginning and some early confessional poems were being written. Yet I was rather unaware of what was going on in the field of poetry except for the privacy of my study of those poems.

"Did you learn how to write modern poetry in that class?"

"I learned how to appreciate modern poetry and what it consisted of. I was completely absorbed by it then."

"Was the teacher pleased with your work?"

"He gave me a good grade, and an appropriate comment."

"Did your parents like your work?"

"I knew my parents wouldn't understand my work, so I never showed it to them or discussed it with them. For them it was part of another world they didn't feel part of because for the most part they were physical immigrants struggling to get by and mentally having a hard time adjusting. Evidently, mental immigration is a different thing and has much to do with abandoning previous associations."

"Were they interested that you liked poetry?"

"They never said so."

"Were they interested in your studies?"

"They never said so, but once when I complained about the hostility of some people, my father said I should leave school. However, he continued to support me and never said that again."

"Did you blame him?"

"No, because there had been trouble before. It seems that everyone was suspicious of everyone else, and as usual I was caught in the middle."

I would look back into that past to search out what had meant so much to me then, to find facts, names, references, meanings that were almost lost and some of these would become more precious in that recovery. And time would forgive and forget.

I would also regret not pursuing that interest in image and language when it was fresh. The road of my personal poetic inspiration opened in front of me much later, seemingly in a blaze of light at a time when I had more leisure. Then I realized how far I had traveled since the days of studying "Pied Beauty" by Gerard Manley Hopkins and "The Raven" by Edgar Allan Poe. Or fallen in love with the quote "A poem is an enchanted thing" by Marianne Moore.

The Supermarket of Word-Values

The quantity and variety of poetry in magazines and books these days are like a supermarket with endless aisles catering to many different gastronomical tastes. The dedication stimulates as food for the mind, fresh or frozen or boxed. Chewing on metaphors has always been a pleasure for me, but one does have to be used to or trained in peering behind the surface of the words to realize this third dimension that bursts with flavor in the mind and emotions like a food bursts with flavor in the mouth.

Poetry has soul and various personalities, reflecting the various people who write it or who conceive of the various schools of writing. It plumbs a great human need, which is not always recognized by the public at large. It is non-materialistic, even anti-materialistic as it gives vibrant life to moon, stars, sun, buildings, plants, earth, water, fire, people's actions as interpretations that will influence thinking and broaden its scope. Materialism in itself has no soul and has only monetary considerations. Without a counterbalance of any art form, it can leave people feeling empty.

Poetry is completely ethical in teaching language, use of language, sounds of words, mental exercise of a kind, shades of emotions, all ways that could lead to euphoria or mystical experience. It communicates on this extraordinary level when its meaning gets across. It requires the utmost concentration for writing and reading and as such exercises the thinking faculties. In its great variety of feelings expressed, it can be sublime or the opposite in the service of delineating subjective experience. But it should not read like a plucked parody with rather shallow meaning or like an apt apology for itself or any other poem in question.

To me the new narrative style is a return with a difference to the story with all the indirections and word plays modern poetry likes. I see it as a possible restoration of some of the popularity poetry has enjoyed in the past when more people understood it. Dana Gioia, poet, winner of the American Book Award for *Interrogation at Noon* and author of the prose study *Can Poetry Matter* as well as former chairman of the National Endowment for the Arts, states that some of Robert Frost's poems were narrative and have influenced the new narrative efforts. He states in a review of Robert McDowell's *Diviners*:

> Contemporary narrative poets not only have the challenge of creating lyric stories; they must also invent cogent forms and intrinsically heightened styles in which to tell them.

McDowell's book is an example he cites for style and originality in structure. The descriptions are compressed by eliminating the usual transitions. The plot stretches across generations rather than being a single lyrical moment. Different from Frost's narrative, this work sprawls across five generations. Gioia presents the idea that there is at present a revival of narrative poetry incorporating modernist forms. I welcome the movement because I write narratives and like to read them.

How wonderfully ethical it is to progress with what seems like a regression, a backward look at an old form that is suddenly unwrapped, taken out from its plastic bag and used in new formulations. I don't mean this to be a plastic pun but rather to be a real image with importance to readers. I've known people who don't usually read poetry to peruse a book of poems and pick out the narratives as the ones they like, simply because they understand them better. The action and the characterizations propel them along to realizations of motivations dressed in images of beautiful mental clothing.

The human imagination produces greater bounty than most of us realize. It is not something in a cardboard box that can be easily opened. It is not a silken flower but a real one. It is a star fruit, a blackberry, an abundance of cheese, color in acceleration, cleanliness of mood and whatever else you can think of that is apt. So much variety for so many people, the growing populace of America and the world. The moral fragrance of perfume. The politics of the calendar and of endless time.

We don't take for granted the words we put forth and throw around. Our considerations reflect our minds and reach out to other people, writing modern poetry to be recited or to be printed. It is disappointing not to be related to in this way. As poets we have options and work according to what we choose as style and subject, subjecting ourselves to being rated by teachers and editors. We visualize more and conceptualize to give each object or person an emotional value, so that the world can seem a more living and lovelier place than it usually is with more of this real and deep level of communication.

We are not extraordinary people, but only perceive the world around us a bit differently. The old adage that "poets are crazy" need not apply. Mental and emotional problems are truly democratic and cut across all fields of endeavor, professional or non-professional, rich or poor or middle class, young or old, middle aged or ethnic. Poets put a great deal of love or anger into their work and sometimes even negative emotions because they show intensity. Even the intensity of sexual aberrations at times works, and please note that I am not sitting on the throne of judgment to sharpen a sort of insight that is often misplaced.

As Louis Ginsberg stated: "Love that is hoarded molds at last." Imagination that is hoarded also molds. Food that is not eaten when fresh, molds. We mold if we hoard our talents without providing for ourselves and others. We mold if we do not invent, if we do not serve, if we do not express ourselves.

As T. S. Eliot, the famed poet, stated in "Four Quartets": "Humankind cannot bear very much reality." If poetry creates unreality with its fantasies and colorful expressions, then we should have a feast that could satisfy any curious mind. We can bear quite a bit of that and with such styles of expression that would please many readers and editors. It certainly challenges me to indulge and to spread the word.

Prose is without question noble in saying loudly what poetry says in silence. It is a necessary explanation where poetry is a constant rediscovery and invention of new metaphors and forms. Prose is a practical consideration where poetry is a survival technique. One often complements the other.

A mental calculator or a real one would do nicely, but approximation is alright when reading poetry or publishing it as hundreds of literary magazines do yearly. Editors and reviewers can be acute analysts. Many readers depend on their opinions of the poetry at hand and of course the prose explications to be able to follow the sense and intentions of any piece of writing.

The crux of the content and what it delivers is this: I write, therefore I am. A familiar parody. I think, therefore I am. I eat, therefore I am. I work, therefore I am. I sleep, therefore I am. A further digression would read like this: I swim, therefore I am an athlete or simply entertained. I sniff perfume, therefore I am transported, happy, sexy or whatever. I taste rose jam, therefore I am a rose. Real poetry in its improbability draws a meaningful or lovely picture in the mind if not in actuality.

"I think the supermarket analogy is the best I've ever thought of."

"Are you writing analogies or poetry?"

"Right now I am writing prose about poetry."

"Why do you use a supermarket analogy?"

"I think the context of my life would explain that."

"And what is that?"

"For much of my life my father worked in the grocery section of a supermarket and then in his own grocery store."

"And talked about it a great deal."

"Yes, so I got the message early on."

"Then what?"

"To take this matter step by step, the next step is that I have been going grocery shopping all my married life. And since I love food and I love to cook so much, it follows that I would use the sights and sounds and colors and textures of the goods in a supermarket."

"Is there another step?"

"Yes, working in my father's store with the candy and the ice cream and the milk and bread, and so forth."

"You mean you've been hypnotized by all this?"

"With my senses and in my memories."

In other words, all of one's senses are involved in the process of writing, especially poetry, which demands sensual awareness. To take the supermarket analogy to new heights, let's say the fish is very fresh. I know because I sniff it deliberately, and this freshness means a good meal to come. Joy lasts for something fresh or well done, and avoidance lasts for lack of freshness.

The sense of sight is very well served in a supermarket with all the colors of fruits and vegetables like persimmons and avocados contrasted with lemons and limes, the bright lights, the order with which everything is placed in cubicles and labeled, the price tag which communicates a practical awakening, the cleanliness all around, the bustle of the employees. Consider the sweetness of a jam mood and the petulance of peapods, the crunch of cereal, the munch of bread, the melodies of alliteration floating over the aisles and raining a tender mist over heads like the soft sprays upon the vegetables to keep freshness. The excitement of all this heightened color is analogous to the excitement of various combinations of words that spark various effects on the mind.

The mind, a sly agent, tastes first, then the mouth in the case of food. So also with words, it tastes and accepts or tastes and rejects. It advances with preference only. Before writers jot down with pen or with computer any sentence or paragraph, they think and rethink in the same manner and write and rewrite accordingly. The mind seeks the equilibrium and enthusiasm of what it accepts as a good decision with which someone else might agree or disagree.

Further, I can say I meditate, therefore I am. I find the process of waiting for inspiration, of thinking out ideas, of plunging into the past to recover certain experiences, of rethinking and rehashing endlessly, a meditative process. The mind is working and the emotions are trying to catch up. They didn't react adequately at the time of the experience, but in reliving it they do and result in a poem or two or more.

The advantage of an education in the humanities is that it teaches analysis of life and its vagaries with literature, art, psychology and philosophy. One can wring meaning out of every block of existence that builds a life, seeing what has always been with us continuing at a different pace and with more complexity or changing. Poetry goes through similar changes.

It has existed since the beginning of civilization and in all cultures in one form or another. It has thrived and it has seemed sometimes on the verge of expiring, but since it has importance and value, it has not expired. Ancient Sappho and Virgil are still well remembered and read. Shakespeare and Dante are treasured and celebrated. Eliot and Pound no less. The moderns add much interest with many vibrant workshops and readings, of poetry slams and courses, of buying books or getting them from libraries, which fortunately buy their books.

It is not likely that poetry will go from us any time soon or anytime. I believe I can safely predict that if and when the moon and the planets become slightly populated with humans, and that is the projection, this cursor of civilization will go with them, being so ingrained in our mentality. Where there is paper and pen or laptop, someone will be sitting on the ground or on a chair thinking of appropriate images to scribble and share with someone there or back on earth.

It echoes our lives back to us to show us what we are and how or what we think and feel. Only civilized human beings can do this sort of thing psychology calls sublimation — a projection and reformation of feelings in a socially desirable manner. It's all baked into the mind, a most precious commodity, like a nourishing meal if one knows how to get nourishment from it.

There are many apt quotes on the subject. Edgar Guest wrote in *The Package of Seeds*, "In this bright little package, now isn't it odd? You've a dime's worth of something known only to God." John Colville repeats his statement on Winston Churchill in *The Fringes of Power*, "He fertilizes a phrase or a line of poetry for weeks and then gives birth to it in a speech." Then in regard to some necessary details, "Vulgarity is the garlic in the salad of life" from Cyril Connolly quoted by Joseph Epstein in *The Middle of My Tether*.

Imagination hovers over us, though we don't always realize it. Practicality going along with creativity, there is no chocolate cake in the basket. We have to make it before we put it there.

Bibliography

Armenian Legends and Poems. Compiled by Zabelle Boyajian. London, New York: Columbia University Press, 1959.

The Armenian Mirror-Spectator. Watertown, Massachusetts: Baikar Press, Nov. 24, 2007.

The Art Book. London: Phaidon Press Limited, 1994.

Bartlett's Familiar Quotations, compiled by John Bartlett. Boston: Little Brown, 1919.

Internet Sources, especially Wikipedia.

Images of America: Watertown. Friends of the Watertown Free Public Library and the Historical Society of Watertown.

Jones, Howard Mumford. *Guide to American Literature and its Backgrounds since 1890*. Cambridge: Harvard University Press, 1953.

Keirsey, David. *Please Understand Me: Character and Temperament Types*. Del Mar, California: Prometheus Nemesis Book Col., 1984.

Kouyoumjian, Hagop. *Bloody Desert*. Boston: Baikar Press, 1949.

Lang, David Marshall. *The Armenians: A People in Exile*. London: George Allen & Unwin Ltd., 1981.

Mooradian, Karlen. *Arshile Gorky Adoian*. Chicago: Gilgamesh Press Limited, 1978.

Mardiganian, Aurora. *The Auction of Souls* (third English edition). Beirut, Lebanon: Doniguian Press, 1966.

Pilibosian, Helene. *History's Twists: The Armenians*. Watertown: Ohan Press, 2008.

———. *At Quarter Past Reality: New and Selected Poems*. Watertown: Ohan Press, 1998.

———. *Carvings from an Heirloom: Oral History Poems*. Watertown: Ohan Press, 1983.

Pilibosian, Khachadoor and Helene. *They Called Me Mustafa: Memoir of an Immigrant*. Watertown: Ohan Press, 1992, 1999.

Raffi. *The Fool*. Translated from the Armenian by Jane Wingate. Boston: Baikar Press, 1950.

Reading Modern Poetry. Edited by John Gerber. State University of Iowa, Key Editions, c. 1955. New York and San Francisco: Scott, Foresman & Co.

Sarkissian, Hagop, *The Sarkissian and Pilibosian Families: A Guide for the Curious*, Watertown, Ohan Press, 2009.

Ussher, Clarence D. *An American Physician in Turkey*. Boston and New York: Houghton Mifflin Company, 1917.

Index

Books by Ohan Press

Helene Pilibosian
Carvings from an Heirloom: Oral History Poems, 1983

Khachadoor Pilibosian and Helene Pilibosian
They Called Me Mustafa: Memoir of an Immigrant, 1992

Hagop Sarkissian (trans.)
From Kessab to Watertown: A Modern Saga, 1996

Helene Pilibosian
At Quarter Past Reality: New and Selected Poems, 1998

Khachadoor Pilibosian and Helene Pilibosian
They Called Me Mustafa: Memoir of an Immigrant, 1999
        (Second Edition)

«Վարժապետի Խելf» — Յօդուածներ Յ. Յ. Սարգիսեանի գրչէն
հրատարակուած հայ մամուլի մէջ, 1935–1961, 2000

Խաչատուր Փիլիպոսեան
Տարիներու Հաւաքածոյ — Հայ մամուլի մէջ տպուած եւ անտիպ
գրութիւններ, 2002

Հեղրի Վարնըմ
Նկարագիր կամ Կեանքի Ուղեցոյցը, 2003
Հայացուց՝ Յ. Յ. Սարգիսեան

Helene Pilibosian
History's Twists: The Armenians, 2008

Hagop Sarkissian
The Sarkissian and Pilibosian Families: A Guide for the Curious, 2009

Helene Pilibosian
My Literary Profile: A Memoir, 2010